YOU CAN HAVE IT ALL—WEALTH, WISDOM, AND PURPOSE

Strategies for Creating a Lasting Legacy and Strong Family

KIP KOLSON

Family Wealth Leadership

Contents

YOU CAN HAVE IT ALL—WEALTH, WISDOM, AND PURPOSE

ENDORSEMENTS

"This thoroughly researched approach to the integration of the qualitative and quantitative aspects of wealth brings a unique and important twist to the conversation by including quotes from scripture. I would recommend this book to anyone who wants to include their Christian values in the transfer of their valuables to their loved ones."

Emily Bouchard, Wealth, Money, and Family Coach Managing Partner, Wealth Legacy Group

"What comes to mind first when you hear the term 'wealth'? How about this term: 'significance'? Now, connect these two terms and consider how wealth can actually help you achieve significance. How can this be? The responses to this question are likely as varied as the number of people considering it. We all want our lives to be considered as significant, don't we? Yet, according to some, wealth can be a stumbling block to getting there. In his book *You Can Have It All—Wealth, Wisdom, and Purpose*, Kip Kolson does a masterful job of helping individuals and families of wealth tackle this interesting combination of having wealth alongside living a life of significance. These pages are filled with practical processes and steps to walk you through understanding how to have wealth coexist with significance and not just today, but also in the generations that follow you. Read this book. You will be glad you did."

Bob Karcher, Author, *Who Are the Joneses Anyway?* Life Coach & Transformational Speaker

"I am very, very pleased that Kip Kolson has poured his life into this extremely important topic by writing this book, *You Can Have It All— Wealth, Wisdom, and Purpose*. Kip has had considerable experience in helping families think through all of the issues around wealth, wealth management, and wealth transfer. This is a book that you want to keep on your bookshelf and constantly refer to. It is a book that is going to challenge much of what the world would tell you about wealth and wealth transfer. It is also a book that is extraordinarily practical and encouraging. It gives me great pleasure to give my endorsement of *You Can Have It All*."

Ronald Blue, Founder of the Ronald Blue Company and
Kingdom Advisors

"*You Can Have It All—Wealth, Wisdom, and Purpose*: what a unique title Kip Kolson has chosen for this timely book on family wealth issues we are facing today within our families and family businesses. For years Kip has lead an outstanding practice in working through all kinds of family wealth endeavors, obstacles related to wealth, and wealth transfer. He gets it! Now he has produced a great book that is leveraging his practical experience, knowledge, in depth research, and even bringing to the family table use of technology. A very deep dive and thought provoking read."

David L. Elliott, President/CEO Santa Ana Chamber of commerce;
Founder of the Institute for Influential Community Impact;
Founder/ President of David Elliott & Associates, Inc.

"What do you do if you've been given a lot? Since that applies to most of us blessed to live in North America, it's incumbent upon us to act with intentionality with our time in order to pass along our values and our resources to the next generation. Your family and all of its members can be a vehicle for good in the world. Family legacy must be intentional; it will not happen by itself. Kip Kolson has created a Family Legacy Roadmap to ensure your family can have lasting impact. Kip's experiences helping families develop and implement their legacy plans is the foundation for the principles in this book that will show you how your family can too."

Greg Leith; CEO, Convene: Business Performance + Eternal Perspective

"As a family therapist for over 30 years, I have worked with hundreds of families and family owned businesses that have 'blown up' over the distribution of parent wealth before and after their deaths. Many times, the wealth that had been formed over the life of the parents, and with much hard work and innovation, is gone in just a few years with frivolous spending by the adult children. Some of the saddest stories are when the money fuels an addiction that leads to a death. In many cases it is a complete shock to parents and family who would never have imagined that family relationships would and could be damaged by the gifts of the parents. Sometimes it is a known fact of some family squabbles, but they never would have dreamed it would end in permanent estrangement. Parents who have had this happen are heartbroken because the last thing they would want is pain and destruction over something that should be a wonderful gift. How can you ensure that what you pass along to your children will be a blessing and not a curse?

Kip Kolson's book, *You Can Have It All—Wealth, Wisdom, and Purpose,* is a blueprint for a reliable positive outcome of distributing parental wealth. The good news of this book is that it goes way beyond the money aspect. As early as childhood years and as late as full adult children years, his strategy helps parents continue to teach character building, strategy, good communication and problem-solving skills, responsibility, the joy of giving to worthy causes, and how to assess the best ones to give to. As a family participates in managing the wealth with structure and rules, they are building good financial and stewardship practices. Kip also vividly explains the importance of the family developing a team of support as an athletic team has coaches for each aspect of the team so that the family improves what they do and can better deal with any relational and financial problems right away so they do not turn into damage.

This book would be good for young couples through empty nesters. Young people can get help to conceptualize what to do with the wealth they begin to accumulate and to begin teaching their children out of the gate. The hope of this book is that you are never too old to make these changes in your life and estate. It could save your family, the heritage you want to pass onto many generations ahead, and, in some cases, the lives of your children."

Larry J. Hamilton, MFT, California Licensed Marriage and
Family Therapist

"I, on a personal and business basis, highly recommend Kip's new book, as well as the services his successful company offers. His track record speaks for itself and anyone interested in protecting and growing their estate in ways that demonstrate love toward their family, needs to read this book. I am proud of both our personal and business relationship over the years and glad it continues to this day and beyond."

John T. Carr, Founder & CIO, Charitable Giving Foundation

"Building wealth for our family was a fun, rewarding challenge, but learning how to take my family on a journey beyond success to significance is proving to be even more complex. *You Can Have It All— Wealth, Wisdom, and Purpose* is providing me with an array of interesting ideas and approaches . . . opening the door for important conversations and concrete action steps."

Lloyd Reeb, Halftime Institute and author,
From Success to Significance

Prologue

As a Christian, I have found that the principles in the Bible are the soundest and wisest advice of any book or article I have read about how we should live every aspect of our lives. All financial and self-help books, seminars, life coaches, and promoters of ways to improve your life subscribe to biblical principles even if their authors have never opened a Bible or adhere to Christian beliefs.

People would not need any more self-improvement or financial advice books if they would apply biblical wisdom to their lives. The reason so many people utilize and promote these principles— intentionally or not—is that the principles are right and true and are successful when followed properly.

I realize I have just suggested you need not read another self-help book, but I am asking that you read this one on the assumption that most people have neither the time nor experience to read Scripture or know where to find verses that provide the wisdom I share here. I do encourage you to do so if for no other reason than to verify its accuracy.

That said, this is not a "Christian" book intended to be read only by Christians. Nor is its purpose to promote my personal faith or convert anyone, although I confess to being pleased if a reader comes to know personally the God who guides my life and has given me so much. It is a book about money and people because they are inseparable and, more often than not, a destructive formula! Whether money causes conflicts in a family or if it is relational issues, struggles, or personal behaviors and addictions that erode the financial fabric, statistics and the law of entropy will ensure that most families will lose their wealth, effectiveness, and closeness within three generations.

I have included many scriptural references, but I ask readers to think of these not so much in their religious context or to automatically dismiss them as theology only but to embrace them for their life instruction value as if they had been written by someone providing the wisdom and knowledge needed to live the life they want.

No matter their religion, faith, or beliefs, readers will identify what will bring them a life of significance and joy. In my relatively long time on this planet, I have found that very few people understand what a significant life looks like much less actually live one. This is even more accurate when applied to families.

Once upon a time, families and their names endured for hundreds of years and impacted our world in many ways. In America, we have the Getty, Rockefeller, Kennedy, Morgan, and Mellon families that built railroads, fabricated steel, held political offices, and built financial empires that are still around today. These significant families passed down much from generation to generation. Where are the modern-day dynasties, and how were the families I just mentioned able to endure while so few families today last more than one, maybe two, generations as unified, impactful forces? How and why do some families achieve significance whereas most do not?

My son, Kevin, and I manage Family Wealth Leadership; we founded it to answer these questions by addressing the conflict between wealth and family members. We have repeatedly witnessed wealth create conflicts that families are unable to overcome—this is a historical and global fact. People and their accompanying issues destroy wealth rather than allow the family and its members to use it in ways that strengthen and perpetuate the family through multiple generations.

We have found two absolutes are required to resolve conflicts. First, families must diligently and religiously adopt and live by shared sound, reliable, and replicable values and principles that work every time—that is, biblical principles. Second, the family must have a shepherd, or in today's vernacular, a coach, to guide its members through the minefields and mazes of life. A coach can teach and educate and provide an objective ear and wisdom that all family members can rely on. A coach will speak truth with love and honesty always with the betterment of the entire family as the objective.

The Bible refers to God as one in three persons: Father, Son, and Holy Spirit. I felt this relationship of the three persons of God to be a perfect example of what a legacy family is, so the original title of this book was, *The Legacy Family—Father, Son, and "Holy Coach,"* the latter describing the role the Holy Spirit plays in humans. The Holy Spirit conveys and interprets God's words through humans to humans in ways that they can apply it to make their lives fruitful, purposeful, and significant. That is, to be a coach, the Holy Coach, who will be your guide as you read each chapter and says,

Wisdom begins with respect for the Lord, and understanding begins with knowing the Holy One. (Proverbs 9:10 NCV)

For the Lord gives wisdom; from his mouth come knowledge and understanding. He holds success in store for the upright, he is a shield to those whose walk is blameless, for he guards the course of the just and protects the way of his faithful ones. Then you will understand what is right and just and fair—every good path. For wisdom will enter your heart, and knowledge will be pleasant to your soul. Discretion will protect you, and understanding will guard you. (Proverbs 2:6–11 NIV)

On the assumption that readers of this book want to know what is true and reliable—no matter what they believe regarding God—I would be remiss if I did not use the one source I know to be so.

Holy Coach: Their purpose is to teach people wisdom and discipline, to help them understand the insights of the wise. Their purpose is to teach people to live disciplined and successful lives, to help them do what is right, just, and fair. These proverbs will give insight to the simple, knowledge, and discernment to the young. Let the wise listen to these proverbs and become even wiser. Let those with understanding receive guidance by exploring the meaning in these proverbs and parables, the words of the wise and their riddles. Fear of the Lord is the foundation of true knowledge, but fools despise wisdom and discipline. (Proverbs 1:2–7 NLT)

Get the truth and never sell it; also get wisdom, discipline, and good judgment. (Proverbs 23:23 NLT)

The Bible is considered a religious book by most people. In fact, it is a love letter from a Father to His children who, like all good fathers, wants His children to live productive, joyful, fulfilled, and significant lives. The Holy Coach says,

All Scripture is inspired by God and is useful to teach us what is true and to make us realize what is wrong in our lives. It corrects us when we are wrong and teaches us to do what is right. (2 Timothy 3:16–17 NLT)

When the Spirit of truth (the Holy Coach) comes, he will guide you into all truth. He will not speak on his own but will tell you what he has heard. (John 16:13 NLT)

If you do not share my belief that God has a master plan and a unique plan for each of His children, I hope you will at least accept that the principles and concepts are true and will work in your life and your family if put into practice. The family relationship between God and His children described in Scripture provides the model for us for a successful transfer of true wealth to each generation.

Accepting that there is a heaven and a hell, we can understand how that symbolizes what will happen to our heirs depending on how they are prepared. Our time on Earth is a training ground for what we will inherit for eternity. Life is preparation for the afterlife. God gave us a prototype, an example of Himself and what He wants us to become— His Son. He gave us His instruction manual—His Word. And He gave us His Spirit to be our guide—His Holy Coach. While we walk this planet, our purpose is to correctly prepare our children for what they will inherit in the same way God is preparing His children for what they will inherit. As family leaders, we must be the examples and prepare our children to be exceptional examples of service and stewardship. We must utilize and teach the right rules and principles and provide an instruction manual for them to follow. And we must learn the wisdom we need from coaches. Not following His model and watching a family destroy itself is not heaven on earth whereas adopting His model can result in at least a small measure of heaven on earth.

Then you will know the truth, and the truth will set you free. (John 8:32 NIV)

You cannot achieve and enjoy a significant life unless you have acquired truth and wisdom.

SECTION I

In the Beginning

CHAPTER 1

Significance

This is a book about families and significance, and it is about the wisdom necessary to effectively use wealth to unite your family rather than destroy it. Although money and finances play a major role in the discussion, this is not an instruction book on how to budget, buy real estate, manage an investment portfolio, plan for retirement, save on taxes, draw up a will, or set up a trust.

Additionally, this is not intended to be a self-help book. This subject has so many moving parts—many being about people's feelings and emotions—that it would be dangerous to attempt to fix family issues on your own. The issues themselves will be different for every family and will have different degrees of intensity and severity that require varied approaches and professional counsel.

In fact, my primary purpose for writing this book is to make the reader aware that there are or will be family challenges and struggles while the matriarch and patriarch are alive and in control of the family wealth, and more so after their passing, that can irreparably damage the family structure. The best chance for successfully avoiding problems and increasing the chance for individual and family significance is to address those problems and challenges when everyone is alive and able to communicate their individual needs, wants, and desires. This also gives everyone the time to gain the training, experience, and maturity they need to be emotionally, functionally, and financially prepared to preserve and increase the family wealth with help from a coach or coaches skilled in dealing with family and financial conflicts before they become uncontrollable.

I wrote this in the belief that my readers want to be significant. I start from the position that everyone has a need to feel needed and important, but not all people are. If that were the case, everyone would be successful, happy, content, and important. That not everyone embodies these characteristics tells me not everyone wants to be significant—or they want to be but do not know how to achieve significance. This book is for the latter group; their families are too important to leave their futures to chance!

So why do some people and only a few families achieve significance while most do not? Even if one person in a family has achieved significance, it does not mean that other family members will or that the family as a whole will be successful much less significant. In fact, history tells us that very few families achieve significance.

Significance can be good or bad. Hitler was significant in a very bad way. Abraham Lincoln and Mother Teresa were significant in very good ways. Significance is a choice—achieving it must be intentional. I don't believe there is accidental significance. There can be momentary and temporary bouts of significance, or there can be events that seemingly accidentally produce a substantial effect on a person's life, but these are not normally long lasting. Significance can have worldwide consequences or affect only a few people in one geographic or social area. Significance is different for each person, and it is as varied as the number of people who choose it.

What Does Significance Mean to You?

How would you define *significance*? Not just the word, but how would you know if you are significant? Stop reading right now and write down how you would know if you are important.

Significance Defined

Here are some dictionary definitions.

1. strongly affecting the course of events or the nature of things; significant

2. having or likely to have a major effect; important

3. having a meaning or purpose, "a meaningful explanation," "a meaningful discussion," "a meaningful pause"

Significance is being important, having value and influence, and making a difference. There is one important concept that, if adopted and embraced, can change your life. Significance cannot be acquired, earned, inherited, or transferred. It is not wealth, celebrity, fame, or position. These may provide a momentary influence on people and events, but they do not confer long-lasting significance.

These definitions tell us what significance is but not how to achieve it. My own definition is more about how than what: it is doing what you need to do to make other people feel and be significant.

Holy Coach: Then he said, "Beware! Guard against every kind of greed. Life is not measured by how much you own." (Luke 12:15 NLT)

Choose a good reputation over great riches; being held in high esteem is better than silver or gold. (Proverbs 22:1 NLT)

Honor the Lord from your wealth and from the first of all your produce; so your barns will be filled with plenty and your vats will overflow with new wine. (Proverbs 3:9–10 NASB)

Significance is bestowed! You will be significant only when someone else says you are significant to him or her or to society. You are significant when you add value to someone else. You may think you are significant, but that does not make it so.

That means significance can also be individualized. I can be significant to my family but not to yours. I would like to believe I am significant to my clients because I help them become significant, but I provide no value to people who are not my clients. I hope you are beginning to understand that significance is achieved through the service you provide to others and society. If other people and society find no value in what you bring to the table, you have no value no matter how many poker chips you have in front of you, no matter how proficient you are at the game, or no matter how skilled you are at bluffing.

Here are two critical points. First, you cannot be significant by yourself! Without someone or something to give your life away to, it is impossible to be significant. Even if you give everything you have to an institution or cause rather than directly to humans, you will be significant only when that thing or cause serves other people and makes their lives better.

The other reason you cannot be significant by yourself is because to be great requires the help of others. All great business, education, political, and sports leaders achieved significance because they had teams. A boxer still needs a trainer, a promoter, and an opponent when he steps into the ring. You must have people who help you, and you must have people you help. You can be significant only when you are part of a team. This is why families achieve significance only when they consciously choose to stay and work together for shared purposes. Even Jesus had twelve disciples. Judas failed badly, but the remaining eleven went on to positively influence the world with the Gospel.

This leads to the second point: the difference between success and significance. Success can be achieved by yourself, it can be defined by only you if you wish, and it can be measured—but it doesn't last. You may have had straight A report cards, multiple sports trophies on the shelf, or became CEO of a large corporation, but twenty or thirty years later, the report cards have been thrown away, the trophies are in storage somewhere, and maybe your picture hangs on a corporate wall near the restroom, but no one gives it a second glance. Over the years, more and more will ask, "Who is that?" Significance, however, has a long-lasting effect—it is usually so big as to be immeasurable, and others define it. So, by default, you cannot be significant by yourself.

Self to Significance

Sorry, it really is not about you! Let me throw out some words to see if you react to them positively or negatively: self-sufficient, self-absorbed, selfish, selfless, selfness, self-centered, self-asserting, self-assured, self-conscious, self-control, self-determination, self-gratification, self-fulfillment, self-discipline, self-involved, self-satisfaction, self-seeking, and self-serving. Sorry for the linguistics test, but I wanted to highlight that my following discussion is not suggesting that the concept of self is good or bad. Like many things in life, it depends on what we choose to do with it.

If you make your life all about you, you will need to like yourself a lot because no one else will. I am not being mean, just honest. It is somewhat of a paradox, but we are all naturally self-centered, self-absorbed, and selfish. To some extent, we must be if we are to survive. The question is whether our pursuit of self requires others suffer for that. We actually increase our chance of survival by doing what we can to help other people survive.

It is called the Law of Reciprocity, or as the Bible puts it, you reap what you sow. Sow anger, greed, and jealousy and you will reap loneliness and an unfulfilled life. Sow kindness, generosity, integrity, and love and family, friends, peers, and colleagues will help you acquire wealth, wisdom, and purpose. The best thing we can do for our self is to take the focus off our self and place it on something or someone else.

Remember my definition of significance? Significance is doing what you need to do to make other people feel and be significant. Playing on the paradox, because we are all interested in ourselves, we can achieve significance by satisfying other people's desires to have what they need and want. You cannot be significant by yourself—you need people, and they need you. I also said that significance is bestowed, not acquired or inherited. If there is no one to whom you are significant, there is no one to bestow it on you. The American Heritage dictionary definition of bestow is, "To present as a gift or an honor; award; confer." And the same dictionary defines confer as, "To invest with." Let me offer my interpretation, a *Kipism*, if you will: "You will be honored and rewarded when you invest in and with other people."

Over the last ten or more years, the idea of going from *success to significance* has become a common phrase. I understand and agree with the intent, but I also believe it skips an important step. The phrase has become popular, and a friend and colleague, Lloyd Reeb, wrote the book of the same title, which I encourage you to read because it focuses on people who had successful business or professional careers in the first half of life but then find themselves at halftime facing a quandary of how they will spend the second half of life.[1] The question, *Is that all there is?* haunts them. The step I see being missed is the correct starting point. We need to start with you, or as I call it, self. Success is a relative term that can be defined by an individual. We can easily feel like we are failing, yet our friends and colleagues would consider us successful. Someone with a million-dollar net worth might feel extremely successful whereas someone else would put themselves in the failure category if they had anything under twenty million.

Additionally, success and failure can live in the same person, just not in the same areas. There are abundant examples of successful businesspeople having failed marriages and being failures as parents. I also believe, in some instances, success was achieved but not earned. Does winning the lottery make one successful or only lucky? Does a $10,000 investment in a stock that grows to $1,000,000 make that investor

---

[1] Lloyd Reeb, *Success to Significance* (Grand Rapids, MI: Zondervan, 2004).

a successful investor? Not everyone is successful in everything and, in many cases, a person doesn't know what personal success much less significance would look like for them. Assuming a person is successful and using success, however one describes it for themselves, as a starting point for defining and attaining significance might not be the right tactic.

Although it is unstated, I know that halftime training does start with "self." Halftime is an organization that coaches and mentors individuals who have been successful in the first half of their lives, and now want to use that success to make the second half more charitable and purposeful in making the world a better place. Another truth is that not everyone can handle success. For reasons known only to them, success becomes uncomfortable and they sabotage themselves to remain in an unsuccessful state. They may have the trappings and demeanor of success, but they are anxious and depressed inside. There can be many sides and dimensions to self that must be dealt with before success can be confirmed and significance pursued.

Why am I so concerned about self? Because everything starts with self. *When we first meet with new clients, our Investigation phase starts with learning about the people sitting across the conference table from us.* Who are they? What have they done? Where have they been? Why and how have they suffered and survived? What have they celebrated? What worries them and what moves them? What do they want for their families' futures? What is important to them about their wealth?

By digging deep in this interview, we accomplish our second objective. We learn whether they have the ability to give up self in favor of service to others. We can still provide financial planning and investment management for them, but guiding them along a path that will lead them from Self to Significance is not likely if they are concerned only about themselves. Take a look at Figure 1.1, a graphic representation of what we do. Notice that "Self" is at the bottom and "Significance" is at the top. The point is that significance is a journey. Those stuck in the self box will never reach the significance box. In Chapter 4, I introduce a train metaphor as an example of two primary components, money and people, that normally conflict with each other as their family train steams off in search of a successful and prosperous future. The train will never leave the station if the focus is only on keeping it shiny and adding more equipment and unnecessary cars that make it bigger and heavier. A train is useful only when it adds cars that carry and provide what other people need. We believe you have been uniquely designed and equipped for your journey, one that only you can accomplish.

You have or will be given the skills, tools, and equipment you need along that journey at the right time but only if and when you leave the station. Trains are specifically designed for delivering what people need where and when they need it. Trains also carry people to where they want to go. A train that does not deliver what people need or help them get to their desired destinations has no value. It might be shiny and impressive, but ultimately, it becomes a museum exhibit with a plaque that reads, "This train was uniquely designed to serve people but never achieved its purpose because it never left the station."

You get to decide what your journey will be like. That is the journey you must discover and carry out for yourself and your family if you hope to reach significance.

Holy Coach: For we are God's masterpiece. He has created us . . . so we can do the good things he planned for us long ago. You made all the delicate, inner parts of my body and knit me together in my mother's womb. Thank you for making me so wonderfully complex! Your workmanship is marvelous—how well I know it. (Ephesians 2:10; Psalm 139:13–14 NLT)

For life is more than food, and your body more than clothing. Look at the ravens. They don't plant or harvest or store food in barns, for God feeds them. And you are far more valuable to him than any birds! (Luke 12:23–24 NLT)

Service

Figure 1.1 graphically represents that moving from self to significance requires going through two boxes called Service and Stewardship. My use of the word *through* is intentional. You cannot get around these essential activities if you hope to be significant. Your value in life and to the human race is directly related to the service you provide the human race. Think about where you are today and how you got here. Assuming you have a reasonably high net worth, how did you get it? Whether you are a CEO of a major corporation, that person's assistant, a musician, an artist, an IT consultant, an actor, a sports professional, a teacher, a firefighter or police officer, a soldier, or a parent, your value as a human being is completely dependent on and determined by the people who need or want the services you offer. If no one wants what you have to offer, I am sorry to say you have no value or significance.

Money is unfortunately the barometer we use to measure a person's value, but it is by no means the most accurate or the only way to measure value. Some of the most important people for maintaining a productive and stable society are paid the least. Teachers, civil servants, military personnel, and stay-at-home parents play critical roles yet receive low or no compensation when compared to actors and athletes who in my mind are nonessential. I am not suggesting the latter group has no value, just that the compensation they receive is disproportionate to the service they provide the world. The service a surgeon provides is more important than catching a football or putting a basketball through a hoop.

For all you stay-at-home parents and homemakers, please keep doing and take great pride in what you do because it is the most important service anyone can provide. As the American Express card commercial says, the work you do is priceless. Your value is not a reflection of the dollars you earn but how much other people need your service no matter the price they can or will pay. Your value is also a function of your passion and personality. If you cannot be excited about what you are doing or want to do, don't do it because you will not be good at it. Too often, people work at jobs only to make money and go home every night depressed and discouraged. You will never feel or be significant no matter what service you provide the world if you hate performing that service—you will not give it your best.

We strive to help our clients find significance so they can feel important, feel good about themselves and the work they are doing, and be joyful. When they are able to bring joy into other people's lives, it always comes back to them. Finding passion and purpose is not always easy, especially for women who have raised children rather than pursued careers, but I can assure you it is possible to have joy and be significant, as you define it, if you are willing to make the effort and work with someone who has the experience and expertise to guide you in discovering what you are most passionate about.

Holy Coach: But it should not be that way among you. Whoever wants to become great among you must serve the rest of you like a servant. Whoever wants to become the first among you must serve all of you like a slave. (Mark 10:43–44 NCV)

Stewardship

That word is normally associated with financial things as in taking good care of possessions and being careful how we spend money. Here, I want to discuss being good stewards of our children. We do a good job of feeding, clothing, educating, and providing for our children in other ways and making sure they have everything we never had.

But, amazingly, we try to ensure they do not have to struggle as we did. I mowed lawns in high school to have enough money to buy my date a burger and a shake. I worked evenings and summers to pay for my education. My first car cost me $500. The mortgage payment on my first home purchase took a chunk out of my meager salary from my first job out of college, and my wife had to work until we had our firstborn. The only reason we could afford a home was because of my GI benefits and a favorable employee interest rate from my lender employer. I share this not to brag or whine but to ask why we want to protect our children from these wonderful, life-teaching experiences. If we are to be good stewards of our children, we should send them to Parris Island, the Marine boot camp, not Paradise Island.

Here is a story about one man who gave his son too much too early.

Holy Coach: To further illustrate the point, he told them this story: A man had two sons. When the younger told his father, "I want my share of your estate now, instead of waiting until you die!" his father agreed to divide his wealth between his sons. A few days later this younger son packed all his belongings and took a trip to a distant land, and there wasted all his money on parties and prostitutes. About the time his money was gone a great famine swept over the land, and he began to starve. He persuaded a local farmer to hire him to feed his pigs. The boy became so hungry that even the pods he was feeding the swine looked good to him. And no one gave him anything.

When he finally came to his senses, he said to himself, "At home even the hired men have food enough and to spare, and here I am, dying of hunger! I will go home to my father and say, 'Father, I have sinned against both heaven and you, and am no longer worthy of being called your son. Please take me on as a hired man.'"

So, he returned home to his father. And while he was still a long distance away, his father saw him coming, and was filled with loving pity and ran and embraced him and kissed him. His son said to him, "Father, I have sinned against heaven and you, and am not worthy of being called your son—" But his father said to the slaves, "Quick! Bring the finest robe in the house and put it on him. And a jeweled ring for his finger; and shoes! And kill the calf we have in the fattening pen. We must celebrate with a feast, for this son of mine was dead and has returned to life. He was lost and is found."

So, the party began. Meanwhile, the older son was in the fields working; when he returned home, he heard dance music coming from the house, and he asked one of the servants what was going on. "Your brother is back," he was told, "and your father has killed the calf we were fattening and has prepared a great feast to celebrate his coming home again unharmed."

The older brother was angry and wouldn't go in. His father came out and begged him, but he replied, "All these years I've worked hard for you and never once refused to do a single thing you told me to; and in all that time you never gave me even one young goat for a feast with my friends. Yet when this son of yours comes back after spending your money on prostitutes, you celebrate by killing the finest calf we have on the place." "Look, dear son," his father said to him, "you and I are very close, and everything I have is yours. But it is right to celebrate. For he is your brother; and he was dead and has come back to life! He was lost and is found!" (Luke 15:11–32 TLB)

This dad probably never made his youngest son work hard for anything. He never had to compete for a job because, right out of college, Dad rolled him into a cushy position in the family business. Did the son appreciate it? Evidently not. It certainly doesn't sound like the son started in the mailroom and worked his way up. Judging by how he handled money once he got his hands on it, he certainly had not received any financial training. However, he knew how to have a good time. Finally, he obviously had no transferable skills since the best he could do was slop pigs. Dad wanted his son to have it better than he had had it growing up. That begs the popular question, "How's that working out for you?"

This father got lucky in that his son was able to swallow his pride and come back home. It would have been a happy ending except for the impact on the older son. Can you blame him for his reaction? He must have asked himself, *How is this fair?*

Jesus told this story as an example of how God responds to us when we have gone astray, and I do not want to diminish that message, but looking at it in human terms and acknowledging that I am reading a lot into the story, did the father do the right thing by removing all the consequences of his son's poor stewardship? Did his reaction help or hinder his relationship with his older son or between the two brothers?

I know I am going beyond the message Jesus intended, but I think the story of the Prodigal Son is a good example of what happens when we are not good stewards over our children and do not teach them to be good stewards of their inheritances and instead give them too much too soon. By the way, although this parable uses money as the catalyst, inheritance also includes stewardship of our Time, Talent, and Training as well as Treasures. Dad did not teach his son how to use his time effectively. Whatever talent the young man had was not developed. We don't know what the son did before leaving Dad's business, but Dad failed if the only training the young man could fall back on was on-the-job pig slopping.

Lloyd Reeb, author of *Success to Significance* and primary spokesperson for the Halftime Institute, says, "Every time you give something to your child, you take something else away. What is your giving depriving your child of?"[2] That should be put on your

---

[2] Lloyd Reeb's statement at a Halftime Summit.

refrigerator to be read every day. From another source, I learned the concept of toxic giving.

The First Gift Creates Appreciation: A person thanks you and truly appreciates receiving a gift from you.

The Second Gift Creates Anticipation: Although there is no assurance that a gift is forthcoming, someone believes it could happen and looks forward to it, still expressing appreciation when received.

The Third Gift Creates Expectation: This is like the birthday, anniversary, or Christmas gift. When received, there will still be an expression of appreciation, but don't ever forget to give it! (Husbands, remember that time you forgot your anniversary?)

The Fourth Gift Creates Entitlement: Instead of appreciation, it now moves into the "I deserve it" mentality. If the gift is not forthcoming, the result will be indignation, anger, and possibly rejection and termination of the relationship.

The Fifth Gift Creates Dependency: Not only is there zero appreciation, this person also demands what is "rightfully" his or hers and expresses resentment that the pipeline is not filled. They know they are being controlled and manipulated, but they will not turn off the pipeline. They fear what they believe they have a "right" to will disappear, and they wonder how they will survive without it. They have lost their dignity and feel they are trapped by their circumstances. It is not their fault when things go wrong—it is your fault.

Stopping the flow will almost assuredly end the relationship because dependent people must seek someone else to feed their addiction. Make no mistake—financial dependency is every bit as toxic as drug and alcohol addiction. *Every time you give something to your child, you take something else away. What is your giving depriving your child of?*

Purpose

What are you good at? Some people can easily answer that question whereas others will struggle to answer it. Some think there is nothing they do well, and that is just not true.

Holy Coach: God has made us what we are. In Christ Jesus, God made us to do good works, which God planned in advance for us to live our lives doing. (Ephesians 2:10 NCV)

Not coincidentally, whatever you are good at provides a clue to your life purpose. However, do not confuse talent with purpose. Your talent is simply a tool that will help you accomplish your purpose. We may assume that because athletes have athletic skills, their purpose is to become professional players. That's a job, not a purpose. A far greater number of high school and college athletes never make it to the big leagues. If talent is thought of as purpose, those athletes will have no purpose.

Likewise, it is natural to think that someone with persuasive skills should be a salesperson or trial attorney or that creative ability means a person should be an architect, designer, writer, or artist. Professional athletes play between eight to twenty years at their games, leaving them maybe forty or fifty years to find their real purpose, which cannot be playing the game.

During the summer Olympics in Rio de Janeiro, Michael Phelps won more medals, solidifying his position as the highest Olympic medal winner in history. But that is not the important story. In an ESPN video, Michael shares the depression and suicidal thoughts he experienced after the 2012 Olympics when he decided to retire from swimming. Since childhood, swimming competitively was his sole purpose; but in retirement, he had no purpose even though he had money and fame. His life went into a downward spiral of parties, drugs, and alcohol abuse, resulting in two arrests for DUI, and being committed to a rehabilitation center. There, he was approached by Ray Lewis, a retired NFL player, who gave him a copy of *The Purpose Driven Life*, by Rick Warren; a book I have referenced several times and include on my recommended reading list.

It changed Michael's life. He went back into training to compete in Rio. After winning the relay race, the interviewer questioned him whether this would, in fact, be his last Olympics. His teammates teased and encouraged him to come back again, but I picked up something in his response that I suspect others missed. He said, "I believe there are other purposes for my life now that I need to pursue." We will have to wait to see if he competes again in four years, or pursues whatever those purposes might be, but his story exemplifies that purpose is not necessarily found in one's profession. Michael now has a baby and a fiancée who he can give his life to, and, although he did not say it, I think he knows that God has a bigger, more important and fulfilling plan for his life.

I have talked about the Halftime concept, the time when people who used their talent for work finally understand that work was not their purpose. The halftime experience—what we do at Family Wealth Leadership—is helping people identify how to use their God-given talents for a purpose greater than only adding more zeros to their net worth. Purpose requires the involvement of a minimum of two people. Your purpose will never be about benefiting self. Significance needs purpose, purpose is a factor of service, and service requires someone to serve.

I identify four major areas (some with subsets) in which you need to develop purpose if you desire significance for your family. You should have a personal mission statement, and I give ideas about how to develop a personal mission statement in a later chapter if you do not already have one.

Next, you need a family mission statement. This will probably seem foreign because few families are cohesively aggregated around a purpose. The third major area is work. Work should not be just a paycheck. Owning a business is not only about independence and your name on the door. Business owners understand that their businesses need mission statements. We see families as—and we encourage our families to become—enterprises. By doing this, we can naturally develop a mission statement that combines family and work. This can be done whether or not there is an actual business in place.

Finally, the purpose of the family wealth must be agreed upon. Money should never be the end-all. Treasures too are only tools and should never be elevated to any more than that. Everyone must be clear on what the purpose of the family wealth is so it will be used to achieve the family purpose.

We always ask new clients, "What is important to you about wealth?" Can you answer that question? Your personal and family mission statements should include an answer. Is your balance sheet simply a way to keep score, a way to measure whether you are successful however you have defined personal success? I see a possible problem if that is true. Success is relative, but it also implies there is a finish line. Is success a matter of crossing the finish line first or in record time? Making a big sale or closing a major business or real estate deal? Then what? When the last deal or race is over, are you no longer successful? The solution is that you must run another race or close another deal. How many races do you have to run, how many deals do you have to close before you consider yourself successful? How many zeros do you have to add to your net worth to put yourself in the successful category? Those are all moving targets that are never ultimately hit.

Consider these folks who didn't have mission statements for their wealth.

Holy Coach: Hezekiah was very wealthy and highly honored. He built special treasury buildings for his silver, gold, precious stones, and spices, and for his shields and other valuable items. He also constructed many storehouses for his grain, new wine, and olive oil; and he made many stalls for his cattle and pens for his flocks of sheep and goats. He built many towns and acquired vast flocks and herds, for God had given him great wealth. Then he (Jesus) told them a story: A rich man had a fertile farm that produced fine crops. He said to himself, "What should I do? I don't have room for all my crops." Then he said, "I know! I'll tear down my barns and build bigger ones. Then I'll have room enough to store all my wheat and other goods. And I'll sit back and say to myself, 'My friend, you have enough stored away for years to come. Now take it easy! Eat, drink, and be merry!'" But God said to him, "You fool! You will die this very night. Then who will get everything you worked for?" Yes, a person is a fool to store up earthly wealth but not have a rich relationship with God.

And it is a good thing to receive wealth from God and the good health to enjoy it. To enjoy your work and accept your lot in life—this is indeed a gift from God. There is another serious tragedy I have seen under the sun, and it weighs heavily on humanity. God gives some people great wealth and honor and everything they could ever want, but then he doesn't give them the chance to enjoy these things. They die, and someone else, even a stranger, ends up enjoying their wealth! This is meaningless—a sickening tragedy. (2 Chronicles 32:27–29; Luke 12:15–21; Ecclesiastes 5:19, 6:2 NLT)

When your balance sheet is a scorecard, its primary purpose is to measure yourself against other people. It is called pride, and there are only two possible outcomes. Either you will feel superior to those you know have less or inferior to those you know have more. If the latter, you will believe you are unsuccessful and will have to run faster on the hamster wheel. If you feel superior, you may feel successful but will treat others as inferior and probably have shallow relationships. Those you call friends may be in name only because they are more interested in what your wealth can do for them than in your friendship. It may be hard to trust others because you suspect their motives.

Holy Coach: For when you have become full and prosperous and have built fine homes to live in, and when your flocks and herds have become very large and your silver and gold have multiplied along with everything else, be careful! Do not become proud at that time and forget the Lord your God, who rescued you from slavery in the land of Egypt. Do not forget that he led you through the great and terrifying wilderness with its poisonous snakes and scorpions, where it was so hot and dry. He gave you water from the rock! He fed you with manna in the wilderness, a food unknown to your ancestors. He did this to humble you and test you for your own good. He did all this so you would never say to yourself, 'I have achieved this wealth with my own strength and energy.' Remember the Lord your God. He is the one who gives you power to be successful. (Deuteronomy 8:12–18 NLT)

Use your money as a tool—invest it in long-lasting and eternal things.

Retirement

It may seem strange to talk about retirement in a chapter about going from self to significance, especially coming from a financial advisor who helps clients prepare for retirement. Regardless, my advice is simple: Don't do it! I'm talking about the type of retirement that looks forward to going to the beach or playing golf every day. If that is your goal, your second half will be boring, routine, and unfulfilling. Worse, it may be cut short because people who do not have a purpose for getting out of bed in the morning don't. Without stimulation and purpose, their health and social connections deteriorate and their lives end sooner than later.

Retirement should be a time for redirection and rebirth, not a time for going into a downward spiral. This is actually the best opportunity you will have to create significance for yourself and your family. You have your health, time, talent, training, and treasures at the ready. You can now reinvent yourself and accomplish the purpose you were created for since you need not be distracted or encumbered by trying to make a living. Someone once said, "Work is what you do to make a living. Purpose is what you do to make a life."

What Is Your Purpose?

You have been designed and blessed with a combination of skills, talents, and attributes to accomplish a purpose and a mission only you can fulfill. This combination is not an accident, nor are you.

Holy Coach: "For I know the plans I have for you," declares the Lord, "plans to prosper you and not to harm you, plans to give you hope and a future. (Jeremiah 29:11 NIV)

God has made us what we are. In Christ Jesus, God made us to do good works, which God planned in advance for us to live our lives doing. (Ephesians 2:10 NCV)

Finding one's purpose is not a simple task. Additionally, a person's purpose may change over time and is not necessarily a person's career, profession, or role. We all have many roles that overlap, and we play them out simultaneously. We are spouses, parents, sons or daughters, grandparents, employees, employers, citizens, Little League or soccer coaches, friends, neighbors—the list goes on. But none of these is a life purpose.

There are critical questions that humanity has struggled with for thousands of years. Why are we here? How did we get here? What is life all about? Is this all there is? Is there life after death? What would give my life significance? I realize readers of this book will represent many religions and faiths or may not be associated with any religion and not adhere to a belief in any god. The only way I have been able to answer these questions to my satisfaction is to believe in the creator God, but again, I am not trying to convince anyone to believe in the God I follow. I do suggest, however, that for the material I cover in the book and for life to have meaning and joy, you at least take the position that it is possible God exists and has a plan for your life even if you choose not to believe in Him.

If you can accept this premise, then this quote from *The Purpose Driven Life* will help you understand everything I discuss regarding the relationship between people and money within the family unit and the meaning of significance for each individual and the family unit: "Life is a *test*, life is a *trust*, and life is a *temporary assignment*."[3] The test is a series of lifelong events that build character and integrity and make us strong and ready for the battles we will fight. Think of it like boot camp for the Marines. That suggests this life is preparation for a bigger, more- permanent assignment, which gets back to the question of life after death. Only you can decide what you choose to believe, but since I've asked that you at least consider God's existence as possible, we can understand that this life is a temporary assignment and everything we do now is preparing us to be successful in that next assignment. It also means, just like the military, all the equipment we have — our Time, Talent, Training, and Treasures — were given to us, and we are to take care of everything meticulously. That is the trust part. We own nothing. It is all government issue; when basic training is over, we give everything back to the owner. We are merely trustees.

---

[3] Warren, *Purpose Driven Life*, 42.

Finally, each one of us is responsible for every member in our unit—our family. We protect, prepare, preserve, and care for each other and our equipment so we can be a tight, well-trained SEAL team and win the battles we fight every day and, like the Marines, never leave anyone to die on the battlefield. We bring everyone home.

CHAPTER 2

Your Family's Story

Establishing significance for yourself and your family, for generations to come, is not an accident—it takes solid planning and careful consideration. To assist families in crafting and capturing their individual stories, we ask them to share their past and present victories, failures, and challenges as well as their hopes and objectives for the future. Understanding where you have been, where you are now, and where you want to be in the future is the first step in creating significance.

Where Have You Been?

History provides valuable lessons, experience, knowledge, and wisdom. In our country, Native Americans revered their elders. This was also true in biblical times, especially in Old Testament history. Stories were a way of life; a good storyteller then was the equivalent of a good author today.

Holy Coach: So Joshua called together the twelve men he had chosen—one from each of the tribes of Israel. He told them, "Go into the middle of the Jordan, in front of the Ark of the Lord your God. Each of you must pick up one stone and carry it out on your shoulder—twelve stones in all, one for each of the twelve tribes of Israel. We will use these stones to build a memorial. <u>In the future your children will ask you, 'What do these stones mean?' Then you can tell them, 'They remind us that the Jordan River stopped flowing when the Ark of the Lord's Covenant went across.'</u> These stones will stand as a memorial among the people of Israel forever." (Joshua 4:4–7 NLT)

Storytelling is a lost art. I daresay most of us know little about our family heritage much beyond our grandparents. Rather than honoring our elders, we avoid them, and that is a real shame because each new generation is losing the experiences and wisdom of the previous generations. Our younger generations are growing up in a world of privilege and abundance. They have no idea of the risks and difficulties their grandparents and great-grandparents had to overcome to provide the wealth the younger generations now get to enjoy. There is no one to bring reality into their lives.

Once, multiple generations lived on the same farm or ranch or within a five-mile radius of each other. When the children and grandchildren married, it was probably to someone on the next farm, or down the road, or maybe the adjoining town. On Sundays, family and friends got together to share a meal, play games, and listen to grandpa and grandma spin a little bit of fiction in with the truth of their personal histories.

Today, families are geographically dispersed and everyone is too busy to spend much more than Thanksgiving and Christmas together. Kids marry people they meet in an out-of-state college in a city a thousand miles away where they now work or live, and the new spouse has family in other parts of the country or world. Gathering the entire family on even holidays is next to impossible. The storytelling, the history, the wisdom, the values, and principles that made families and America great are lost forever.

Is the family's past that important? Would children learn about commitment, honor, loyalty, love of country, and bravery if someone could share personal experiences from wars in Europe, Korea, Vietnam, and now the Middle East? Would they benefit from hearing how difficult life was during the Great Depression or how the little grocery store on the corner or car repair shop turned into the business that created the wealth they are enjoying right now and will receive in the future?

And what about the model grandpa and grandma and maybe you and your spouse demonstrated by being married to each other for fifty years, raising children and grandchildren, dealing with diseases and old age, and laying to rest brothers, sisters, parents, and children? What wonderful stories and life development lessons will not be heard because we have lost the art of storytelling?

Many families can't find the time to have dinner together because everyone is going in different directions. If they are together, the television is on or everyone is staring at a cell phone or tablet. Conversation is nonexistent. They don't know what went on in each other's day much less what happened twenty, thirty, or forty years before they were born.

Did I strike a nerve? History is not just about what happened, it is preparation for each new generation so its members will know how to deal with what will happen, and it will happen because history does repeat itself.

Holy Coach: Tell your children about it in the years to come, and let your children tell their children. Pass the story down from generation to generation. (Joel 1:3 NLT)

What can you do? If the children are still at home, retain the sanctity of mealtimes and prohibit electronic distractions. For young children, use bedtime as storytelling opportunities. You can read books, but how about sharing some, "When I was your age . . ." or "When I was a kid . . ." stories? You know you skinned a lot of knees and probably had at least one broken bone doing something crazy but exciting. Tell them some secrets about grandpa and grandma. Be creative. Nostalgia can be fun.

If the kids are out of the house, plan family vacations. On holidays, add an extra day at the front or back for family activities other than eating, watching football, or napping while the kids entertain themselves. Encourage the younger kids to talk within the group about what is happening in their lives. Bring an "around the campfire" process into the family room or actually go camping. Having three generations intentionally sharing stories strengthens family bonds and creates stories the grandchildren will tell their grandkids.

Don't think the younger children will not be interested. They do want to participate because it makes them feel a part of something much bigger than themselves. It gives them a sense of belonging and roots.

Holy Coach: Always remember these commands I give you today. Teach them to your children, and talk about them when you sit at home and walk along the road, when you lie down and when you get up. Write them down and tie them to your hands as a sign. Tie them on your forehead to remind you, and write them on your doors and gates. (Deuteronomy 6:6–9 NCV)

You can do a lot. It is your responsibility to protect your children and teach them what is right rather than what society wants them to believe. You just need to be intentional and a little creative.

Where Are You Now?

As a financial advisor and family coach, we spend a great deal of time interviewing dad and mom for our Family Wealth Significance

Statement (see Chapter 9 to learn how to craft this statement for your family) to learn and document their childhood, how they met, their married life, their years of raising children, how they started and built a business, their careers, their hardships, struggles, challenges, victories, and successes. We need this information to help identify where the family and its members are today and why and how they got where they are so we can do our job as the family coach.

The other reason we document the past, present, and desires for the future is to capture the current family's values and principles, what was important to them, and the wisdom they want to pass on so future generations can appreciate and take pride in their heritage. In some cases, we can create a DVD of an interview with dad and mom so they can verbally and visually share their family values and legacy with great-great-grandkids. Dad and mom may have relational issues that have strained or are straining the marriage. There is almost always some discord, hurts, and dissatisfaction between siblings and between parents and children. Everyone and every family have baggage they brought with them into the present and will carry into the future. Significant families understand there will always be problems, but they address them head-on and immediately. That doesn't mean everyone gets everything he or she wants or that issues are solved to everyone's satisfaction, but they can use these difficulties to strengthen relationships and family bonds.

We must understand what happened in the past and how it impacts family dynamics today. Only then can we move forward successfully. Whether wealth is affecting relationships or people are creating money problems, it is critical to know the causes and reasons so we can identity and implement the right solutions.

Where Do You Want to Be?

Clients come to us for many reasons, but the primary reason is that their pasts have dictated where they are presently and they are not satisfied with the results and do not want to repeat their mistakes. We can do nothing about the past, but we can control our future, and that is what they want to do. Even families fortunate enough to be in a good spot now know they cannot maintain that happiness unless they plan to do so, especially when so many people are involved in the family.

There is a good question we learned from Dan Sullivan, who founded Strategic Coach, and we use it every time we meet with a new client for the first time. "If we are sitting here three years from today, what has to have happened in those three years for you to feel good about your progress?" Most advisors engaged in financial planning ask clients when they want to retire, where they plan to send the kids to college, or when and how much they need to fund other savings goals. They ask these questions so they can input the data into their computers and produce twenty- and thirty-year projections. The truth is that no one can even come close to knowing what will happen and how lives change in a twenty- or thirty-year span. We prefer to stay within three-year increments and update every year because that period is at least somewhat predictable and much easier for clients to visualize and buy into. It is also more easily measured to see if we are progressing or falling behind.

When long-term plans are created, clients and the advisors tend to put them on the shelf and forget about them. Even when there are significant life changes such as births, deaths, marriages, divorces, and job changes, most clients do not update their planning and the planners might not be aware of the changes. Remember, the purpose of planning is to anticipate future events and determine those that will help and those that will hurt us and take what action we can take today to prepare.

There are many current and possible future dangers that could keep our clients from achieving progress. Dangers can be financial—a bad economy, job cutbacks or termination, or a large one-time expenditure. They can be physical like medical or health issues, intellectual due to a lack of education or training, or relational such as a divorce. If the dangers are within your control, strategies and tactics can be developed and enacted immediately or over time to overcome them. If they are outside your control, protective measures must be instituted.

Next, we explore the opportunities available that increase the probability of you reaching your objectives. Just because opportunities exist and can be identified does not mean they will be captured. For example, you may have the assets and cash flow to buy a nice home that will increase in value, but you will also need to secure financing you can handle. Qualifying for a loan could be a strength or weakness. One client wanted to fund a charitable trust with stocks from his investment portfolio. He had made a lot of money on them, so he would have been taxed heavily if he sold them. Contributing them to a charitable trust would eliminate the taxes, and the charitable contribution would reduce the taxes he owed on his regular income. However, he had used the stock as collateral for a loan, and a charitable trust cannot hold debt; therefore, the loan had to be paid off first. Again, selling the stock to pay the loan would create taxes and reduce the amount of contribution—an unacceptable solution.

Sometimes, opportunities must be created when it seems none exists. We were able to fund a bank loan that paid off the margin loan, thus freeing up the stock and allowing it to be donated to the charitable trust, giving the client a nice deduction that reduced income taxes in the year of the contribution. The income the client was allowed from the charitable trust was sufficient to pay off the bank loan over five years. The client did not need the income for living expenses, so this created opportunity achieved benefits for the client, the bank got a profitable loan, and the client's alma mater would eventually receive a substantial financial gift.

The final question associated with the three-year question is, "What strengths exist that will help you achieve your objectives?" Like opportunities, these can be a combination of our four Ts of True Wealth; Time, Talent, Training, and Treasures. Usually, the first three are more important than the treasures. Additionally, these do not necessarily have to be limited to one person. Because we work with the entire family, we can identity and tap into strengths available in the entire team. Someone might have the legal or tax training needed or the training and education in buying and selling businesses or investment real estate. Or we have a teacher or educator in the family to help younger children prepare for their future roles in the family enterprise.

But, as is the case with opportunities, strengths are useful only when applied and used properly—and I emphasize *properly*. It is like a torque wrench tightening a bolt: not enough pressure and the bolt could come loose, too much force and the bolt will snap. Dad or one of the children may have leadership experience, but if they dominate and manipulate people and are unwilling to give up some control, they will stifle and dis-incentivize the next generation's ability to properly manage the family's wealth; they will snap the head off the bolt.

Holy Coach: Fathers, do not nag your children. If you are too hard to please, they may want to stop trying. (Colossians 3:21 NCV)

What is important to you about wealth? Have you ever thought about that? Is it a scorecard to see if you are better than or falling behind other people? Is it so you can have expensive toys and showy possessions to impress other people? Maybe wealth is for you all about having fun, partying, traveling, and engaging in thrills and spills activities. There is nothing wrong with any of these, but I can assure you, those pursuits ultimately lead to discontentment and unhappiness because there will never be enough. The new toys or possessions grow old or go out of style quickly, and the newer models becomes must haves.

Think about Apple's phones, tablets, and now watches. We must give Apple's marketing team credit for convincing people they have to spend thousands of dollars every year to own something they don't need and isn't all that different from the one they already have.

But maybe you are someone who understands that money is a tool to achieve goals and not the goal itself. When I describe "treasures" to clients and prospects, I say it is earned and burned—earned in that we either work or invest it to receive a return on our labor or risk taking. But burned has a dual meaning. Unfortunately, the first meaning is the more likely. It is like throwing dollar bills into the fireplace. Money is wasted and improperly used or foolishly invested and disappears into a heap of ashes. Or money can be used like fuel in a car's gas tank to get us to our destination. It's a choice, and inherited money too often winds up in the hands of children who had zero driving lessons and have never been behind the steering wheel of a go-kart much less the metaphorical eighteen-wheeler they will ultimately be responsible for steering and controlling.

If True Wealth is seen as a resource to help family and others become what they are best suited to be and to discover and fulfill their purpose, wealth will be multiplied many times over. As an investment advisor, I encourage clients to invest in sound and prudent financial investments, but as a family coach, I know they will receive a far greater return if they invest their Time, Talent, Training, and Treasures in others. Look around your community, your industry, and your peers and I am sure you will discover that joyful and successful people have learned to engage in people investing.

Holy Coach: I realized the reason people work hard and try to succeed: They are jealous of each other. This, too, is useless, like chasing the wind. (However) Two people are better than one, because they get more done by working together. If one falls down, the other can help him up. But it is bad for the person who is alone and falls, because no one is there to help. If two lie down together, they will be warm, but a person alone will not be warm. An enemy might defeat one person, but two people together can defend themselves; a rope that is woven of three strings is hard to break. (Ecclesiastes 4:4, 9–12 NCV)

If you have not or cannot define what is important to you about wealth and its purpose for your life, you must take the time and get help if necessary to do so. In *Alice in Wonderland*, Alice asks the Cheshire cat for directions because she is unsure where she is going or supposed to go. His response: "If you don't know where you are going my dear, then any road will get you there." If you have no idea what your purpose is, how will you ever know if you have accomplished what you were designed to accomplish? If you have not clarified in your own mind the purpose for your wealth, you will go down many dead-end roads or roads that take you to where you should not and do not want to go.

Holy Coach: There is a way that seems right to a person, but eventually it ends in death. (Proverbs 14:12 GW)

Enter through the narrow gate. For wide is the gate and broad is the road that leads to destruction, and many enter through it. But small is the gate and narrow the road that leads to life, and only a few find it. (Matthew 7:13–14 NIV)

If you are married, gaining clarity about your purpose and how you will use your wealth to achieve personal significance is not enough. A husband and wife must be homogeneous; they both must ask, "Are we together or apart in this effort?" Does your spouse share your purpose for your combined wealth? Through client interviews, we learn quickly where spouses are in agreement or vastly apart. The Holy Coach said, "A rope that is woven of three strings is hard to break." Husband and wife must be united in purpose and very clear about their joint mission if their family is to be significant. They must then unify the others in their family around that mission and purpose. That does not mean everyone is in lockstep like robots. In reality, family members have different goals, objectives, missions, and purposes; the challenge is to meld the individuals into the overall family.

But that is hard. It takes time, insight, patience, training, and coaching. The overall mission and purpose must provide the latitude and flexibility to allow everyone to optimize his or her and the entire family's Time, Talent, Training, and Treasures to be all they were created to be.

A military SEAL team is the epitome of unification. Every member is extremely clear about the team's primary mission, but each soldier is given—in fact must have—the responsibility and authority to execute a specific role to react and adapt to any situation in a split second. A significant family has a SEAL team mentality!

A primary area of disagreement centers on how the children and grandchildren will inherit the family wealth. Although the roles can be reversed, we usually find that mom is the family diplomat and peacemaker and wants all the children to be treated equally. Three sons and daughters, each gets a third; four, and each gets a quarter. Dad is usually more pragmatic and judges his sons and daughters based on their abilities and maturity. Is equal fair? And who defines what is fair?

Holy Coach: The landowner who went out early one morning to hire workers for his vineyard. He agreed to pay the normal daily wage and sent them out to work. At nine o'clock in the morning he was passing through the marketplace and saw some people standing around doing nothing. So he hired them, telling them he would pay them whatever was right at the end of the day. So they went to work in the vineyard. At noon and again at three o'clock he did the same thing. At five o'clock that afternoon he was in town again and saw some more people standing around. He asked them, "Why haven't you been working today?" They replied, "Because no one hired us." The landowner told them, "Then go out and join the others in my vineyard."

That evening he told the foreman to call the workers in and pay them, beginning with the last workers first. When those hired at five o'clock were paid, each received a full day's wage. When those hired first came to get their pay, they assumed they would receive more. But they, too, were paid a day's wage. When they received their pay, they protested to the owner, "Those people worked only one hour, and yet you've paid them just as much as you paid us who worked all day in the scorching heat." He answered one of them, "Friend, I haven't been unfair! Didn't you agree to work all day for the usual wage? Take your money and go. I wanted to pay this last worker the same as you. Is it against the law for me to do what I want with my money? Should you be jealous because I am kind to others?" (Matthew 20:1–15 NLT)

Does equal mean fair? While Dad may be more analytical about who should get what, he might tip the scales through favoritism or manipulation. Again, there is no right or wrong, just differences that must be addressed. It is imperative to understand that the words *equal* and *fair* are not synonyms. Mom wants equal because she believes that is fair. If one out of the three or four children is the leech mentioned in Chapter 1 and every child receives an equal inheritance, I can assure you the remaining children will not feel that was fair. In the above story, equal was certainly not viewed as fair by the workers. Your sons and daughters might be no different from those workers.

The reason heirs make attorneys prosperous is because equal was unfair in someone's mind. Especially when large sums are involved, equal almost always results in destroying the family because it fails to recognize the uniqueness and importance of each person. There is nothing as unequal as the equal treatment of unequals. The uniqueness and individualism of each person and his or her role must be considered.

Holy Coach: Wealth gained through injustice dwindles away, but whoever gathers little by little has plenty. An inheritance quickly obtained in the beginning will never be blessed in the end. (Proverbs 13:11, 20:21 GW)

If you cannot be trusted with worldly riches, then who will trust you with true riches? And if you cannot be trusted with things that belong to someone else, who will give you things of your own? (Luke 16:11–12 NCV)

Likewise, favoritism and manipulation will be resented and rejected; it too will be a catalyst for destruction. As I said in the previous paragraph, significant families constantly observe, analyze, and align rewards with need, ability, responsibility, and leadership.

In this passage, I substituted *child* for *servant* and *man*.

Holy Coach: The kingdom of heaven is like a man going on a trip. He called his children and entrusted some money to them. He gave one child ten thousand dollars, another four thousand dollars, and another two thousand dollars. Each was given money based on his ability. Then the man went on his trip. The one who received ten thousand dollars invested the money at once and doubled his money. The one who had four thousand dollars did the same and also doubled his money. But the one who received two thousand dollars went off, dug a hole in the ground, and hid his master's money.

After a long time, the master of those children returned and settled accounts with them. The one who received ten thousand dollars brought the additional ten thousand. He said, "Sir, you gave me ten thousand dollars. I've doubled the amount." His master replied, "Good job! You're a good and faithful child! You proved that you could be trusted with a small amount. I will put you in charge of a large amount. Come and share your master's happiness." The one who received four thousand dollars came and said, "Sir, you gave me four thousand dollars. I've doubled the amount."

His master replied, "Good job! You're a good and faithful child! You proved that you could be trusted with a small amount. I will put you in charge of a large amount. Come and share your master's happiness." Then the one who received two thousand dollars came and said, "Sir, I knew that you are a hard person to please. You harvest where you haven't planted and gather where you haven't scattered any seeds. I was afraid. So I hid your two thousand dollars in the ground. Here's your money!" His master responded, "You evil and lazy child! If you knew that I harvest where I haven't planted and gather where I haven't scattered, then you should have invested my money with the bankers. When I returned, I would have received my money back with interest. Take the two thousand dollars away from him! Give it to the one who has the ten thousand! To all who have, more will be given, and they will have more than enough. But everything will be taken away from those who don't have much." (Matthew 25:14–29 GW)

Finally, everything I have just said must be documented. There are at least four primary reasons for this and why we draft a Family Wealth Significance Statement for our families. One is to capture the family history. Two is to document what is happening right now and set the stage for where the family needs to go. Three is laying out the plan in detail as to the roles needed, who will fill those roles, and the blueprint for accomplishing the plan. The fourth purpose is to provide information to everyone—family and advisors—as to the values, principles, and purpose that are important to the family so every generation will have clarity on what is expected of them and most of all that they are expected to carry on the mission.

Let me use the Bible as my example. The Bible has two major sections with four subsections. God constructed the Bible linearly— past, present, and future. The Old Testament is the past section. God identified the Israelites as His chosen people, His family, and their mission and purpose was to set up and implement God's plan for spreading His Word and love throughout the world and pass it on from generation to generation. It provides rules and laws (the Commandments) that if followed would prosper and benefit the entire family of God. It also describes how the family consistently self-destructed every time it failed to obey the plan.

The second component in the Old Testament is prophecy, which enabled every generation of Israelites then and the reader today to understand the overall plan and what to expect will happen in the future as the plan unfolds; it provides metrics that confirm that the plan is real and being achieved as each prophecy is fulfilled. In effect, it is an action plan that we can follow and check off as each action is completed.

The New Testament too has two subsections. The first four books, the Gospels, are the present section, chronicling the life and mission of Jesus Christ, God's Son, from His birth to His crucifixion.

The rest of the New Testament is the future section. Its purpose is to provide details for how the family (the church) should prepare family members for their roles in the family. It helps them define, develop, and implement their purpose using their God-given Time, Talent, Training, and Treasures to accomplish the overall family purpose and again how to transfer those values and principles to subsequent generations. In doing so, each person will find significance.

The Family Wealth Significance Statement is effectively the family's bible.

CHAPTER 3

Your Family's Conflict

Now that we've developed your family's story, we have to confront a danger that threatens to destroy your family's legacy: conflict. Much of this would have been uncovered when we revisited past and present family relationships, but now they must be addressed and reconciled if possible. Families and wealth are often in conflict for many reasons. There is no perfect family because families are made up of imperfect people with different personalities, desires, education, and experiences, and that is just in the blood family. Then the sons and daughters grow up and marry and they bring strangers into the family who come from their own dysfunctional families.

Of course, they start having children and, in a relatively short time, three generations representing different environments and cultures are expected to like and support each other. The probability of that happening is extremely low unless there is a purposeful, well-designed, and well-executed plan in place as well as a willingness by everyone to make it successful and invest the time, energy, emotions, and resources necessary.

The First Family

No, I am not referring to our president's family. Let me defer to the Holy Coach.

Holy Coach: Then God said, "Let us make mankind in our image, in our likeness, so that they may rule over the fish in the sea and the birds in the sky, over the livestock and all the wild animals, and over all the creatures that move along the ground." So God created mankind in his own image, in the image of God he created them; male and female he created them. The Lord God took the man and put him in the Garden of Eden to work it and take care of it. And the Lord God commanded the man, "You are free to eat from any tree in the garden; but you must not eat from the tree of the knowledge of good and evil, for when you eat from it you will certainly die." The Lord God said, "It is not good for the man to be alone. I will make a helper suitable for him." (Genesis 1:26–27, 2:15–18 NIV)

God created Adam and Eve for two primary purposes: to be good stewards of the resources He put in their care, and to build a family that would be a legacy for all humanity. But humans do not always heed wisdom. Immediately there was conflict between good and evil, man and God, a need to control versus obedience, husband and wife, and brother with brother, and families have been torn apart ever since trying to deal with these same conflicts, as you will see later.

Worry & Fear

We worry a lot; we naturally think of the worst-case scenario. Psychologists' couches are occupied by patients suffering from worry and anxiety. One reason we gather and hoard wealth is because we are afraid we will lose it, or it will be taken away, or it will run out too soon. That fear turns money into our master. It starts using us rather than us using it for our enjoyment and to help others. Who owns whom? We do not own anything because we came into this world with nothing and will leave it in the same way. Why then do we worry about what is not ours?

We live in a world filled with risks. Fear might cause me to stay in bed rather than driving to work. Many people are so fearful of losing money that they do nothing with what they have, and inflation will eat it away. Parents might worry that divulging their net worth and estate plan to their children will dis-incentivize them to be productive but still have the conversation. Contrast that to parents who do nothing and avoid the conversation. When their heirs get control of the wealth, they are unprepared to manage it properly and their parents' fears become reality—they squander it!

Here is a paradox. People pursue wealth and buy things in the belief that it will make their lives worry free. Then they spend more money buying safes, security systems, and insurance and even hiring guards because they worry their things will be lost or stolen. They spend money they did not have to spend had they not spent money on those unnecessary and expensive things in the first place. They invest in the stock market, commodities, collectibles, and businesses and lay awake at night worrying whether their stocks will decline, their businesses fail, or the economy will go into the tank. Since I am an investment advisor, I want my clients to be invested prudently, and the things I just itemized are good and valid investments. But my point is that wealth does not eliminate worry, it increases it.

Holy Coach: The rich can be sued for everything they have, but the poor are free of such threats. (Proverbs 13:8 MSG)

This is not to say we should not plan for the unknown or save up for that rainy day or the time when we can no longer produce income because of disability or age. Being good stewards requires that we use what we have been given wisely and judiciously. The fear creeps in when we are unwise and spend frivolously, when we realize our assets are dwindling rapidly.

Another worry that is becoming more prevalent is parents concerned about what inherited wealth will do to their children and grandchildren. Because of my work with coaching families, I concur that this is a legitimate fear, but it can be eliminated by getting the proper help and instituting the right solutions.

Holy Coach: Don't store up treasures here on earth, where moths eat them and rust destroys them, and where thieves break in and steal. Store your treasures in heaven, where moths and rust cannot destroy, and thieves do not break in and steal. Wherever your treasure is, there the desires of your heart will also be. And why worry about your clothing? Look at the lilies of the field and how they grow. They don't work or make their clothing, yet Solomon in all his glory was not dressed as beautifully as they are. And if God cares so wonderfully for wildflowers that are here today and thrown into the fire tomorrow, he will certainly care for you.

Why do you have so little faith? So don't worry about these things, saying, "What will we eat? What will we drink? What will we wear?" These things dominate the thoughts of unbelievers, but your heavenly Father already knows all your needs. Seek the Kingdom of God above all else, and live righteously, and he will give you everything you need. So don't worry about tomorrow, for tomorrow will bring its own worries. Today's trouble is enough for today. (Matthew 6:19–21, 24–34 NLT)

We worry about what we cannot control, but we control nothing except our reactions to events in our lives. We worry about tomorrow because we have no idea what tomorrow holds, and even if we could know, we cannot control it. We can control only how we react to it. What value is there in worrying about what we can do nothing to change? We can and should prepare properly; this is the right reaction for what we can know and what is unknown. If we have prepared properly, anxiety goes away.

Worry is a negative only when it turns into fear. Worry can be a positive when it induces action to keep the worry from turning into fear. If in my example of the heirs, the worry causes the parents to get help in designing and executing a sound plan for the wealth transfer, that is a good thing.

Holy Coach: And He said to His disciples, "For this reason I say to you, do not worry about your life, as to what you will eat; nor for your body, as to what you will put on. For life is more than food, and the body more than clothing. Consider the ravens, for they neither sow nor reap; they have no storeroom nor barn, and yet God feeds them; how much more valuable you are than the birds! And which of you by worrying can add a single hour to his life's span? If then you cannot do even a very little thing, why do you worry about other matters? Consider the lilies, how they grow: they neither toil nor spin; but I tell you, not even Solomon in all his glory clothed himself like one of these. But if God so clothes the grass in the field, which is alive today and tomorrow is thrown into the furnace, how much more will He clothe you? You men of little faith! And do not seek what you will eat and what you will drink, and do not keep worrying. For all these things the nations of the world eagerly seek; but your Father knows that you need these things. But seek His kingdom, and these things will be added to you." (Luke 12:22–31 NASB)

The key words in this passage are in the last sentence. After describing all the worry-related issues, we are told to seek the right solution. Though we are told not to worry, I have found that to be impossible. In Scripture, worry and faith are considered opposites. I think this is valid if worry leads a person to fear. However, I also believe that worry can lead us to a stronger faith. It may even be said that without worry, faith is not required.

Whether in a spiritual, relational, or financial sense, worry can cause us to identify where and in what or whom we should correctly place our faith. Trust in a family can easily be destroyed and faith can be lost. However, if our worries cause us to seek wisdom and assistance from family members or friends, our faith in those persons and possibly the entire family structure will be reinforced considerably.

There is another form of fear I've seen in families. Dad and Mom fear their children will not like them if they don't buy them everything they want. They don't state it that way, but that is what it is. Usually, they will rationalize it as love. "I demonstrate my love for my children and grandchildren by buying them everything they want." Or they give their children a very large inheritance because they want the children and grandchildren to fondly remember them. Love cannot be measured in dollars. Often, inheritances produce the opposite effect, especially if the sons and daughters disagree with how the estate was allocated. If one son or daughter gets more than another or gets an asset a brother or sister wanted, they believe their parents loved one more than the other, and they will resent it. Even if everyone gets an equal share, some inevitably believe they deserve more and will carry dislike and discontent, not love, for Dad and Mom for not doing so.

Deception & Mistrust

The person we should worry about the most when we think about being deceived is often ourselves. We have a tremendous ability to lie to ourselves and believe that everything is fine when in fact we are self-destructing. We don't necessarily do it intentionally, but we can be our own worst enemy. We believe we know more than we do and don't ask for advice or guidance because our egos get in the way.

Holy Coach: The seed falling among the thorns refers to someone who hears the word, but the worries of this life and the deceitfulness of wealth choke the word, making it unfruitful. (Matthew 13:22 NIV)

While we can deceive ourselves, we also lie to each other. By far, the primary reason families break down is because trust has been destroyed and communication is minimal, if not nonexistent. Spouses make decisions about shared assets and income without consulting each other often with devastating financial results. One person buys an expensive luxury that the other person doesn't want, and money that was supposed to provide a comfortable retirement is gone, essentially robbing that person's future. One child lies about his or her needs, getting the parents to fund a lifestyle that is unhealthy physically, emotionally, and spiritually. They also steal from siblings and grandchildren who should have received an inheritance.

When they are small, siblings tell lies about each other all the time to gain an advantage over the other for something. Every parent has heard, "That's not fair!" or "Why does she get to have that and I don't?" Unfortunately, those same attitudes and rivalries carry over into adulthood in most families.

Holy Coach: You must not steal. You must not testify falsely against your neighbor. (Exodus 20:15–16 NLT)

The primary reason relationships at any level and especially in families are destroyed is due to a breakdown in trust. Trust is an attribute that is easily lost and very difficult to regain. Trust is more easily achieved in a new relationship before anyone has the occasion to stumble, but once lost, it might never be found again. This is especially true in families whose members live together intimately for so many years. We know each other's strengths and weaknesses, and we learn how to manipulate and use those to our own advantage to get what we want.

There can be more trust between friends than between family members. Dad assures his son he will be at his little league or soccer games but repeatedly doesn't make it or shows up for the last few minutes, so the son learns he cannot trust Dad to do what he says he will do. Siblings fight over something they both want; Mom says neither can have it, but later, one of them works Mom into giving it to him or her rather than the other. That sibling's trust in Mom and the brother or sister will be destroyed. Trust is a fragile commodity that is easily destroyed by what might seem to be small, inconsequential, and sometimes unintentional actions and events that occur over many years. They get buried and hidden, but they do not die. They erupt in the future, especially when there is money and valuable assets on the line.

Holy Coach: The trustworthy person will get a rich reward, but a person who wants quick riches will get into trouble. (Proverbs 28:20 NLT)

One would think the family should be a safe haven in which its members could express their fears and weaknesses without worrying someone in the family will take advantage of them for his or her personal gain, but unfortunately, we know that is more often not the case. There can be many reasons, but I believe it boils down to the fact that we are all self-centered; caring more about others—even our own family members—does not come naturally.

Trust is an attitude that convinces me to think I can be confident you will never do anything intentionally that will hurt me. Trust is eroded when I fear this is not true or you hurt me physically or emotionally. Building trust requires intention, discipline, and work. You must be constantly on guard and aware of dangerous attitudes, actions, and unkind words in yourself and others and reveal them immediately. If undiagnosed, distrust is a cancer that spreads quickly, but it can be cured when identified and properly addressed, and the earlier the better.

Holy Coach: The one who was my friend attacks his friends and breaks his promises. (Psalm 55:20 NCV)

Beware of your neighbors. Don't trust your relatives. Every relative cheats. Every neighbor goes around slandering. (Jeremiah 9:4 GW)

The people of Judah will be put to shame because that nation can't help them. That nation can't give aid or help to them. It can only offer shame and disgrace. (Isaiah 30:5 GW)

Trust has five essential components all of which must be in place. If even one is missing or weak, trust will not be achieved. I talk about these in a later chapter, but one is competency. Have you ever heard, "Don't let your mouth write a check your body cannot cash"? We sometimes say we will do something we have no ability to do. It may be because we do not want to look bad or we want the other person to do something for us or get us something we want, so we make a promise we know we cannot keep. Do that a couple of times and people will learn quickly not to trust what you say.

Holy Coach: It is better not to promise anything than to promise something and not do it. (Ecclesiastes 5:5 NCV)

Think about a relationship and a time when you were involved in a breakdown of trust whether as offender or offended. What was the cause? If you were the offender, were you trying to get something for yourself, win an argument, protect your position or opinion, or had committed a wrongdoing that injured the other person physically or emotionally? Think about your regrets, the words you wish you could retract that were said to a spouse, child, or sibling. Broken trust is almost always the product of our pursuit of self, when we care more about ourselves than about the important people in our lives.

Holy Coach: Don't those who stray plan what is evil, while those who are merciful and faithful plan what is good? (Proverbs 14:22 GW)

I add the words *for others* after the word *good*. You will build and maintain strong trust when you work for others' good rather than your own, and by doing so, you will still get what you want.

As I have said several times, rebuilding trust takes diligence, intention, effort, and a lot of time. Just saying you are a changed person and will do better will not cut it.

Holy Coach: Please swear by the Lord that you'll be as kind to my father's family as I've been to you. Also give me some proof. (Joshua 2:12 GW)

Walking the talk consistently and constantly must become a way of life for the historically untrustworthy person who wants to regain trust. He or she must give lots of signs along the way. The good news is that we all start out with other people assuming we are trustworthy. The bad news is that that stops when we do something to break that trust. We may even receive some latitude for a couple of failures, but usually, the three-strike rule applies. Better to be conscious of how easily we can all strike out and work hard on our batting skills so we get to keep coming up to the plate than be thrown off the team (family).

Communication

Trust and communication are inseparable. We have all been the recipient or perpetrator of saying or hearing a promise to do something only to be disappointed, so from then on, we do not trust or are not trusted. In such cases, we were not focused on our interests and did nothing evil; we just didn't communicate well, so our expectations and the other person's expectations were different. We did exactly, at least in our own minds, what we said we would do. However, the other people had different perspectives and images of the anticipated outcomes, so trust was lost. No one did anything wrong. It was just a misunderstanding!

Holy Coach: Anyone with ears to hear should listen and understand. (Mark 4:23 NLT)

Listen as Wisdom calls out. Hear as understanding raises her voice! (Proverbs 8:1 NLT)

Better to hear the quiet words of a wise person than the shouts of a foolish king. (Ecclesiastes 9:17 NLT)

"Honestly!" Like many of you, I will preface a statement with that word. When I do that with one client, he always responds, "Oh, now you're going to be honest? I guess you weren't being honest before!" He knows I am always honest with him, but he likes to give me a hard time—it's a game we play. My part is to remind him that I use the word *honestly* when I am about to tell him something I think he doesn't want to hear. The question is not about my honesty but whether he is willing to accept some honest criticism, suggestion, or instruction I am about to drop on him. So now it is your turn. Honestly, you don't listen very well! Now that I got that off my chest, neither do I nor anyone else.

This is becoming an even bigger problem in a world in which people can't take their eyes off their smartphone screen long enough to see if the person talking is even moving his or her mouth. Even if we do make eye contact, do we hear and understand what others are trying to communicate to us? The reason we do not hear is because we are thinking about ourselves and are more concerned about what is happening in our lives than what the other person is dealing with, what he is thinking or feeling, or the need or hurt she is sharing in hopes of having found a friendly and compassionate ear.

Honestly (there is that word again), we love to hear ourselves talk about ourselves. Or we become more concerned about defending our position, our actions, or something we said than truly trying to understand what others are saying or feeling. I will confess that the disagreements I have with my wife, though they are few, can go on longer or grow bigger because I get defensive rather than hearing her feelings. Sound familiar? Feelings aren't right or wrong, but they determine our actions and reactions to circumstances and people. They may not even be valid, but if we are not hearing and understanding the feelings behind the words, we will be unable to mend a damaged relationship. Do you really listen to your children? Will they even try to communicate with you, or have they given up because their words fall on deaf ears?

Holy Coach: Why can't you understand what I am saying? It's because you can't even hear me! (John 8:43 NLT)

My dear brothers and sisters, take note of this: Everyone should be quick to listen, slow to speak and slow to become angry, because human anger does not produce the righteousness that God desires. (James 1:19–20 NIV)

How long before you stop talking. Speak sense if you want us to answer! (Job 18:2 NLT)

Should I continue to wait, now that you are silent? Must I also remain silent? No, I will say my piece. I will speak my mind. For I am full of pent-up words, and the spirit within me urges me on. I am like a cask of wine without a vent, like a new wineskin ready to burst! I must speak to find relief, so let me give my answers. I won't play favorites or try to flatter anyone. I speak with all sincerity; I speak the truth. (Job 32:16–21, 33:3 NLT)

Another component of trust in communication is confidentiality, the direct opposite of gossip. Confidentiality means whatever someone shares with another person stays with that person; gossiping means we tell everyone. In addition to the obvious destruction of trust, another devastating result of gossip is much of what is passed on is not true. If you ever played the telephone game when you were a child, you will understand what I am saying. In the telephone game, the first person whispers something to the next person, who then passes on what they heard to the next, and the next, and so on. When the last person in the lineup states what they have heard, it is usually quite different from what was said at the start.

Gossips don't tell just one person; they spread their gossip like manure, and they always tell these secrets to other gossips in hopes of hearing gossip in return. Even if the first conveyance of a piece of gossip was somewhat accurate, by the time it works its way through numerous iterations, the message will have been distorted, and this can result in rejection, shame, destroyed reputations, divorce, and damaged personal relationships that can never be mended. Sadly, this is another virus that infects many families, especially wealthy families in which financial gains can be the reward for a little "innocent" gossip. Siblings talk about each other to each other, sometimes ganging up on one. Or they talk about the other person's spouse, or sometimes they pit one parent against the other. This is often the case in blended families.

Holy Coach: A gossip goes around telling secrets, but those who are trustworthy can keep a confidence. Those who control their tongue will have a long life; opening your mouth can ruin everything. A troublemaker plants seeds of strife; gossip separates the best of friends. There is more hope for a fool than for someone who speaks without thinking. (Proverbs 11:13, 13:3, 29:28 NLT)

My experience shows that those who plant trouble and cultivate evil will harvest the same. (Job 4:8 NLT)

Dissatisfaction, Desires, and Greed

We are never satisfied. Marketing firms rely on discontent to sell us everything we do not need. I was once told, and I believe it is true, that a luxury once acquired becomes a necessity.

Houses and cars are meant to shelter and transport us. Cars are a necessity in our world today, but does a $100,000 vehicle get us to our destination faster than a $25,000 one? Sure, the more expensive car has more gimmickry and comfort features and probably burns more fuel, but as long as they both have air conditioning, power steering, and power windows is all that other stuff really worth another $75,000? I have obviously just clued you in to at least three of my biases. I'm sure you are thinking about arguments right now about why that price tag is justifiable. But ask yourself, "Really?"

Does a 4,000- or 5,000-square-foot home provide more protection from the elements than a 2,000-square-foot home does? Does a sixty-inch flat screen get shows we can't get on a thirty-seven-inch screen? I am not suggesting it is wrong to own nice things, only that we should ask ourselves why we are buying expensive examples of this or that when less-expensive alternatives exist and whether we have better uses for the money.

Holy Coach: Those who love money will never have enough. How meaningless to think that wealth brings true happiness! The more you have, the more people come to help you spend it. So what good is wealth—except perhaps to watch it slip through your fingers! (Ecclesiastes 5:10–11 NLT)

Going back to my car example, assuming you hold the $100,000 car for ten years and sell it; perhaps you would get $25,000 for it. However, investing the $75,000 you kept by buying the less-expensive car at that 6 percent annual return would have given you $134,000 in ten years.

Spending $100,000 and having $25,000 at the end of ten years instead of $134,000 certainly sounds like watching it slip through your fingers.

Holy Coach: The leech has two suckers that cry out, "More, more!" There are three things that are never satisfied—no, four that never say, "Enough!" (You can fill in the four you chose) (Proverbs 30:15 NLT)

You can fill in the four things that are never satisfied as you wish. Okay, "leech" is a little severe, but it is not necessarily a description of a person as much as a person's attitude, unless it describes those people in the previous verses who become your best friends when they know you will pay the tab. The point is we can easily succumb to "The more I have, the more I want" attitude if we are not diligent.

Holy Coach: Don't be obsessed with getting more material things. Be relaxed with what you have. (Hebrews 13:5 MSG)

Key in this statement is that word *relaxed*. Ask yourself, does life get more complex or simpler the more things I own? Do I worry more the more I own? If I have less to lose, do I worry less? Again, owning things is not bad unless they start to own you!

Holy Coach: For I have learned to be content whatever the circumstances. I know what it is to be in need, and I know what it is to have plenty. I have learned the secret of being content in any and every situation, whether well fed or hungry, whether living in plenty or in want. I can do all this through him who gives me strength. (Philippians 4:11–13 NIV)

Question here: are you content right now with what you have and where you are in life? If not, will owning more things bring you contentment? If you answer yes to this last question, then please describe exactly what you need to own or how much more money you must have to bring you contentment and why it would do that. Finally, ask these same questions as to how you think your spouse and your children would answer them.

"I want it!" The questions are, What do you want? Why? Will it help or hurt you or anyone else? Within a family, satisfying one person's desires means someone else in the family must give up something he or she wants or needs. Depending on the severity of everyone's wants and needs, conflicts are almost sure to ensue.

Holy Coach: What is causing the quarrels and fights among you? Don't they come from the evil desires at war within you? You want what you don't have, so you scheme and kill to get it. (James 4:1–2 NLT)

Uncurbed desire is hazardous to a person's physical, mental, and spiritual health. Children who get everything they want most often become spoiled brats and grow up to be leeches. We unfortunately live in a world that caters to every sensual desire a person can experience—drugs, alcohol, food, sex, fame, fun, work, and money to name a few.

None of these is bad in itself (illegal drugs excluded), but when indulged in to excess, they can destroy marriages, families, careers, relationships, and lives. Wealth, or more accurately the pursuit of wealth for selfish reasons, is a subtle drug that can easily addict anyone not equipped to manage it wisely as a tool rather than worshipping it as a god.

Holy Coach: So prepare your minds for action and exercise self-control. So you must live as God's obedient children. Don't slip back into your old ways of living to satisfy your own desires. You didn't know any better then. (1 Peter 1:13a, 14 NLT)

The *American Heritage Dictionary* defines *greed* as "an excessive desire to acquire or possess more than what one needs or deserves, especially with respect to material wealth." The first four words are *excessive desire, needs,* and *deserves.* Excessive desire implies being out of control. We all want what we need and deserve and maybe even more, but excessive desire is obsession, "a compulsive, often unreasonable idea or emotion (*American Heritage Dictionary*). The *Collins English Dictionary* adds that *greed* "often is associated with anxiety and mental illness." Needs are relatively identifiable and quantifiable. Food, water, air, clothing, shelter, and in today's world, transportation and communication are viable needs; but we should be careful we don't move into the "excessive desire" zone on clothes, shelter, transportation, and communication. What we deserve is more subjective and possibly more deceptive.

Who decides what we deserve? Do we decide for ourselves? If so, who says that what we believe we deserve is what we deserve? Socialist governments decide what its citizens deserve. In a capitalist society, others decide. Our employer and our clients dictate our income. Lenders determine how much we can borrow, how and when we must repay it, and how much it will cost us. Some evidently deserve better terms and availability than others. Oh yes, the country club may or may not accept you, but that probably depends on what you are willing to pay. And the big one, the IRS, believes it deserves what we have more than we deserve it. We call it income, estate, inheritance, and gift taxes. It is a great deal. The government didn't earn it, didn't take any risk, but it gets about 50 percent of what we have when we die.

The words I think need to be added are, "at the detriment to someone else." Yes, we are all subject to greed. Honestly (remember, this means I'm about to tell you something you may not want to hear), you have an excessive desire to acquire what you do not need or deserve. It gets dangerous and destructive to your family and yourself when it becomes wanting and taking what you do not need or deserve at the detriment of someone else. This is what happens when dad and mom's estate is being settled and the children are hiring their own attorneys to get what they each believe they "need and deserve" and their siblings do not "need or deserve." Wait a minute! If greed is taking what someone else has worked for and deserves away from them so I can have what I didn't work for and do not deserve, is that a definition of taxes? The Holy Coach has a lot to say about greed.

Holy Coach: Greed brings grief to the whole family, but those who hate bribes will live. An angry person starts fights; a hot-tempered person commits all kinds of sin. (Proverbs 15:27, 29:22 NLT)

Holy Coach: Then Jesus said to them, "Beware, and be on your guard against every form of greed; for not even when one has an abundance does his life consist of his possessions." And He told them a parable, saying, "The land of a rich man was very productive. And he began reasoning to himself, saying, 'What shall I do, since I have no place to store my crops?' Then he said, 'This is what I will do: I will tear down my barns and build larger ones, and there I will store all my grain and my goods. And I will say to my soul, "Soul, you have many goods laid up for many years to come; take your ease, eat, drink and be merry.'" But God said to him, 'You fool! This very night your soul is required of you; and now who will own what you have prepared?' So is the man who stores up treasure for himself, and is not rich toward God." (Luke 12:15–21 NASB)

There is only one solution to greed.

Holy Coach: Give, and you will receive. Your gift will return to you in full—pressed down, shaken together to make room for more, running over, and poured into your lap. The amount you give will determine the amount you get back. (Luke 6:38 NLT)

Do nothing from selfishness or empty conceit, but with humility of mind. Regard one another as more important than yourselves; do not merely look out for your own personal interests, but also for the interests of others. (Philippians 2:3–4 NASB)

I used the Eden story as an example of how pride can ruin our lives, but it also demonstrates the problems we create when we act on our emotions rather than taking the time to think through the consequences of our actions and decisions. What if Eve, instead of immediately reacting to the temptation, had said, "Serpent, I need some time to give this more thought, talk it over with Adam, and run it by God. If everyone thinks it's a good idea, I'll get back to you and we can move forward"?

A teenage shepherd boy picked up five smooth stones from a brook and went off to challenge a giant in a duel between armor and a sword and a slingshot. The smooth rock sunk deep into the giant's forehead, and the teenager was victorious over Goliath as he collapsed and died at David's feet. David later became a warrior and commander and was appointed by God to be the second king of the Israelites. But kings are men, and all men give into the temptation of wanting what they should not have.

Holy Coach: Now when evening came David arose from his bed and walked around on the roof of the king's house, and from the roof he saw a woman bathing; and the woman was very beautiful in appearance. So David sent and inquired about the woman. And one said, "Is this not Bathsheba, the daughter of Eliam, the wife of Uriah the Hittite" David sent messengers and took her, and when she came to him, he lay with her; and when she had purified herself from her uncleanness, she returned to her house. The woman conceived; and she sent and told David, and said, "I am pregnant." Then David sent to Joab, saying, "Send me Uriah the Hittite."

So Joab sent Uriah to David. When Uriah came to him, David asked concerning the welfare of Joab and the people and the state of the war. Then David said to Uriah, "Go down to your house, and wash your feet." And Uriah went out of the king's house, and a present from the king was sent out after him. But Uriah slept at the door of the king's house with all the servants of his lord, and did not go down to his house. Now when they told David, saying, "Uriah did not go down to his house," David said to Uriah, "Have you not come from a journey? Why did you not go down to your house?" Uriah said to David, "The ark and Israel and Judah are staying in temporary shelters, and my lord Joab and the servants of my lord are camping in the open field. Shall I then go to my house to eat and to drink and to lie with my wife? By your life and the life of your soul, I will not do this thing."

Then David said to Uriah, "Stay here today also, and tomorrow I will let you go." So Uriah remained in Jerusalem that day and the next. Now David called him, and he ate and drank before him, and he made him drunk; and in the evening he went out to lie on his bed with his lord's servants, but he did not go down to his house. Now in the morning David wrote a letter to Joab and sent it by the hand of Uriah. He had written in the letter, saying, "Uriah in the front line of the fiercest battle and withdraw from him, so that he may be struck down and die." So it was as Joab kept watch on the city, that he put Uriah at the place where he knew there were valiant men. The men of the city went out and fought against Joab, and some of the people among David's servants fell; and Uriah the Hittite also died.

So the messenger departed and came and reported to David all that Joab had sent him to tell. The messenger said to David, "The men prevailed against us and came out against us in the field, but we [g]pressed them as far as the entrance of the gate. Moreover, the archers shot at your servants from the wall; so some of the king's servants are dead, and your servant Uriah the Hittite is also dead. Then David said to the messenger, "Thus you shall say to Joab, 'Do not let this thing displease you, for the sword devours one as well as another; make your battle against the city stronger and overthrow it'; and so encourage him." Now when the wife of Uriah heard that Uriah her husband was dead, she mourned for her husband. When the time of mourning was over, David sent and brought her to his house and she became his wife; then she bore him a son. But the thing that David had done was evil in the sight of the Lord. (2 Samuel 11:2–7 NASB)

The baby born of this unholy union would die at birth. David's commander and friend confronted him, and David confessed and repented, but there was no way to right the terrible wrong he had done. A momentary breakdown in integrity and reason coupled with the desire for immediate gratification, and numerous lives were forever changed.

Like Adam and Eve, David had everything he could ever need or want. He had wealth, power, and position, but immediate gratification for what he could not have infected his soul. He didn't go up to the roof that night looking for trouble, but he just let his emotions take over. While we cannot say his wealth was the cause, if he had not been the king, he would not have been on a palace roof that night. Wealth is not the problem, but it does create opportunities to make bad decisions to satisfy the desire for immediate gratification.

Holy Coach: Those who want to become rich bring temptation to themselves and are caught in a trap. They want many foolish and harmful things that ruin and destroy people. The love of money causes all kinds of evil. Some people have left the faith, because they wanted to get more money, but they have caused themselves much sorrow. (1 Timothy 6:9–10 NCV)

They are looking for profits and do not control their selfish desires. (Psalm 73:7 NCV)

Wealth can make people feel they deserve something they would not be able to buy if they did not have the wealth!

Ungratefulness

People who believe they are entitled to or owed something are not grateful when they receive it. Kids showered with gifts and everything they want throughout their lives will not appreciate an inheritance in the sense of understanding it is a gift and not something they have a right to. As I said previously, parents will go out of their way and will sacrifice what they may need to keep for themselves to win the favor of their children and grandchildren—all they ask for is a thank you. They may hear the words, but that does not mean the recipient is truly grateful.

A good way to test this is to stop giving. Grandma is paying the monthly cell phone or iPad fee. Dad is putting gas in junior's car. Well, it isn't junior's since Dad paid for it. Stop paying for it and see how much gratitude grandma gets from her granddaughter or dad gets from junior. It will probably sound more like indignation and resentment. "How could you?" or "You can't do that!" will be the more likely responses. Before we pass judgment on these ungrateful kids, we should ask ourselves, *Did my generosity create this?*

Holy Coach: Some people curse their father and do not thank their mother. They are pure in their own eyes, but they are filthy and unwashed. They look proudly around, casting disdainful glances. They have teeth like swords and fangs like knives. They devour the poor from the earth and the needy from among humanity. (Proverbs 30:11–14 NLT)

Are you a grateful person? Do you acknowledge that everything you have—air, good health, children, freedoms, and ability to work, imagine, and pursue your goals—are all gifts? I am sorry to tell you this, but you do not deserve or have a right to anything you have. You will say, "Wait a minute! I worked hard for what I own. I got an education, I worked my way through college, I got a job, and I climbed the ladder of success because of my skills and intelligence. I am a self-made person." I applaud you, but how did you get the intelligence and inborn skills that make you you? Who brought you into this world, nurtured you, cared for you, and imparted wisdom to you? If you were born in America, what role did you play in securing the freedom to do whatever you want when and where you want? Who made it possible for you to pursue the career you chose and your dreams?

Look around you. Visit a country in the developing world where poverty, disease, squalor, and death are daily realities. How different might your life and that of your family be if you embraced gratitude rather than having attitude? In my experience, people who are truly thankful for everything they have been given become givers and in return receive more than they ever expected and are happier and have more fulfilled and joyful lives.

Holy Coach: While Jesus was on his way to Jerusalem, he was going through the area between Samaria and Galilee. As he came into a small town, ten men who had a skin disease met him there. They did not come close to Jesus but called to him, "Jesus! Master! Have mercy on us!" When Jesus saw the men, he said, "Go and show yourselves to the priests." As the ten men were going, they were healed. When one of them saw that he was healed, he went back to Jesus, praising God in a loud voice. Then he bowed down at Jesus' feet and thanked him. (And this man was a Samaritan.) Jesus said, "Weren't ten men healed? Where are the other nine? Is this Samaritan the only one who came back to thank God?" Then Jesus said to him, "Stand up and go on your way. You were healed because you believed." (Luke 17:11–19 NCV)

Would you be counted with the one or the nine?

I am concluding this section with a real-life story that sums up much of what I have discussed above. King David had everything anyone could want. If anyone could successfully transfer his kingdom and his wealth to his children, he should have been the one.

Holy Coach: David had a son named Absalom and a son named Amnon. Absalom had a beautiful sister named Tamar, and Amnon loved her. Tamar was a virgin. Amnon made himself sick just thinking about her, because he could not find any chance to be alone with her. Amnon had a friend named Jonadab son of Shimeah, David's brother. Jonadab was a very clever man. He asked Amnon, "Son of the king, why do you look so sad day after day? Tell me what's wrong!" Amnon told him, "I love Tamar, the sister of my half-brother Absalom." Jonadab said to Amnon, "Go to bed and act as if you are sick. Then your father will come to see you. Tell him, 'Please let my sister Tamar come in and give me food to eat. Let her make the food in front of me so I can watch and eat it from her hand.'" She went to him so he could eat from her hands, but Amnon grabbed her. He said, "Sister, come and have sexual relations with me." Tamar said to him, "No, brother! Don't force me! This should never be done in Israel! Don't do this shameful thing!

But Amnon refused to listen to her. He was stronger than she was, so he forced her to have sexual relations with him. After that, Amnon hated Tamar. He hated her more than he had loved her before. Amnon said to her, "Get up and leave!" When King David heard the news, he was very angry. Absalom did not say a word, good or bad, to Amnon. But he hated Amnon for disgracing his sister Tamar. Two years later Absalom had some men come to Baal Hazor, near Ephraim, to cut the wool from his sheep. Absalom invited all the king's sons to come also.

Absalom said, "If you don't want to come, then please let my brother Amnon come with us." King David asked, "Why should he go with you?" Absalom kept begging David until he let Amnon and all the king's sons go with Absalom. Then Absalom instructed his servants, "Watch Amnon. When he is drunk, I will tell you, 'Kill Amnon.' Right then, kill him! Don't be afraid, because I have commanded you! Be strong and brave!" So Absalom's young men killed Amnon as Absalom commanded, but all of David's other sons got on their mules and escaped. (2 Samuel 13:1–5, 11–12, 14–15, 21–23, 26–29 NCV)

One of King David's commanders, Joab, learned of the murder, but knowing how difficult it would be to directly break the news that his son had raped his daughter, he devised a scheme using a surrogate woman.

Holy Coach: King David asked her, "What is the matter?" The woman said, "I am a widow; my husband is dead. I had two sons. They were out in the field fighting, and no one was there to stop them. So one son killed the other son. Now all the family group is against me. They said to me, 'Bring the son who killed his brother so we may kill him for killing his brother. That way we will also get rid of the one who would receive what belonged to his father.' My son is like the last spark of a fire. He is all I have left. If they kill him, my husband's name and property will be gone from the earth."

Then the king said to the woman, "Go home. I will take care of this for you." King David said, "Bring me anyone who says anything bad to you. Then he won't bother you again."

The woman said, "Please promise in the name of the Lord your God. Then my relative who has the duty of punishing a murderer won't add to the destruction by killing my son." David said, "As surely as the Lord lives, no one will hurt your son. Not one hair from his head will fall to the ground." The woman said, "Let me say something to you, my master and king." The king said, "Speak." Then the woman said, "Why have you decided this way against the people of God? When you judge this way, you show that you are guilty for not bringing back your son who was forced to leave home. We will all die someday. We're like water spilled on the ground; no one can gather it back. But God doesn't take away life. Instead, he plans ways that those who have been sent away will not have to stay away from him! (2 Samuel 14:5–8, 10–14 NCV)

Meanwhile, Absalom, Ahithophel, and all the Israelites arrived at Jerusalem. Absalom said to Ahithophel, "Tell us what we should do." Ahithophel said, "Your father left behind some of his slave women to take care of the palace. Have sexual relations with them. Then all Israel will hear that your father is your enemy, and all your people will be encouraged to give you more support." So they put up a tent for Absalom on the roof of the palace where everyone in Israel could see it. And Absalom had sexual relations with his father's slave women. Ahithophel said to Absalom, "Let me choose twelve thousand men and chase David tonight. I'll catch him while he is tired and weak, and I'll frighten him so all his people will run away. But I'll kill only King David. Then I'll bring everyone back to you. If the man you are looking for is dead, everyone else will return safely."

This plan seemed good to Absalom and to all the leaders of Israel. "This is what I suggest: Gather all the Israelites from Dan to Beersheba. There will be as many people as grains of sand by the sea. Then you yourself must go into the battle. We will go to

David wherever he is hiding. We will fall on him as dew falls on the ground. We will kill him and all of his men so that no one will be left alive. If David escapes into a city, all the Israelites will bring ropes to that city and pull it into the valley. Not a stone will be left!" Absalom and all the Israelites said, "The advice of Hushai the Arkite is better than that of Ahithophel." (The Lord had planned to destroy the good advice of Ahithophel so the Lord could bring disaster on Absalom.) (2 Samuel 16:15, 20–22, 17:1–4, 11–14 NCV)

David counted his men and placed over them commanders of thousands and commanders of hundreds. He sent the troops out in three groups. Joab commanded one-third of the men. Joab's brother Abishai son of Zeruiah commanded another third. And Ittai from Gath commanded the last third. King David said to them, "I will also go with you." But the men said, "You must not go with us! If we run away in the battle, Absalom's men won't care. Even if half of us are killed, Absalom's men won't care. But you're worth ten thousand of us! You can help us most by staying in the city." The king said to his people, "I will do what you think is best."

David's army went out into the field against Absalom's Israelites, and they fought in the forest of Ephraim. There David's army defeated the Israelites. Many died that day—twenty thousand men. The battle spread through all the country, but that day more men died in the forest than in the fighting. Then Absalom happened to meet David's troops. As Absalom was riding his mule, it went under the thick branches of a large oak tree. Absalom's head got caught in the tree, and his mule ran out from under him. So Absalom was left hanging above the ground. When one of the men saw it happen, he told Joab, "I saw Absalom hanging in an oak tree!" Joab said to him, "You saw him? Why didn't you kill him and let him fall to the ground?

I would have given you a belt and four ounces of silver!" The man answered, "I wouldn't touch the king's son even if you gave me twenty-five pounds of silver. We heard the king command you, Abishai, and Ittai, 'Be careful not to hurt young Absalom.' If I had killed him, the king would have found out, and you would not have protected me!"

Joab said, "I won't waste time here with you!" Absalom was still alive in the oak tree, so Joab took three spears and stabbed him in the heart. Ten young men who carried Joab's armor also gathered around Absalom and struck him and killed him. Then the Cushite arrived. He said, "Master and king, hear the good news! Today the Lord has punished those who were against you!" The king asked the Cushite, "Is young Absalom all right?" The Cushite answered, "May your enemies and all who come to hurt you be like that young man!" Then the king was very upset, and he went to the room over the city gate and cried. As he went, he cried out, "My son Absalom, my son Absalom! I wish I had died and not you. Absalom, my son, my son!" (2 Samuel 18:1–4a, 6–15, 31–33 NCV)

Discontent, deceit, jealousy, hypocrisy, self-centeredness, pride, greed, immediate gratification, competition, infighting, incest, revolt, and ingratitude are just a few of the character flaws that infected one of the most important families in the history of the world. The nation of Israel uses the Star of David on its flag and reveres King David in much the same way Americans think of George Washington.

The lesson in this true story is that no family is exempt from the problems and trials wealth and power can cause. Was wealth the sole cause of the dysfunction? Of course not. Remember, David was just a shepherd boy until he took down Goliath. If he had stayed a shepherd, we would probably not be reading this story today.

Jealousy & Competition

Sometimes, our desires are founded in jealousy.

Holy Coach: Never desire to take your neighbor's household away from him. Never desire to take your neighbor's wife, his male or female slave, his ox, his donkey, or anything else that belongs to him. (Exodus 20:17 GW)

Jealousy is simply wanting what someone else has.

Holy Coach: Then I observed that most people are motivated to success because they envy their neighbors. But this, too, is meaningless—like chasing the wind. (Ecclesiastes 4:4 NLT)

Typically, it is not a case of needing something because I probably already have something equally as good or better, but I want what the other guy has just because he has it and I don't. As my pastor, Rick Warren, says, "We buy things we don't need, with money we don't have, to impress people we don't like." Jealousy is a cancer that eats away our bodies, minds, and souls. It can cause us to sacrifice our integrity on the altar of greed, or worse, to commit crimes against other people, maybe even a family member.

Holy Coach: Adam made love to his wife Eve. She became pregnant and gave birth to Cain. She said, "I have gotten the man that the Lord promised." Then she gave birth to another child, Abel, Cain's brother. Abel was a shepherd, and Cain was a farmer. Later Cain brought some crops from the land as an offering to the Lord. Abel also brought some choice parts of the firstborn animals from his flock. The Lord approved of Abel and his offering, but he didn't approve of Cain and his offering. So Cain became very angry and was disappointed. Then the Lord asked Cain, "Why are you angry, and why do you look disappointed? If you do well, won't you be accepted? But if you don't do well, sin is lying outside your door ready to attack. It wants to control you, but you must master it." Cain talked to his brother Abel. Later, when they were in the fields, Cain attacked his brother Abel and killed him. (Genesis 4:1–8 GW)

Anger is cruel, and fury is overwhelming, but who can survive jealousy? (Proverbs 27:4 GW)

But if you have bitter jealousy and selfish ambition in your heart, do not be arrogant and so lie against the truth. (James 3:14 NASB)

Jealousy and competition are often the reason many families have never been or will never be significant. I am talking about competition with the world and interfamily competition. Competition has its place if it encourages someone to constantly improve, but not if it's based in jealousy. Competition that requires someone else to lose so that I win will create anger, fighting, jealousy, and other bad things families endure. We all know of a family or have heard of families fighting over mom and dad's estate. It is like a boxing match. When the bell rings, everyone comes out swinging with a legal team in tow. Let the competition begin!

Competition with the world is the keeping up with the Jones syndrome. Again, there is nothing wrong with our having more material possessions, income, or extravagant lifestyles as long as our spending is on necessities and we are not going heavily into debt to do so. We all have different needs, wants, desires, and circumstances. One family may feel a motor home for family vacations is right for them while another family prefers flying to vacation spots and staying in hotels. However, if one family's purchase of a new motor home prompts the neighbors to buy a bigger one, that jealousy and one-upmanship becomes destructive. We have all done this to greater or lesser degrees with cars, houses, and toys.

When my grandchildren were younger, I observed how the neighbors tried to one-up each other with their kid's birthday parties. When I was a kid, it was a cake, noisemakers, funny hats, and pin the tail on the donkey. Now, it's water slides, bounce houses, amusement parks, and other big-bucks diversions in order not to be outdone.

Holy Coach: As Jesus and the disciples continued on their way to Jerusalem, they came to a certain village where a woman named Martha welcomed him into her home. Her sister, Mary, sat at the Lord's feet, listening to what he taught. But Martha was distracted by the big dinner she was preparing. She came to Jesus and said, "Lord, doesn't it seem unfair to you that my sister just sits here while I do all the work? Tell her to come and help me." But the Lord said to her, "My dear Martha, you are worried and upset over all these details! There is only one thing worth being concerned about. Mary has discovered it, and it will not be taken away from her." (Luke 10:38–42 NLT)

Competition prompts us to compare ourselves to other people, and that is a losing proposition in that it causes us to become prideful or depressed. There will be only two outcomes. If we believe ourselves to be better than others, we become prideful. If we assess that we are not as good as others, we can become depressed and withdrawn from the world.

Holy Coach: Pay careful attention to your own work, for then you will get the satisfaction of a job well done, and you won't need to compare yourself to anyone else. For we are each responsible for our own conduct. (Galatians 6:4–5 NLT)

Do not judge others, and you will not be judged. Do not condemn others, or it will all come back against you. Forgive others, and you will be forgiven. Give, and you will receive. And why worry about a speck in your friend's eye when you have a log in your own? How can you think of saying, 'Friend, let me help you get rid of that speck in your eye,' when you can't see past the log in your own eye? Hypocrite! First get rid of the log in your own eye; then you will see well enough to deal with the speck in your friend's eye. (Luke 6:37–38, 41–42 NLT)

Lack of Wisdom

Doesn't everyone want wisdom? Unfortunately, no. On the premise that it is wise to do what is best for one's self, it would seem that everyone would welcome wisdom into his or her life, but we know not everyone does.

The reason is that gaining true wisdom requires effort, but there is an even bigger problem: it might require a change in lifestyle, habits, behaviors, and relationships. It is certainly not wise for people to remain in abusive relationships, yet they do. Even when those relationships come to an end, they become involved in another and another.

Obesity is a major health problem in America. Carrying more weight than a body is designed to carry is unwise, but who wants to give up candy, chips, ice cream, and bakery goods and start exercising? Not as many people as need to.

Although I titled this section "Lack of Wisdom," I think it is more an unwillingness to accept wisdom. When we coach individuals and families, we provide them sound strategies, tactics, and actions they can use to improve their lives and relationships and help them learn how to successfully manage and optimize their financial wealth. Most will readily apply what we recommend and teach them, but not everyone. We can demonstrate the logic and financial benefits of spending less and saving more, but to do so may mean giving up something they are unwilling to give up. They reject wisdom so they can cling to what is unwise.

Holy Coach: My child, listen to what I say and remember what I command you. Listen carefully to wisdom; set your mind on understanding. Cry out for wisdom, and beg for understanding. Search for it like silver, and hunt for it like hidden treasure. Then you will understand respect for the Lord, and you will find that you know God. Only the Lord gives wisdom; he gives knowledge and understanding. (Proverbs 6:1–6 NCV)

Breaking the Rules

This is so obvious, I'm not sure I need to devote a lot of space explaining the problems that result when rules are not followed. You already know this! I think I will let the Holy Coach do all the talking on this one.

Holy Coach: God blesses those who obey him; happy the man who puts his trust in the Lord. (Proverbs 16:20 TLB)

The serpent was the shrewdest of all the wild animals the Lord God had made. One day he asked the woman, "Did God really say you must not eat the fruit from any of the trees in the garden?" "Of course we may eat fruit from the trees in the garden," the woman replied. "It's only the fruit from the tree in the middle of the garden that we are not allowed to eat. God said, 'You must not eat it or even touch it; if you do, you will die.'" "You won't die!" the serpent replied to the woman. "God knows that your eyes will be opened as soon as you eat it, and you will be like God, knowing both good and evil." The woman was convinced. She saw that the tree was beautiful and its fruit looked delicious, and she wanted the wisdom it would give her.

So she took some of the fruit and ate it. Then she gave some to her husband, who was with her, and he ate it, too. At that moment their eyes were opened, and they suddenly felt shame at their nakedness. So they sewed fig leaves together to cover themselves. When the cool evening breezes were blowing, the man and his wife heard the Lord God walking about in the garden. So they hid from the Lord God among the trees. Then the Lord God called to the man, "Where are you?" He replied, "I heard you walking in the garden, so I hid. I was afraid because I was naked." "Who told you that you were naked?" the Lord God asked. "Have you eaten from the tree whose fruit I commanded you not to eat?" The man replied, "It was the woman you gave me who gave me the fruit, and I ate it." Then the Lord God asked the woman, "What have you done?" "The serpent deceived me," she replied. "That's why I ate it." Then the Lord God said to the serpent, "Because you have done this, you are cursed more than all animals, domestic and wild. You will crawl on your belly, groveling in the dust as long as you live. And I will cause hostility between you and the woman, and between your offspring and her offspring. He will strike your head, and you will strike his heel." Then he said to the woman,

"I will sharpen the pain of your pregnancy, and in pain you will give birth. And you will desire to control your husband, but he will rule over you."

And to the man he said, "Since you listened to your wife and ate from the tree whose fruit I commanded you not to eat, the ground is cursed because of you. All your life you will struggle to scratch a living from it. It will grow thorns and thistles for you, though you will eat of its grains. By the sweat of your brow will you have food to eat until you return to the ground from which you were made. For you were made from dust, and to dust you will return." So the Lord God banished them from the Garden of Eden, and he sent Adam out to cultivate the ground from which he had been made. (Genesis 3:1–19, 23 NLT) Wow! Breaking the rules is a really bad idea!

Holy Coach: "This is the fate awaiting the wicked from the hand of the Almighty. If he has a multitude of children, it is so that they will die in war or starve to death. Those who survive shall be brought down to the grave by disease and plague, with no one to mourn them, not even their wives. "The evil man may accumulate money like dust, with closets jammed full of clothing—yes, he may order them made by his tailor, but the innocent shall wear that clothing and shall divide his silver among them. Every house built by the wicked is as fragile as a spider web, as full of cracks as a leafy booth! "He goes to bed rich but wakes up to find that all his wealth is gone." (Job 27:13–19 TLB)

People who accept discipline are on the pathway to life, but those who ignore correction will go astray. (Proverbs 10:17 NLT)

The eye that mocks a father and despises a mother's instructions will be plucked out by ravens of the valley and eaten by vultures. (Proverbs 30:17 NLT)

Only a fool despises a parent's discipline; whoever learns from correction is wise. Whoever abandons the right path will be severely disciplined; whoever hates correction will die. If you reject discipline, you only harm yourself; but if you listen to correction, you grow in understanding. (Proverbs 15:5, 10, 32 NLT)

When people do not accept divine guidance, they run wild. But whoever obeys the law is joyful. (Proverbs 29:18 NLT)

What shall I say about the homes of the wicked filled with treasures gained by cheating? . . . Therefore, I will wound you! I will bring you to ruin for all your sins. You will eat but never have enough. Your hunger pangs and emptiness will remain. And though you try to save your money, it will come to nothing in the end. You will save a little, but I will give it to those who conquer you. You will plant crops but not harvest them. You will press your olives but not get enough oil to anoint yourselves. You will trample the grapes but get no juice to make your wine. (Micah 6:10a, 13–15 NLT)

Arrogance

Holy Coach: Before a downfall the heart is haughty, but humility comes before honor. (Proverbs 18:12 NIV)

It is impossible for us to achieve significance if our world revolves around ourselves.

The Holy Coach said above that, "humility comes <u>before</u> honor." He also says, "Blessed are the meek, for they will inherit the earth." (Matthew 5:5 NIV)

What do you think of when you hear the words *meek* and *humble*? Most people associate meekness with weaknesses or being timid and fearful. The *Collins English Dictionary* gives these definitions. "1. Patient, long-suffering, or submissive in disposition or nature; humble. 2. Spineless or spiritless; compliant. 3. An obsolete word for gentle." Another definition I have heard for meek is, "strength under control." I am reasonably sure the "spineless and spiritless" are not going to inherit the earth, but why would the meek and humble do so? Would you rather be in the company of those who focus all their attention on themselves or on you?

We give our time, talent, and treasures to people who make us feel important, and we avoid those who constantly talk only about themselves. We do business with people and institutions that improve our lives, and we shun those who only want to take advantage of us. We prefer to work for employers who are looking out for our interests, not just their own. And employers hire people they believe will be loyal and committed to the company and their customers, not just drain the company's resources to feather their own nests.

The self-centered have few friends, few loyal colleagues, and even fewer supporters. They have no support system and very little power and ultimately face an uphill battle because conflict and adversity are the fruits of self-centeredness. Humble people put more value on others than on themselves, and in return, those people will do whatever they can to raise up the humble and help them become successful. The humble achieve significance by making others feel important and significant. Is it any wonder why the meek will inherit the earth?

Perhaps you have heard the term *original sin*, but do you know what it is? Was Adam and Eve's sin real? Was biting into a piece of fruit they were not to eat that big a deal that it required their banishment from the garden of Eden and all the other bad things mentioned previously? We've all done something "minor" like that.

The issue was not only that they disobeyed, it was the reason they disobeyed. The serpent played on their pride. Remember his words: "God knows that your eyes will be opened as soon as you eat it, and you will be like God." In my experience with advising individuals and families, I have found that pride is the primary reason their financial houses are not in order, and that creates strife and conflict. Remember, "We buy things we don't need, with money we don't have, to impress people we don't like." That's pride, and it leads to relational discourse. When the heirs start fighting over their share of the estate, the symptom is greed but the disease is pride.

Adam and Eve had everything they could have possibly needed or wanted, yet they desired the one thing they didn't need but wanted. You probably have everything you need and many of your wants. The same is true for your heirs, so why do the heirs go to battle? A friend of mine is in a legal battle with her sister over their mother's house. My friend has her own home, and the sister has no intention of moving into the home. My friend is okay with selling the house and dividing the proceeds but not the sister. She might argue there is sentimental value because she grew up in that house, but if she is not going to live there, and turning it into a rental is not practical, then what is her real issue? I submit it is pride in that she just doesn't want her sister to have it or any of the benefits from a sale. Pride is never logical or reasonable.

Holy Coach: When pride comes, then comes disgrace, but with humility comes wisdom. Pride goes before destruction, a haughty spirit before a fall. Pride ends in humiliation, while humility brings honor. (Proverbs 11:2, 16:18, 29:23 NLT)

Through your wisdom and understanding you have made yourself rich. You have gained gold and silver and have saved it in your storerooms. Through your great skill in trading, you have made your riches grow. You are too proud because of your riches. (Ezekiel 28:4–5 NCV)

Who says you are better than others? What do you have that was not given to you? And if it was given to you, why do you brag as if you did not receive it as a gift? You think you already have everything you need. You think you are rich. You think you have become kings. (1 Corinthians 4:7–8 NCV)

Hypocrisy

Hypocrisy is the condition of a person pretending to be something he is not. It goes on to say, "See lying and lies." It can be revealed through inconsistencies, selective choices, or the "That doesn't apply to me" attitude.

In a marriage, one spouse spends on anything he or she wants while the other is restricted to a limited budget. Or they say they will or will not do something and then do the opposite. They do not walk the talk. Or the husband says his wife should only have a basic, fuel-efficient car since she just needs it for local, short trips, but he deserves a BMW or Mercedes because he needs to maintain a certain business image. The "doesn't apply to me" attitude is where the wife says her husband must brown-bag his lunches while she has a closet full of shoes she seldom has occasion to wear. The rule of maintaining a budget only applies to him, not her.

Holy Coach: Why do you look at the speck of sawdust in your brother's eye and pay no attention to the plank in your own eye? How can you say to your brother, 'Let me take the speck out of your eye,' when all the time there is a plank in your own eye? You hypocrite, first take the plank out of your own eye, and then you will see clearly to remove the speck from your brother's eye. (Matthew 7:3–5 NIV)

Hypocrisy causes us to think better of ourselves than of others. Like pride, we think we are better or more deserving. When it comes to settling dad and mom's estate, the heirs may say everything should be equal, but then they fight over everything, even inconsequential items. Worse, they find reasons why their siblings are undeserving and unworthy of receiving anything. Yes, "See lying and lies."

When we coach individuals and families, we find one area of hypocrisy that is a struggle for almost everyone. Our objective in coaching is to help each person and the family as an entity discover what would make them significant and to implement strategies and actions that can make that happen. We help them define and clarify their passions and the services they can offer the world and how to be good stewards of the resources they have been given. We begin the process by helping them identify and define their personal values— what is important to them. These can be values such as love, faith, trust, consistency, and honor, to name just a few. We then ask them to explain how they will bring these values to their family. What we often discover is that the stewardship of the money and possessions is 180 degrees from the values they claim are important to them. They say they love their children, but they use money as a way to control and manipulate them or as a reward or punishment for the behaviors or performance they expect from their children. Sometimes, it is subtle and done with good intentions, but at other times, it is blatant control.

A child asks a parent for something. The parent says no. So the child asks again. And again. The game continues until the parent finally gives in. Or the child plays one parent against the other: "Mom said I could have it!" Dad would not have allowed the child to have whatever it is, but mom already said he or she could, so dad goes with it. Remember the serpent's words, "Did God really say?" This trick works well when the child is trying to get one parent to do something the other parent said he or she could not do. When children succeed at these gambits, they learn their parents are hypocritical. You may not have thought of it that way, but remember the definition of hypocrisy: "The condition of a person pretending to be something he is not." When a parent pretends to be tough but turns out to be a softie, that is being hypocritical. It may have minor consequences when the kids are young, but what they learned in their youth will be used to their advantage as adults.

Undisciplined Indulgence

Think about a time when your finances were tight. I got married between my junior and senior year in college. I paid personally for my education by working part-time in the evening and during summer breaks, and my wife worked full-time. Macaroni and cheese was a staple, and public transportation supplemented our very used car. A lot of thought went into every expenditure because we had to stretch a somewhat inelastic and minimal income over our basic needs. Somehow, we never wanted for anything even though there were things we wanted.

Lack of wealth created a self-imposed discipline on us, a governor to keep our spending under control. That discipline early in our marriage helped us maintain control over our finances as our income and net worth grew. Unfortunately, too many young adults, children, and grandchildren in the last thirty or forty years have been raised in economic conditions that have not taught them the lessons we learned out of necessity.

Growing up with wealth has robbed them of the discipline they need to keep their spending and even their lives from spiraling out of control. Wealth has caused them to believe they are entitled to have things they do not deserve. They have not had to earn the money the hard way to pay for what they want. We deserve only what we have personally worked for. If others did the work, we do not deserve to have what they worked for and we did not.

Holy Coach: A wise child accepts a parent's discipline; a mocker refuses to listen to correction. If you listen to constructive criticism, you will be at home among the wise. If you reject discipline, you only harm yourself; but if you listen to correction, you grow in understanding. (Proverbs 13:1, 15:31–32 NLT)

Did you enjoy being disciplined when you were a child? Okay, I know that was a silly question. But do you agree now that you can see the wisdom in the discipline you received and are thankful for it? Not so silly, right? Our parents provided discipline for us when we were growing up. The question is whether we were wise enough to accept and learn from it. It is hard to accept discipline and criticism, but when they are offered in love and concern for our betterment, it is foolish to reject or ignore the wisdom they represent.

The most loving thing parents can do for their children is to teach them discipline because one day they will not be around to provide it. The most harm they can do to a child and themselves is to eliminate controls in their lives. Sound discipline is simply applying positive controls while they are young so they will know how to apply them themselves when they are adults. Not teaching them self-discipline will almost assuredly ruin them.

Holy Coach: Those who spare the rod of discipline hate their children. Those who love their children care enough to discipline them. Discipline your children while there is hope, otherwise you will ruin their lives. (Proverbs 13:24, 19:18 NLT)

Children need and want discipline. I am not talking about physical punishment but about teaching and mentoring children to adopt positive and productive behaviors and to take responsibility for themselves and their actions so they will be able to take care of themselves and gain the respect of other people. Too often, parents do not discipline their children because they think they are protecting or sheltering them from failure, disappointment, and the disapproval of other people. Doing so becomes a self-fulfilling prophecy. The child becomes the very thing they are trying to avoid.

Handing substantial wealth to others that they have not earned is like giving them a drug without telling them all the negative side effects or preparing them for the experiences that can destroy them and their relationships. The reason 70 percent of wealth is lost every time it passes from one generation to the next, and completely gone by the end of the third generation, is because parents have not equipped the next generation with the discipline they need to manage wealth effectively and appropriately.

Holy Coach: To discipline a child produces wisdom, but a mother is disgraced by an undisciplined child. Discipline your children, and they will give you peace of mind and will make your heart glad. Words alone will not discipline a servant; the words may be understood, but they are not heeded. A servant pampered from childhood will become a rebel. (Proverbs 29:15, 17, 19, 21 NLT)

It is not a surprise that combining a lack of discipline with a desire for instant gratification results in spending what we don't have for things we don't need to impress people we don't like.

Holy Coach: The wise have wealth and luxury, but fools spend whatever they get. (Proverbs 21:20 NLT)

In America, anyone can become a millionaire. We have heard the stories of the millionaires next door. If this is true, why do so many people, even well-educated people, barely get by and die penniless or live a minimal retirement? Why is so much wealth completely gone in three generations? The reason is a lack of discipline to control the desire for immediate gratification that leads to spending rather than saving.

We are born selfish and self-centered. Babies do not care about anyone but themselves. "Feed me! Change me! Drop everything to meet my needs and wants!" We all know the first word babies learn to say is "mine." Learning to share is just that. It must be learned because it is unnatural to our nature. This is the buying what we don't need.

Holy Coach: Those who love money will never have enough. How meaningless to think that wealth brings true happiness. The more you have, the more people come to help you spend it. So what good is wealth—except perhaps to watch it slip through your fingers! (Ecclesiastes 5:11 NLT)

If our focus is always on things, we will never have enough money, so to quench our spending addictions, humanity invented a special drug—debt! Who needs cash when credit cards are so easy to obtain and credit card companies are so eager to entice us into using them? This is the "money we don't have" part.

Holy Coach: The rich rule over the poor, and borrowers are servants to lenders. (Proverbs 22:7 NCV)

Does getting into debt make you feel good? What you bought with debt might have provided some excitement and satisfaction for a time, but those feelings disappear relatively soon, and what you buy wears out or is broken long before the corresponding debt is paid off. Why are credit card companies able to charge 20 percent or more? Because once you are hooked, you are now an indentured servant; you are in bondage. Hundreds of years ago, you would have been jailed or forced to work for a master to whom you owed money. Today, the masters have institutional names, and they can take everything you have if you cannot pay what you owe them.

The Holy Coach also said, "The more you have, the more people come to help you spend it." Most people have a need to be liked and accepted by other people. What better way to do so than to buy it? Now we not only spend on ourselves, but we can spend two, three, four, or more times what we would spend only on ourselves because we are now buying for a crowd. That means we burn through wealth two, three, four, or more times faster. This is the "impress people we don't like" part. Actually, it is probably the reverse. The people we are trying to impress do not care about or like us; they care about themselves and just use what we have to help themselves.

Procrastination

"Don't do today what you can put off till tomorrow!" This attempt at humor is unfortunately too true and too sad. You are a procrastinator! If you are disagreeing with me right now, good for you, that puts you in a small percentage of the population. For the rest of us, welcome to the club. By the way, our monthly club meeting scheduled for tomorrow evening has been moved to next month. We can joke about it, but most of the time, procrastination is not a laughing matter. Someone once said the saddest words ever heard were, "Oh, what might have been."

The type of procrastination I am talking about is the missed opportunities to do something good, to go somewhere you have never been, to try something new, and to be kind and generous to a family member or friend or someone you do not know but you can tell needs encouragement and a helping hand. Of all those regrets you carry around in your mind and spirit, many of them are the product of procrastination.

Holy Coach: Farmers who wait for perfect weather never plant. If they watch every cloud, they never harvest. (Ecclesiastes 11:4 NLT)

Let me rephrase what the Holy Coach said that updates it for Americans today. People who wait for their perfect situation will never plan for their future until it is too late to do what they need to do to ensure they will have a future. They were going to get that life insurance policy in place, but never got around to it, so their survivors are struggling to pay the bills, send the kids to college, or pay the estate taxes.

They also put off seeing the attorney to draft their wills and trust so the survivors are having to deal with probate, paying estate and gift taxes that could have been eliminated or reduced, and the assets are distributed in ways that do not adequately provide for or protect the heirs—especially when there are special needs children or a blended marriage.

They thought social security, that little pension amount, and foregoing contributions to a 401k or IRA would still provide the retirement income they needed, but now know it will not. They discussed meeting with a financial planner many times, but life was just too busy and retirement was a long way off, so there would be plenty of time to do it later. There never will be!

Let's sweep those family conflicts under the rug rather than facing them head on and they will somehow magically go away. They won't!

It has been said the only certainties in life are death and taxes. Taxes can be minimized, possibly eliminated, but they can be planned for. Everyone does a certain amount of tax planning. Growing older, and the life conditions associated with aging, and death are the only real certainties. Amazingly, the things everyone knows will happen, and should be planned, never are, so their life and family situation becomes chaotic, anxious, fearful, depressing, and unfulfilling.

The Remedy

Wealth is power, and can bring out the worst in people, making them believe they have the right to do whatever they want to whomever they please, and take whatever they desire without judgment or consequences. Wealth can dull morality; it is like a virus you don't realize you have until you break out in a rash or pockmarks, and then it overwhelms your body, causing death.

Influenza is a virus I am sure you know well, but when do you know you have it? When you have a fever, the chills, runny nose, and a headache and arching muscles—when the symptoms become apparent. Next time those same symptoms appear, you know immediately you need to get to the doctor for treatment. Even better, since we know the probability is high we will get the flu when that season rolls around, we can take preventive measures by getting a flu shot.

In my industry, "affluenza" is an illness caused by the improper use of wealth, and it can infect and devastate a family even to the point of being terminal. Like the flu, there are symptoms we can recognize and treat, but we prefer to inoculate our "patients" before they catch the disease. The reason I spent a lot of space covering the negatives related to wealth is so you will be able to spot the symptoms and get treatment before the infection takes over the entire body. Better yet, I hope this book will encourage you to get your vaccination shot so you will avoid the disease altogether.

Unfortunately, affluenza is not easily cured. It is preventable, but it is not as simple as administering a shot or antibiotics. Here are some of the antidotes.

Holy Coach: Supplement your faith with a generous provision of moral excellence, and moral excellence with knowledge, and knowledge with self-control, and self-control with patient endurance, and patient endurance with godliness, and godliness with brotherly affection, and brotherly affection with love for everyone. The more you grow like this, the more productive and useful you will be in your knowledge of our Lord Jesus Christ. But those who fail to develop in this way are shortsighted or blind, forgetting that they have been cleansed from their old sins (2 Peter 1:5–9 NLT)

While this passage obviously has a Christian message, I ask you to consider the application of these principles regardless of your beliefs or faiths. Are they not the attributes you want for yourself and your children? Moral excellence, knowledge, self-control, endurance, and love.

Holy Coach: Children, obey your parents because you belong to the Lord, for this is the right thing to do. "Honor your father and mother." This is the first commandment with a promise: you honor your father and mother, "things will go well for you, and you will have a long life on the earth." (Ephesians 6:1–3 NLT)

That is actually the fifth commandment of the big Ten Commandments Moses received. What I have always found interesting about this is that you might think it would say that the parents' lives would be extended, but instead, it says that by obeying and honoring your parents, you get the benefits.

Holy Coach: Don't speak evil against each other, dear brothers and sisters. If you criticize and judge each other, then you are criticizing and judging God's law. But your job is to obey the law, not to judge whether it applies to you. (James 4:11 NLT)

Remember that part about breaking the rules? The rules are not there to restrict you but to protect you and help you get what you want and need to become successful and significant. Your job is simply to obey, and good things will happen.

By now, you can see that the remedy for keeping a family strong and healthy is to recognize all the things that cause problems in families—the list I provided above—and do the opposite. Be grateful for everything and everyone. Obey the rules. Give freely and generously of your time, talent, training and treasures. Love others and make them more important than yourself. Seek and embrace wisdom. Be courageous and vulnerable enough to face the truth. Stop worrying and procrastinating. Take prudent risks and get going!

Not long ago, I saw an old *Saturday Night Live* comedy sketch with Bob Newhart in the role of a psychiatrist. The female patient was telling him all the things that caused her anxiety and fear and kept her from being happy. He said that for five dollars, he would give her two words that would solve her problems and change her life. He blurted out, "Stop it!" She would respond with something like, "But what if I say something to someone and they don't like me?" His response to each of her exceptions was, "Stop it!" Actually, for five dollars, that was pretty good advice. Stop doing what does not work and start doing what does.

After raising many negatives, you should not think the situation is hopeless. I mention several times in this book the names Getty, Rockefeller, Carnegie, and Kennedy as examples of families who have been successful in keeping their wealth within the family and creating legacies we all know. I can assure you there are many less recognizable families that have been, and are being, successful in building legacies.

In my own backyard in Orange County, California, the Samueli family (he is the co-founder of Broadcom) created an academy for underprivileged children in Santa Ana, they have the Samueli Foundation that benefits many causes, and most recently made a $200 million contribution to the University of California, Irvine.

Lawrence and Cindy Field shared their experience of having a family coach work with Cindy's parents and the entire family to prepare future generations to be good stewards of the family wealth. Let me paraphrase one segment that demonstrates this family is on its way to significance. Each child and grandchild was tasked with creating milestones for family members participating in and accessing the benefits of the wealth: "To our surprise, had we established the milestones, they would have been at our level, but the children's milestones were much tougher. We dumbed them down, thinking they would hold a grudge if we held the bar too high, but they were way past that bar."

A final example is the Don and Doris Meyer family. Don built a successful lumber business that created substantial family wealth, but also a lot of debt, some of which was used to buy things that added no financial value to the family, but especially no spiritual, emotional, or relational value. In fact, the materialism was eroding these values.

Don and Doris decided to establish a self-imposed limit on their asset accumulation and spending, and give the rest away to causes they cared about. The bigger decision, however, was to involve the entire family in creating the structures for making this happen, and responsibility for implementing the plan.

Doris used some of the family wealth to build a safe house for abused women and their children affected by that abuse. Doris said, "I pray God will give us more and more profits because I have lots of ideas on how I want to give it away."

Doris goes on to say they decided to give some money, not a lot, to their children immediately, rather than after they die, to see how they would handle it. One daughter used her money to sponsor families moving to their town from other countries who had very little to start a new life in America. She befriends, buys food, and pays their rent until they can become self-sufficient.

A son partnered with a doctor to buy and rehabilitate a small building into a medical facility that provides medical services to local people who cannot afford traditional sources of healthcare. They are continuing to replicate that model.

But the best part of this story are the values the grandchildren are acquiring. One grandson said his parents gave him an allowance starting at age 5, with the caveat he had to use at least ten percent for a tithe or helping other people. A granddaughter said, "It is not only money we are to be generous with, it is more like time." Those are good descriptions of significance.

CHAPTER 4

Why Is This Happening to My Family?

Actually, it isn't all your fault or your brother's, sister's, mother's, or father's fault if your family is struggling with a variety of issues and challenges. When wealth transfers from one generation to the next, it is almost assured that deterioration in the family will occur. It is a law. It is the second law of thermodynamics—entropy. Entropy is the concept that everything in the universe always moves toward its lowest common denominator, its simplest form, unless overridden by another physical or chemical law. An ice cube left at room temperature will melt and then evaporate. We can reverse the process by applying other laws; we can combine two hydrogen atoms with one oxygen atom to get water, then freeze the water by lowering the temperature to get the ice cube.

The law of entropy is just as valid in families. In their natural state, families want to move from a complex to a simple state. Owning expensive, complex things such as businesses, real estate, and investments and trying to divide them equitably among many people with varying needs, wants, motivations, and beliefs is difficult, especially over multiple generations. Unless other laws and principles are intentionally applied over time to overcome family entropy, deterioration will occur.

The problem, like razing a ten-story office building, is that tearing something apart is dirty and destructive and leaves piles of debris.

The Odds Are Stacked

You may be thinking, *Yeah, but my family is different. We have a good family. That won't happen to us.* If that's what you're thinking, please memorize this simple proverb, "Shirtsleeves to shirtsleeves in three generations." It has been proven and documented in every country throughout thousands of years that 70 to 80 percent of wealth is lost as it passes from one generation to the next, so that the fourth generation starts with zero wealth. Italy: "From stalls to stars and back to stalls." Spain: "Who doesn't have it, does it, and who has it, misuses it." Brazil: "Rich father, noble son, poor grandson." China: "Wealth never survives three generations." The message is clear. By the end of the third generation, everything you worked so hard to build and maintain has a 70 to 80 percent probability of being back at zero when your great-grandchildren arrive. Your heritage as well as your wealth will have dissipated. They will probably not know your name much less your struggles, successes, failures, and victories. If they do know anything, will they be proud or ashamed of their family history and heritage? King Solomon told us three thousand years ago what to expect.

Holy Coach: Riches can disappear fast. And the king's crown doesn't stay in his family forever—so <u>watch</u> your business interests closely. <u>Know the state</u> of your flocks and your herds; then there will be lambs' wool enough for clothing and goats' milk enough for food for all your household after the hay is harvested, and the new crop appears, and the mountain grasses are gathered in. (Proverbs 27:23–27 TLB)

Notice the "intention" in his statement.

Interestingly, parents are not as concerned with what will happen to their money as what will happen to their family by the money. U.S. Trust conducted a survey called "Affluent Americans XIX." Here are eight of the top twelve concerns of "What Worries Affluent Parents Most about the Effect of Wealth on Their Children."[1]

- Too much emphasis on material things   60 percent

- Naïve about the value of money   55 percent

- Spend beyond their means   52 percent

- Have their initiative ruined by affluence   50 percent

- Not do as well financially as parents would like   49 percent

- Not do as well financially as parents did   44 percent

- Hard time taking financial responsibility   44 percent

- Will be resented because of their affluence   36 percent

Principles for Overcoming Entropy

These eight concerns are just components of entropy; they are concerns precisely because they can lead to deterioration in a family. Again, the only way to stop this is to use another law or principle that can reverse the effects of entropy. The principles I have identified are purpose, principles, plan, protection, preservation, process, people, preparation, participation, and philanthropy.

Purpose: I use this in two contexts. First, overcoming entropy must be intentional; you have to want to conquer it or intend to keep it from

---

[1] Institute for Preparing Heirs white paper, "Beyond the Money, 2013"; paragraph "Parents Worry Primarily About the Impact of Money on Their Children," U.S. Trust Survey of Affluent Americans XIX, December 2000.

happening in the first place. Second, you and your family must define and clarify what your purpose is in this world. Without a clear purpose that everyone shares and is committed to, there will be nothing to hold your family together. Everyone will go his or her separate way.

Principles and Values: There must be sound moral, ethical, spiritual, social, and financial values, laws, and principles that everyone accepts and strictly adheres to even at the risk of his or her own detriment if it benefits others and the family.

Plan That Protects, Preserves, and Promotes Family Values and Purpose: I have said this several times, but it is important to repeat it. It is critical that there be a relentless commitment by everyone to build up and not let anything tear down the family's capital. That includes financial, human, spiritual, intellectual, and social capital. There must be a constant pursuit of excellence. Anything that depletes or erodes any form of the family's capital should be avoided or quickly killed.

Process: The process is how the plan is implemented. There should be standardized processes and systems that are replicable and repeatable so they can be learned and applied by every generation. However, there also needs to be a process for constantly analyzing, testing, and questioning the continuation of systems and processes and modifying, discarding, and initiating new systems when necessary and beneficial.

People: People are the most important component in a family and the greatest source of joy and conflict. Unfortunately, the conflict too often overrides and destroys the joy. The conflict is usually in two primary areas. The first is in relationships. Starting the day each of us enters this world and must interact with parents and siblings, we experience hurts, fights, disagreements, and insensitivities that damage or destroy relationships, and those conflicts will impact the family's financial wealth negatively.

The second form of conflict centers on money. Even in families with good relationships, money tends to cause those relationships to deteriorate. Whether the people are causing the money problems or the money is causing people problems, if both are not addressed in unison and carefully crafted and coordinated, the family will not achieve significance.

Preparation and Participation: Every job I ever had, and I suspect you will concur, required OJT, on-the-job training. I learned how to push a mower (when I was ten, we couldn't afford a power mower) in straight lines back and forth. When I was old enough to be hired by someone who had a power mower, I learned how to pull the cord to start it, fill the gas tank, check the oil, and attach and detach the grass catcher. When I learned to drive a car, it was under the tutelage of an instructor in my high school drivers' education class. There was classroom instruction, homework, and then time in the automobile learning how to use the clutch to shift gears (if you are under forty years old, you can ask your parents what a clutch is), first driving in the school parking lot, then on city streets, and finally on the freeway. The latter is the preferred method of preparation for life.

Why then do families expect their children and grandchildren to manage money and wealth without preparation and participation under the supervision of people who can guide and teach them what works and what doesn't work? Yet that is exactly what most families do. The kids are unprepared and inexperienced when dad and mom die and transfer millions of dollars to their care. The plan and process mentioned above must incorporate a training program, systems, and structures that teach and offer hands-on experiences—the opportunity to fail and succeed.

Philanthropy: I will talk more about this later, but philanthropy is the one tool that has the greatest opportunity for uniting a family around a common purpose with shared values and principles and a platform for teaching and setting an example for subsequent generations of what brings true joy in life. It is the one area where it is at least possible to avoid conflicts, greed, and jealousy.

The Family Twain

There is a serious deficiency in the financial industry. Some institutions and financial advisors will tout themselves as addressing this deficiency, but in my experience, they offer just lip service to try to distinguish themselves from the thousands of other firms and advisors who all essentially provide the same basic services. The terms *wealth management* and *life planning* have become popular. What they mean is that they want to sell services for financial planning, investments, insurance, estate planning, and retirement and may dig a little bit into your and your spouse's financial goals and objectives but no further and then only because it could lead to the sale of another financial product or service.

What we learned relatively early in working with families is that almost no one in the financial industry focuses on the human side of the family. Yes, some financial advisors talk about life planning, but they never really delve into the relational struggles and issues the money can cause in families. Similarly, there are psychologist and therapists that offer personal and relational therapy, but they will never get into the money side of the family. Therein lies the problem: "Never the twain shall meet."

The word *twain* is old English for the word "two." As I think about families, I am reminded of our forebears coming across the continent in search of their future. What helped open America to these brave explorers and settlers? The railroad. So, the family train became my metaphor of the realities of families trying to hold everything together as they steam off into their future.

The similarity of the words "train" and "twain" is opportunistic in that the family train is comprised of two major components: people and money. On one side, there is the financial track the family train needs to travel to reach its future. By the way, I purposely use the word *future* because families do not have destinations, they have futures. The crew laying the track comprises financial professionals, accountants, attorneys, lenders, and financial planners. Each has a different job.

Staying with my train metaphor, one surveys and establishes the direction, one delivers the track to the jobsite, another delivers the spikes, the third lays the track, and the fourth hammers the spikes. However, none of them is at the jobsite at the same time; they don't work as a team, and they have never met or talked to each other, but they are laying track.

Then there is the "people" crew—psychologists, therapists, relational and marriage counselors, and all those professionals who deal with individual and family "people" problems. Like the financial crew, they haven't met or even know of each other's involvement on their own crew, and each crew is oblivious to the other's existence, but the people crew is laying a parallel track.

The problem is that a train cannot go very far on one track. Families hire the people crew and ignore the financial crew or vice versa. Or they use both at different times and never match them up. Even if they employ both crews, they probably lay their respective tracks at different times and at varying lengths and in divergent directions; nothing is coordinated. Laying track directly on bare ground at varying lengths and nonstandard distances between the two tracks is a disaster in the making. The tracks will shift and twist and cause the train to crash.

You cannot work on the financial track and ignore the impact it will have on the people track. Nor can you work on the people track and ignore the consequences it will cause to the financial track. In both cases, the result is a train wreck.

Obviously, what is required is one coordinated crew working side-by-side with another coordinated crew. Everyone needs to be communicating, competent in their individual roles, and coordinated in activities and timing so that the same length of track is laid at the same time and a standard distance between the two tracks is maintained and going in the same direction. There is one more critical requirement. A railroad track needs railroad ties! Setting tracks on bare ground doesn't work.

Railroad ties serve several very significant functions. First, they provide a solid foundation for the tracks; tracks laid on bare ground can warp and bend. Second, they maintain the integrity of the track; the distance between the two tracks must be consistent. Third, they keep the train on the track. If the tracks move even a little, the train comes off the track. Fourth, they retain the train's direction and mission. Fifth, they tie everything together, and sixth, by accomplishing all the above, a train wreck is avoided.

The family needs a "railroad tie," that is, a coach who works on both the money and people tracks simultaneously. The coaching related to the people track eventually comes to an end. It is normally heavy at the front end, lasting from one to two years depending on the size and issues in the family. However, the financial track never ends. Coaching that works on both tracks as a unified activity can foresee challenges and problems and address them before they can derail the family train. I view coaching as shepherding.

Holy Coach: The one who enters by the door is the shepherd of the sheep. The one who guards the door opens it for him. And the sheep listen to the voice of the shepherd. He calls his own sheep by name and leads them out. When he brings all his sheep out, he goes ahead of them, and they follow him because they know his voice. (John 10:2–4 NCV)

Planning is about preparing for the future. While no one can predict exactly what and when something could derail the train, we can know the types of problems and the solutions that best address those problems. Because the family train goes on in perpetuity, we can be sure there will be storms, mountain, valleys, forests, rivers, and marshes that will impede or grind the family's progress to a halt. Having a trained shepherd who can help the family know when and how to go around, over, under, or through those obstacles can make all the difference in the family's progress and significance.

The Family Wealth Office Team provides ongoing oversight and management of the family's resources and dynamics and brings back the Family Wealth Coaching Team when needed to solve specific problems and people issues as and when the family grows and changes.

A family's resources include financial, human, spiritual, intellectual, and social capital. Obviously, the financial capital is represented by the financial track and the people track represents the human, spiritual, intellectual, and social track of the family. Each track has fourteen primary activities that must be analyzed, and certain strategies and tactics must be implemented if the family is to be united for significance. They are:

People (Human, Spiritual, Social, Intellectual Capital)	Financial (Financial Capital)
1. Develop the family mission/values	1. Balance sheet and cash flow
2. Build trust within the family	2. Liability management
3. Open lines of communication	3. Investment strategies and implementation
4. Identify roles	4. Asset protection and insurance
5. Analyze each individual's abilities	5. Plan for financial independence
6. Determine individuals' suitability for roles	6. Plan for specific savings objectives/needs
7. Analyze and develop competence for roles	7. Business planning/ business progression
8. Train to develop competence	8. Tax and legal planning
9. Offer experience to gain competence	9. Achieve diversification/ manage risk
10. Educate to prepare for responsibilities	10. Family progression/ wealth transfer planning
11. Create measurement standards	11. Pre- and post-death philanthropic planning
12. Accountability tracking	12. Asset structure and titling
13. Resolve conflicts	13. Monitor family governance/management
14. Initiate mentoring	14. Facilitate inter- generational continuity

It's a Lot Like Football

Let me share one more analogy. This one is applicable to life as well as the family unit. American football comes the closest to typifying how we should live our lives. Also, I hope it is the sport most readers can identify with since they have either played football, had or have someone who has or is playing, or has graciously sat next to the football fanatic channel surfing between multiple games on Sundays so as not to miss any of the action.

Ownership: With the exception of a bunch of guys getting together on a Saturday at the local park or high school field, every team is owned by someone or something. Professionally, it is a person or persons, and academically, it is a university or high school. My comparison to life is that ownership lies within the family; the family is the owner. Initially, the ownership rests in the control of the patriarch and matriarch. But since the children are normally going to have control, the family needs to make a paradigm shift to include the heirs as future owners and treat them that way.

Organization: This has two meanings. The first entails a logical, coordinated effort and a plan, processes, and system for efficiency, order, and effectiveness. The second meaning is a legal entity that creates structure and formality and holds everything together. Families are typically unstructured and informal. In that state, they will never be significant. A formal organization, a definitive structure is required.

Capital: Every enterprise requires financial capital. Let's not forget, whether professionally or academically, sports are big business with a definite profit motive. They also involve human, spiritual, intellectual, and social capital that must be invested and used properly in the right ways and roles to gain the most success. Management hires a quarterback to throw the football to a receiver, not kick it through the uprights.

Initially, capital is primarily provided by generation one, but generation two is invited to invest. This is where families planning for significance differ from traditional estate transfers. In the latter, the flow of assets is one way and usually lost. In significance planning, capital flows in multiple directions because investing in the family can produce a significant return on investment for financial and human capital alike.

Management: The players and coaches play the game, but management runs the organization; it handles the finances and ultimately decides whom the players and coaches will be. Without management, the team is in effect that group of guys playing a pickup game on Saturday afternoon. Generation one will be the first president and CEO, but they bring generation two in as their immediate management team and can supplement them with nonfamily personnel, and when appropriate, introduce generation three to the team.

Coaches: Once management is in place, the next hire is the head coach, who fills out the rest of his coaching staff so he can be sure everyone is on the same page, communicates well, knows the systems, and has the experience and expertise to get the best from the players and team.

Each coach has a different role, responsibility, and mission, but every coach's primary mission is to prepare his players for the roles they must perform in the game. Whether in a sports team or a family, management does not coach; it brings in people who have the skills and objectivity to prepare the players and can bridge the gap between management and players. Coaches don't determine players' salaries, but they do counsel management on which players to pick and what they believe each player is worth. How successful would a professional team be without coaches? How successful would your family team be without coaching?

Coaching is not limited to the kind of financial and personal coaching we do. I include accounting, legal, insurance, and lenders to name a few as part of the family coaching team. If there is a family-owned business, there could be many more coaches. The head coach and his direct staff are integral to the team, but others are called upon when needed.

Players: While all the above are necessary, players play the game. They are the implementers, the workers, the "get it done" group. Without the players, nothing happens. All family members are players, and some will also be on the management team. An advantage a family has that sports teams and businesses do not is that in families, each person can pick to be one, both, or none. They can choose to be only a player and have no interest in being on the management team, or they can choose not to play at all; however, they also need to understand there is no chance for a Super Bowl ring if they choose not to be on the team.

Training: I am guessing that a professional three-hour game on Sunday equates to twenty-five to thirty hours of practice per week, not counting preseason and off-season workouts and practices. Training and practice requires at least ten times the effort of the actual activity, and I am probably underestimating. But athletes spend years to perfect their athletic abilities before they become proficient and reach the top or win the gold or the trophy.

Training includes physical, mental, emotional, and spiritual preparation. In fact, the latter three can be more important than the physical preparation. Many teams match up physically, but the win goes to the team that is better prepared mentally and emotionally. Pep talks boost morale and spirit and raise emotions to a fever pitch. We have all heard the coach respond to the sportscaster's question with, "I guess they just wanted to win more than we did." Winners win because they are physically, mentally, emotionally, and spiritually prepared to win; they expect to win, so losing never crosses their minds. As a unified team, families must be in the game to win!

We understand this, yet when it comes to transferring wealth, the recipients have had no training and very little if any playing time in a game. It is literally like taking someone who doesn't know what the game of football is, putting him in a uniform, and lining him up against a three- hundred-pound defensive lineman and expecting him to make a hole for the running back for a hundred or more plays. You can imagine the results! That's what we do to our kids with the family wealth when we drop it on them without preparing them first.

Playbook: On the first day of practice, the coach distributes three-ring binders to every player. He has been working on them for months during the off season. In his mind, he has attempted to imagine everything his opponent will do on the field and to create strategies for his team to deal with whatever is thrown at them. The players are required to make the contents of this binder a way of life from then on. They will run drill after drill executing the instructions in this binder until their reactions become automatic. It is the team's bible, and the outcome of the games and their season depends on how well they have learned and executed the strategies in that binder.

Additionally, the coaching staff prepares a game plan for each game. The game plan considers the environment, the opponent's strengths and weaknesses, the weather, the stadium, the location, and the condition of their own team and its players.

Families need a playbook and game plan. In our terminology, those are a significance plan and an action plan. Without these, they will be an uncoordinated, disconnected, and unproductive group of individuals aimlessly wandering in many directions; they will never be a team. When unforeseen events threaten, they will have no resources or knowledge on how to overcome the threats. They are easily divided.

Practice: Long before game day, players spend hours and hours pretending to play the game. Practice is going through the motions detail by detail as though they were actually playing the game. Practice is another form of training. The problem is that no one likes to train and practice; most want to just play the game and avoid the hard work of practice and a sweaty, stinky, sore, and tired body. There are no fans in the stands clapping and cheering their efforts.

Families need to have practices. Everyone needs to have exposure to the family's playbook along with ample time and repetitions in pretending to play the game so they will be adequately prepared when they step onto the field. The reality is that every generation has an opening day, a day when they must actually play the game. Dad and Mom are no longer able or available to make decisions or execute the game plan. But unlike football, there is no clock winding down to the final seconds. The game of life never ends; it just moves to different stadiums with different players and new opponents. If the new players have not had the opportunity to train and practice, they will have been defeated before the starting kickoff.

Rules, Regulations, and Referees: Imagine the game of football without rules or people to enforce the rules. Football is a dangerous sport. Even with strict rules, enforcement, and state-of-the-art protection, serious damage and career-ending injuries are all too frequent. If there were no rules and referees, 300-pound warriors engaged in physical combat would be equivalent to gladiators in the Roman Colosseum.

Rules create order where there otherwise would be chaos, and they protect the players. Earlier, I said one of the dangers to a family is breaking the rules. Religions give us rules, society makes our rules, government institutes laws and rules, and families have rules. However, there are natural laws that can produce even harsher penalties if we violate them. Included in these natural laws are financial and relational laws. A financial law would be that you cannot spend more than you make. You cannot have so much debt and so little income that you are paying only the minimum on your credit cards. The penalty for breaking those laws is bankruptcy. A relational law is,

Holy Coach: Love the Lord your God with all your heart, and with all your soul, and with all you mind. This is the first and greatest Commandment. The second is like it. Love your neighbor as yourself. (Matthew 22:37–40 NIV)

If you want your children to become responsible, productive adults, you must teach them and model responsibility for them. Teaching them to obey the rules creates order and unification and enhances communication and trust when everyone knows the rules and plays by them. Obeying the rules also protects them from harm.

Good rules do not restrict freedom; rather, they protect and allow people to take prudent risks and expand their freedoms. Think about teenagers learning to drive. They cannot drive until they have learned the rules and passed the test, but once they get their license, their worlds open up to a whole new set of freedoms. And hopefully, obeying those rules will keep them and others safe.

If obeying the rules is such a good idea, why do we need referees? You already know the answer—it is because not everyone plays nice all the time.

Holy Coach: for all have sinned and fall short of the glory of God. (Romans 3:23 NIV)

We like rules when they work to our favor, but we bend or break them when they keep us from doing what we want to do. Rules are a form of control, and we hate being controlled. We crave to have control in our hands, not have it handed to us. We do not want anyone telling us what to do or when or how to do it.

We all break the rules once in a while. That freeway speed limit is meant for the other guy, not me. "Officer, I thought I came to a complete stop at that stop sign. Or at least I slowed down quite a bit." "No Mr. IRS agent, I am pretty sure those are legitimate deductions." You get my point. We all need referees in our lives. While a family can police itself to some degree, it will be better served by having third-party objectivity and truthful advisors who can tell all involved what they need to hear whether or not they want to hear it and can offer accountability. I think this too must be a law of life, but kids do not want dad and mom telling them what to do or holding them accountable. They almost always rebel! Yet as a coach, I can say essentially the same thing and they would be okay with it. True, I might be more diplomatic in how I say it. And, like referees, sometimes, the advisors need to get in the middle of a brawl when tempers get a little hot and unfriendly words are exchanged and bring reason and civility to the debate.

Halftime—In the Locker Room: The whistle blows. The teams go to their locker rooms. The coach of the team that is behind by thirty points will probably be explaining his players' shortcomings with words I cannot use here. But the point is still the same. They will review what they did wrong, what they did right, and how they are going to do it better. They will analyze the conditions they will be facing in the second half. They will go over what the opponent is doing or not doing, what injuries they have, what players should shift to different positions, what plays worked and which didn't, and so on.

Families need to have periodic halftimes. How often depends on the size and geographical dispersion of the family, the complexity of the family holdings, and the family's mission. Like the football team, they need to assess their resources, game plan, everyone's roles, and what is working or not, and then make the necessary adjustments and changes so they can score more points in the second half.

The Super Bowl: The ultimate goal in football is to win the Super Bowl. I would like to use that as symbolic of achieving significance. I don't believe that a sports victory is even close to what I consider personal or family significance to be because it is a single achievement, and in twenty years, many players end up selling their Super Bowl rings on eBay. But a team that wins multiple Super Bowls builds a legacy, exactly what gaining significance does for a family.

Next Year, and Next Year, and Next: Finally, families always have a next season—the next generation. For most teams, the ownership, management, coaches, players, and even the cities where they play now are not the same as when the teams were first formed. Yet we have been fans of our favorite teams for years and raise our kids and grandkids to be Packers, Steelers, or Cowboys fans because those teams have developed systems and processes that transfer the team's time, talent, training, and treasures effectively to future management, coaches, and players. They have developed a legacy and built a heritage of excellence. If families want to stay in the game and win a Super Bowl year after year for fifty or a hundred years, they need to think and execute the way the professionals play the game.

CHAPTER 5

Idea

Holy Coach: Do your planning and prepare your fields before building your house. (Proverbs 24:27 NLT)

Do you think planning your future and your family's future is a good idea? Our firm, Family Wealth Leadership, does financial, retirement, insurance, estate, and asset protection and, more important, significance planning for clients.

When we talk to people about what we do, almost everyone says planning is certainly a good idea. Our next statement is, "Great! Let's get started." But they say, "Things are a little hectic right now" or "We're making some changes in my business right now, so let me get back to you in six months."

I recently had a prospective client send me an email asking if it was possible to keep his business in his family and what would happen if all the kids did not want to be involved. I responded that there were solutions and it was exactly what we did, so asked when we could meet. His response came after several attempts to set a meeting: "I'm simply not interested right now." How does a person go from having very legitimate and potentially damaging concerns to not being interested? Unlike taxes or financial emergencies, financial planning does not have the same urgency, and the negative impact of not planning will not be realized until well into the future, so the "I'll do it tomorrow" mentality takes over. In Chapter 3, I highlighted procrastination as one of the major impediments to achieving significance. It might be the biggest one.

There is also the "bury your head in the sand" effect. "If I don't think about it, it will magically go away." But it never does! The problems just get bigger and more difficult to solve. I have also seen many examples of the philosophy our government uses, the "kick the can down the road" attitude. That way, I don't have to deal with the problems; I'll just pass them off to the next generation and let them deal with them. Not only does that not work, it also becomes a self-fulfilling prophecy by creating a toxic situation that could have been avoided.

On the assumption that you are reading this book because you want to be proactive rather than reactive, I will explain the process we use. Because we believe planning is a good idea, we use the acronym IDEA to describe the process.

Before I explain the acronym, I need to expand on why having a process is important. I mentioned in Chapter 4 that "Process" is one of the seven pillars we use when working with families. Without a repeatable process, no plan will be successful. A process is an orderly, sequential set of steps to achieve a desired result. I enjoy watching a TV show called *How It's Made*. It describes the manufacturing of products from flowerpots to cars, airplanes to wooden pencils, and parking structures to kitchen stoves. The key to manufacturing anything is an assembly line that starts with gathering the necessary materials, combining those materials in exactly the right quantities, molding and shaping them to exact criteria and standards, and assembling and fastening the components in the right sequence and locations at the right times. Then comes filing, sanding, painting, polishing, cleaning, labeling, and packaging the products. If any step is missed, the result will be failure.

Additionally, the process can be accomplished by machines and robots because the steps are repetitive and consistent, making the process faster and more accurate. That is the methodology we use in working with families. By using the right process, we can be confident the desired result will come off the assembly line as and when we expect and ready to perform its intended purpose. That doesn't mean perfection is achieved every time. In manufacturing, testing and quality controls are conducted before the product is shipped. Any defects or errors are corrected. Families and people are not products or machines, but that makes the process even more important so any corrections can be made before reaching the end of the assembly line. Quality controls are instituted every step of the way.

The process can be standardized and then easily tweaked to fit each family's unique and specific needs. If we had to develop a new process every time or make it up as we went along, the activities could go on forever with no end in sight and offer no way to know or measure the result. Here is a simple example of a process.

Holy Coach: We also have joy with our troubles, because we know that these troubles produce patience. And patience produces character, and character produces hope. (Romans 5:3–4 NCV)

Hopefully, you agree that having a viable process is a good IDEA, so here is our process.

Investigation

Holy Coach: You must investigate thoroughly and inquire carefully. (Deuteronomy 13:14 NET)

Pay careful attention to the condition of your flocks, give careful attention to your herds, for riches do not last forever, nor does a crown last from generation to generation. (Proverbs 27:23–24 NET)

For which of you, wanting to build a tower, doesn't sit down first and compute the cost to see if he has enough money to complete it? (Luke 14:28 NLT)

That last verse asks a good question. Why would anyone start a project without first doing the necessary research and discovery? The obvious answer is they wouldn't, but reality tells a different story. If everyone did the necessary homework before starting a project—buying something expensive, getting involved in a relationship, investing in that "can't lose" deal someone recommended, and in my area, making decisions about managing wealth and its impact on the family without getting the proper help—there would be very few do overs. Have you had more do overs in your life than you care to admit?

Many people will spend more time planning their weekend activities than planning their futures. I suspect this is because the future seems a long way off and there will be plenty of time to do it later (remember procrastination); planning requires work, time, energy, and thinking. Remember how enthusiastic you were about writing term papers in school and the research required to get at least a C? How you looked forward to those fun times in the library (this was before the Internet), reading all those books and articles, and staying up to 3:00 a.m. typing on a typewriter? (If you don't know what a typewriter is, ask your parents.)

As covered in Chapter 2, we need to investigate our family history. The old adage, "If we don't study history, we are doomed to repeat it" is one reason. By researching you and your family's history, we learn details about everyone. We learn about the challenges and the successes, the differences and the struggles between those people. We need to learn everything we can about those two tracks—the people and financial sides of the family train. We need to identify how those two tracks have interacted with each other so we can keep them from separating and causing a family train wreck. We cannot move into the design and development phase until adequate research and investigation is completed.

Here are some of the components we use. First, we interview the patriarch and matriarch separately. We do this because we have learned if they are in the room at the same time, we don't always hear the truth. When only one spouse is in the room, we get more honesty and openness. Once we have the results of our individual interviews, we lay out their responses side by side and review them with both people in the room, and then the negotiation begins. All those issues or feelings not aligned must be negotiated until we reach agreement. We cannot move into design and development if we do not have consensus on almost every point. That doesn't mean one person gets what he or she wants and the other does not; it does mean they will have to come to a mutual understanding.

Once we have dad and mom in agreement, we interview all their children and their spouses. If grandchildren are mature and responsible, we may also interview them. In this way, we learn more about dad and mom from the kids' perspective, the issues they see in the family, and their desires for the family's future. This is critical information to have because they will one day be driving the train. Concurrently, we will be reviewing their balance sheet, cash flow, tax returns, estate and legal documents, and their existing advisors to determine if we have a qualified team or need to replace someone on the team.

Another major activity is helping dad and mom identify who they are and who they want to be in order to achieve personal significance, and then what they want the family to be to achieve family significance. In our experience, most people have never identified what significance would look like for them. They can speak to their identities as parents, business owners, workers, and spouses, but they frequently haven't given much thought to what will truly light their fire. This must be clear to them if they hope to have a joyful life.

The purpose of investigation is to become clear on what service and value they bring to the world, to identify the resources they have or are available to them to achieve the first activity, and how to efficiently and effectively use their true wealth to accomplish their personal and family goals and objectives. There are always gaps, and through investigation, we discover where and how wide they are. Then we can begin to identify solutions, which leads us to the design and development phase.

Design and Development

That last passage (Luke 14:28) is applicable here also. What does baking a cake, going on vacation, and building a fifty-story building have in common? They all require a detailed and orderly plan. No one would start construction on a building without having blueprints first. You might say some chefs cook without recipes, but the truth is they use recipes in their heads rather than on paper. They know the required ingredients, the exact amount of each ingredient, and the sequence for adding and combining them; they know the exact amount, sequence, and type of ingredients by memory and repetition so it only seems they are not using recipes.

There is a reason we answer a friend's question about what we are doing this summer with, "We're planning a vacation." Some people might just pack the car and head out, but when they run out of gas or can't find a place to spend the night, they come up with a plan for the next day.

You have decided to build your dream house. One of your first actions will be to hire an architect to create a design on paper based on your goals and objectives. You will be asked many questions about what you envision, what your desired outcome would look like, what you can afford, and where it will be located and when you need it completed. The architect creates a series of illustrations, sketches, and drawings for your review. Alternatives and the pros and cons of each will be discussed, and accepted or rejected, and new options explored until you are satisfied the design achieves your desires. This is the design phase, but a house cannot be built using only these drawings. Likewise, in designing your family's future, all your goals, objectives, needs, and desires must be transferred to paper and reworked until you are satisfied your future is designed as you picture it and you have sufficient resources allocated in the right ways at the right times to achieve it.

Development converts the design drawings into blueprints, which are the documents the builder will use to get the necessary approvals and build the house. There will be specific and very detailed blueprints for electrical, plumbing, air conditioning, structural, interior and exterior, and landscaping components. The contractor will develop a precise and sequential timeline for construction because every component must be put in place in the right order and at the right time. That includes identifying the right subcontractors, bidding out the work, and establishing all the costs that go into the construction contract. You then go to the bank to arrange the construction loan along with that portion of your personal capital you must allocate to the project. If you do not have sufficient personal resources, the lender will not approve the construction loan and the house will not be built. The last thing anyone wants is to start building and then run out of money only to be left with a home that is vacant and unlivable, or a future that falls far short of a dream that was not properly designed and an achievable plan developed. Construction (the execution phase) cannot, and will not, commence until the development phase is complete and approved. To do so will most likely cause the house to collapse during a storm. This is exactly the same process a family must use if their family structure is to withstand the storms and forces it will face, and must overcome, as it progresses through multiple generations.

Holy Coach: But don't begin until you count the cost. For who would begin construction of a building without first calculating the cost to see if there is enough money to finish it? Otherwise, you might complete only the foundation before running out of money and then everyone would laugh at you. They would say,

"There is the person who started that building and couldn't afford to finish it." (Luke 14:28-30 NLT)

I certainly would not rent office space in a building constructed without approved plans and a licensed and experienced contractor building it, but this is exactly what many people do with their lives especially with regard to transferring wealth to future generations. Let me say here that having a trust, wills, and the associated documents is *not* a plan; they are instructions trustees and the court can use to honor your wishes for distributing your assets, but these documents provide zero education, training, and preparation for the people receiving those assets.

Holy Coach: The wisdom of a sensible person guides his way of life, but the stupidity of fools misleads them. (Proverbs 14:8 GW)

Whether your heirs will fall into the clever or foolish camp depends on what you do now to help them become clever or keep them foolish. Using our historical statistic, without preparation we can assume 70 percent will be the "stupid persons," making important decisions with little knowledge and understanding of the consequences and even less real-world training and experience. Impetuous and emotional decisions destroy wealth.

Holy Coach: The plans of a hard-working person lead to prosperity, but everyone who is always in a hurry ends up in poverty. (Proverbs 21:5 GW)

You can make many plans, but the Lord's purpose will prevail. (Proverbs 19:21 NLT)

Again, you must decide for yourself whether there is a greater plan for your life than simply acquiring and hoarding things as opposed to using your life to make the world a better place for others, especially your children and grandchildren. Your example will form your heirs' attitudes about wealth and whether they too will use it for only their own consumption. If you ultimately decide there is a bigger plan, it is foolish not to do everything you can to use what you have been given and to train your family to use what they will receive from you to fulfill that purpose because the bigger plan will prevail no matter what you choose to do. The train is leaving the station. You must decide if you are willing to get onboard and go where it will take you. Of course, the more important decision is to be sure you are on the right train. That's why we start with investigation.

Execution

Nothing happens until something happens! All the research, study, investigation, planning, and designing are worthless if the project never gets off the drawing board. Significant families are motivated, take-action families. It is a mistake to move before planning; it is also a mistake to not move after adequately planning. Planning does not involve risk—executing does. That is why procrastination becomes the action of choice. And making choices requires taking risks. Consider the following event.

Holy Coach: But Moses told the people, "Don't be afraid. Just stand where you are and watch, and you will see the wonderful way the Lord will rescue you today. The Egyptians you are looking at—you will never see them again. The Lord will fight for you, and you won't need to lift a finger!" Then the Lord said to Moses, "Quit praying and get the people moving! Forward, march! Use your rod—hold it out over the water, and the sea will open up a path before you, and all the people of Israel shall walk through on dry ground! (Exodus 14:13–16 TLB)

The Israelites are in a real fix. Pharaoh and his troops are at their backs and bearing down rapidly. The Red Sea is before them. They are trapped! God provides a solution that is rightly scary. They are relying on this guy Moses, who was once the adopted brother of the guy in the chariot leading the charge of what is essentially an execution mob, and Moses is telling them to cross on dry ground between two massive walls of water and not worry about anything. I can hear them saying, "Ah, Moses, no one has ever done this before, and it seems to us there is more than a little risk in what you are telling us to do!"

I wonder if even Moses is having doubts about the risk since he evidently decides one more prayer couldn't hurt. Sometimes, even prayer is an excuse not to take risks. You would think God would have been pleased that Moses wanted to talk to Him a little more about this since God wants us to pray to Him, right? But God knows it is a stall tactic and a lack of faith, so (I love this part) He commands him to stop praying and get moving! Significant families plan, analyze and weigh the risks, determine the best course of action, then go for it. Astronauts walked on the moon because they did just that.

Administration

I used to be a real estate developer, and developing is a perfect example of the process I have been describing. A developer starts with investigation to find out where and what to develop based on what the market will support and the authorities will allow and the condition of the land, the title, and the environment. The engineers and architect are hired to design it, and the contractor builds it.

The final activity is to manage it. Tenants must be found, leases negotiated, rents collected, utilities and services managed, building and landscaping maintained, financing acquired, and all this is repeated constantly. A building not well maintained will lose tenants, be unattractive to new tenants, and deteriorate and lose value. A well-managed building will increase in value. Significant families diligently administer their family's capital—remember that I include human capital in that definition—to ensure their value is constantly increasing. If the family is not administered well, just like the office building, it will be devalued.

Finally, administration is a form of investigation. We all understand it is impossible to think of everything that could possibly happen and create a design that works perfectly. Additionally, there will be construction defects, some visible and some not. It isn't until we operate the building and test the systems and facilities under everyday conditions that we discover those defects and what is working and what is not. We go back to the drawing board to make changes, implement the changes, and administer it all.

The process is circular; it never ends. Families are much more complex than buildings, have many more moving parts, and all those parts (the people) have multiple defects, so you can see why administration is critical to a family's significance.

Holy Coach: The Lord God placed the man in the Garden of Eden to tend and watch over it. (Genesis 2:15 NLT)

But those who won't care for their relatives, especially those in their own household, have denied the true faith. Such people are worse than unbelievers. For if a man cannot manage his own household, how can he take care of God's church? (1 Timothy 5:8, 3:5 NLT)

No Plan Is a Plan to Fail

If you do not know where you are going or how to get where you want to be, you probably will not like where you end up. Once you are clear and have agreement on where you want to go, when you want to get there, and the resources you have or need, the next step is exploring the ways and routes to get there. Since most people will not build homes, let me use an example familiar to us all. When my computer or smartphone map lays out a route for me, I like to review my options and alternate routes when I am going somewhere I have never been. I may want to combine multiple tasks and objectives to save time and avoid unnecessary trips. The shortest distance may not be the fastest choice especially on California freeways.

If I am not in a hurry and can afford the time, I might want to take a more scenic and relaxing route. I also need to decide who is going with me. Some people will be in the car at the start of the trip, whereas others might be picked up or dropped off along the way. I have to plan for the extra time that would require plus mapping the side trips needed to deliver or pick them up. I need to plan whether my vehicle can accommodate everyone joining me. Do I need varying types of vehicles? If I am planning a cruise, I may need some combination of car, bus, train, plane, and ship.

When I take the time to plan, I arrive where I want to be on time. When I do not plan, I arrive somewhere I do not want to be, and I am either late or stressed out if—and when—I get to my desired destination only one minutes before my designated arrival time—or worse, I am late.

This is the reason we plan with our clients. A life is infinitely more complex than a vacation, so it needs careful, thoughtful, and intentional planning if a family is to become significant.

Holy Coach: We should make plans—counting on God to direct us. Steady plodding brings prosperity; hasty speculation brings poverty. A prudent man foresees the difficulties ahead and prepares for them; the simpleton goes blindly on and suffers the consequences. Any enterprise is built by wise planning, becomes strong through common sense, and profits wonderfully by keeping abreast of the facts. Good planning and hard work lead to prosperity, but hasty shortcuts lead to poverty. (Proverbs 16:9, 22:3, 24:3–4 TLB; 21:5 TLB and NLT)

Where Are You Now, and Where Do You Want to Be?

Everyone is in one of three phases of life: survival, success, or significance. Everything we do at our firm is designed to help our clients and their families progress through each phase, with significance being the sought-after prize. How one defines these phases is subjective and individualized for you, your spouse, children, and family. One person's definition of success may be another person's definition of survival. With that understanding, I offer the definitions we use but still with the caveat that my definitions will be customized to each individual and family.

Regarding your financial well-being, we would compartmentalize your financial wealth into these three phases because you cannot move to the next phase until the phase you are currently in is financially secure. Survival is defined as funding your *needs*. I emphasize the word *needs* because needs are too often confused with *wants*. Here again, one person's needs could be another person's wants, so it is important to be clear. A Honda Civic can be a satisfactory need and the Acura a want. But someone who has been driving BMWs for years might not consider an Acura as something that would satisfy his or her need. So however the needs are defined, we first analyze how much financial resources are required to ensure that those needs are met no matter what bad and unforeseen events might happen.

We have found that clients do not always use their wealth wisely because they are in constant fear it will disappear and they will be penniless even when their net worth is in the millions. They have never answered the "How much is enough?" question, so they are always afraid they will run out of money. Once the survival phase is ensured, you can move to the success phase. Again, this is an individual, subjective issue, but our definition is that this is when you fund the *needs* of your family. For our purpose, family is assumed to be your sons and daughters and their children—immediate family members who are not now or will not be dependent on you for their subsistence.

Here, too, how much is enough is the critical question. I discussed previously that equal and fair are not synonymous, and it is critical that this concept be applied here. Warren Buffett said, "A very rich person should leave his kids enough money so that they would feel they could do anything, but not so much that they could do nothing."[1] My interpretation is that you give them enough of your Treasures only if they will combine it with their Time, Talent, and Training to be successful at whatever they want to do assuming it is legitimate and legal.

The amount given will then depend on what each child needs to be successful in his or her own terms. That might include helping them acquire and refine the necessary Training and Talent, and creating the required Time available to accomplish the other two. Giving children more than they need potentially creates dependence and destroys their dignity. Assuming this can be accomplished, the success phase is completed and you can move on to the final phase.

Let me state before going into detail about the significance phase that a measure of significance can be achieved in the survival and success phases. If you are meeting the needs of your family, you are certainly significant to them, remembering that significance is bestowed, not bought or acquired. The significance I am talking about goes well beyond your family. The significance I am describing is when you fund others who are in need. This type of significance is world changing and will be life changing for your family.

How much excess wealth do you have? If that question is directed to anyone with substantial wealth, whether it be ten or a hundred million, how would he or she answer? Normally, the response is, "I don't have

---

[1] Warren Buffett, Kirkland, Richard I. "Should You Leave It All to the Children?" *Fortune*, September 29, 1986. Available at: http://archive.fortune.com/magazines/fortune/fortune_archive/1986/09/29/68098/index.htm.

any excess wealth." Why is this question and its answer important? First, if we have effectively set up your financial structures so the survival and success phases are adequately funded for the rest of your and your children's and grandchildren's lives, what are you going to do with the remaining wealth that is technically not needed? Why do you need to keep growing that amount you will never need and probably never use? There comes a point when you can own only so much stuff, so many homes, so many cars, and so many toys; and go on so many trips and play days, so what is the point? You probably do have excess wealth!

The second reason the answer is important is that excess wealth is the resource for achieving significance. In Chapter 4, I identified the types of capital every person and every family possess. A very important one is social capital, which incorporates relationships internal and external to the family. I go into greater detail in Chapter 6, but you have a responsibility to your family and to society, which includes friends, peers, employers, employees if you are an employer, governments (federal, state, city, etc.), and to people and causes that need what you offer. You have social capital whether or not you realize it. We call it TAXES! Two-thirds of the federal budget is devoted to social programs. Are you confident and happy with how politicians are spending your money? Are the causes you care about being funded? Are your tax dollars funding activities you would prefer not to fund or violate your moral or religious beliefs?

The issue is not whether you have social capital; it is about who controls it. I will assume you would prefer to use your money for the causes you care about. Adding insult to injury, I think we can also be confident that each dollar of our money filtered through government will be reduced to maybe twenty-five cents by the time it can do any good for society. Plus, you get zero recognition and enjoyment for contributing to the government's causes, and there is no benefit for your children and family. In fact, taxes are a detriment to your family and an impediment to achieving significance. The good news is that the IRS encourages us to take on this responsibility ourselves by allowing deductions for charitable contributions. That gives us a platform for achieving family significance.

If we assume for the moment that we are successful in funding to the dollar your survival and success needs and goals so there is in theory nothing left over, you actually still have tax dollars we can convert into excess wealth using the right legitimate and legal strategies. Effectively, you can probably keep your excess wealth and divert what you must send to governments to your favorite charities and church. It is having your cake and eating it too. If properly structured, it can be a win/win/win for you, your children and family, and the beneficiaries of your philanthropy. Beneficiaries are the key to significance. Remember, significance is bestowed by those people and causes that gain value from the service you provide them. Significant families steward their four Ts of True Wealth in ways that positively change people's lives. They use their excess wealth, real and tax dollars, in ways that involve the entire family in helping the sick, the impoverished, the widows and orphans; and the result is their own family grows stronger and closer.

Holy Coach: Take care of any widow who has no one else to care for her. (1 Timothy 5:3 NLT)

Give justice to the poor and the orphan; uphold the rights of the oppressed and the destitute. (Psalm 82:3 NLT)

In truth, caring for these people is OUR responsibility, NOT the government's.

GOSPEL

In Scripture, the word *Gospel* means Good News because it leads to a life of freedom, contentment, and joy. Likewise, adopting the Family

Wealth Leadership's wealth GOSPEL can strengthen a family and lead to financial freedom and contentment. Entropy is inevitable, but the good news is that it can be mitigated with the right process and strategies and a firm determination to fight it.

I believe the right process and coaching is the good news that offers ways to reverse this natural deterioration in families and lower that 70 percent statistic. I use the acronym GOSPEL to lay out the principles and values individuals and families must adopt to move from survival through success all the way to significance.

G—Give

- Tithe a minimum of 10 percent.

- Give to help others.

- Give to help family while alive.

- Give to leave behind a legacy giving (after-death giving)

- Use your true wealth (Time, Talent, Training and Treasures) to serve others.

O–Ownership

- Everything belongs to God; your responsibility is to be a good steward.

- Pass on to others what has been gifted to you better than you received it.

S—Save

- Pay yourself first.

- Save at least 10 percent.

- Invest prudently using wise counsel.

P—Plan

- For emergencies

- For financial independence

- For specific savings goals

- For catastrophic events

- For transferring True Wealth in ways that benefit future generations and society and strengthens the family rather than destroying it

E—Expenses

- Spend only what is left over *after* funding all the above.

- Know how much is enough and commit to spending only that much.

- Before spending, always ask, "Do I want it but do not need it?"

- Maintain a budget diligently.

L—Liabilities

- Use strategies that minimize taxes.

- Pay cash.

- Avoid credit card and personal debt *at all cost unless you pay them off promptly so as to avoid interest charges and late fees. Never, never carry a balance.* If you use credit cards, only use those that offer rewards or have cash-back provisions and no annual subscription fees.

- Borrow only to invest in things that produce reliable income and/or appreciation at a rate that is at least 2 percent greater than the cost of the money, and avoid variable interest. The only investments that should be considered—and only after careful consideration, thought, due diligence, and wise counsel—are investments that require substantial amounts and would be impossible or impractical to pay cash such as

- Primary residences

- Businesses

- Income-producing real estate

- Government and high-quality corporate bonds

In my train illustration, I explain that families are composed of two tracks, the people track and the financial track. Most of the discussion to this point has focused on the people track, so let's see how we can align one component of the financial track with the survival, success, and significance concept.

Most people and most financial and investment advisors aggregate investments into two or three categories. The first division is normally between qualified and nonqualified accounts. Qualified accounts have certain tax advantages in the form of deferred taxes or tax-free growth and income. Pension plans, IRAs, and a 401(k)s are examples of deferred accounts. The taxes are paid when funds are distributed or withdrawn from the accounts. ROTHs and municipal bonds are examples of tax-free accounts and investments.

Nonqualified accounts have no tax advantages. Income taxes must be paid every April 15 on the interest earned and realized gains from sold investments. Designing the portfolio for these assets is based on the assumption that the funds will not be needed for ten, twenty, or more years and can incorporate higher-risk investments. Although the investments will be in different accounts, the design treats it as one account.

A third component might be a liquidity account that is invested more conservatively. What I have just described is somewhat traditional, but it exposes the entire portfolio to the same amount of risk and not necessarily to the client's life objectives. It may be designed around specific goals such as education or retirement but is not a significance objective.

Our approach uses three distinct life objectives. We call it Living, Lifestyle, Legacy, and it aligns with the survival, success, significance format. I recommend that you review your situation in light of this. The Living portfolio is designed to ensure survival if the unimaginable happens. Analyze every consistent and ongoing expenditure from the "How much is enough?" perspective. This is the hard part because, honestly, you will resist doing it, but you must. Ignore your current lifestyle and assume a bare-bones but adequate and comfortable lifestyle. Consider a nice but smaller home, less expensive cars, not eating out every night, and a modest vacation as some examples.

Holy Coach: Keep me from lying and being dishonest. And don't make me either rich or poor; just give me enough food for each day. If I have too much, I might reject you and say, "I don't know the Lord." If I am poor, I might steal and disgrace the name of my God. (Proverbs 30:8–9)

We then compute the amount of investment assets needed assuming a conservative interest rate, an estimated life expectancy (we use age ninety-five), and all sources of reliable and sustainable income. Employment and business income are ignored because this is a survival analysis based on a worst-case scenario and those income sources could disappear quickly in tumultuous economic times.

If the result of this analysis indicates you need a million dollars, a portfolio can be designed for these assets separate from your other assets, which provides the greatest probability of sustaining you and your spouse under any circumstances. The challenge, as I mentioned before, is mentally being able to imagine yourself giving up your current lifestyle expenses and downsizing to a more subsistence-type of living. Obviously, we hope it never comes to this, and it is not an exercise in attempting to convince you that you should. But understand that higher expenses mean more assets must be dedicated to survival, thus reducing their availability for other activities and uses, and it keeps those assets at a lower investment rate since the investments must be more conservative to minimize risk.

Hopefully I didn't depress you too much, but in case you're a little down right now, we will move to the Lifestyle portfolio, which should reinvigorate your enthusiasm and confidence. Because you now have the confidence you can survive Armageddon, we can layer on the restoration of your lifestyle. Whether you want this to be your existing lifestyle or a higher or reduced lifestyle is your call. Just remember, that higher equates to more dollars having to be allocated and lower requires less, which impacts the amount left for success (your heirs) and significance. The analysis is the same as I have already described, so if you needed a million for survival and another million for lifestyle, we now must invest two million in ways that ensures you can weather all economic storms again without any income except that which is stable and sustainable. We can be a little more aggressive with the second million and take additional risk to gain more potential return since the survival portfolio is in place.

Assuming there are available assets in excess of what has already been allocated, the Legacy portfolio can be invested with relatively more risk. We can do this because in theory, you will never need these assets since your lifestyle is reasonably assured for the remainder of your lives.

Depending on your age, the age of your heirs, and at what ages you want your children and grandchildren to have access to their inheritances, these assets could have sufficient time to grow and ride out large market swings. These accounts can be invested more aggressively, and you would want to remove them from your estate to reduce the impact of estate taxes, which can be 50 to 60 percent. For example, $1 million left in your estate could grow to $4.7 million at 8 percent in twenty years. If the estate tax rate is 50 percent, your heirs will receive $2.35 million. If we move the assets out of your estate early, they could receive the entire $4.7 million. If the living and lifestyle analysis had not been completed, you may not know how much you can afford to move out of your estate, therefore exposing more of it to estate taxes.

Again, the question, "How much is enough?" must be answered. Since Warren Buffett is considered one of the wisest businessmen of our time, I think we should heed his wisdom and not corrupt our children with excessive wealth they did nothing to deserve. Honestly, if you think your children are different, you are wrong! But if by chance your children are the exception, you have no way of knowing or controlling what undeserved wealth will do to their children and grandchildren. The financial analysis can give us the right numbers, but employing coaching and proper strategies that teach stewardship and personal responsibility is critical if significance is to be achieved.

So, we've successfully and reasonably assured your survival and success, and there is in fact excess wealth you did not know you had. Now that's opportunity! Significance awaits you if you will grasp it. You and your children and grandchildren can achieve legacy. Since these are per our previous definition assets you will never need or use for you or your family, you can now help others in need. These are the assets you can invest financially, you can use for people-and-causes investments, and more important, you can invest in character building so your family will be strong and able to defend every attack against its integrity.

Holy Coach: Don't you see that children are God's best gift, the fruit of the womb his generous legacy? Like a warrior's fistful of arrows . . . Oh, how blessed are you parents, with your quivers full of children! Your enemies don't stand a chance against you; you'll sweep them right off your doorstep. Good people will inherit the land and will live in it forever. They will enjoy a good life, and their children will inherit the land. (Psalm 127: 3–5 MSG; Psalm 37:29, 25:13 NCV)

Obviously, to accomplish this, we need resources. I have continually stressed that your two primary resources are your financial track and your people track. I go into more detail in Chapters 6 and 10 about these, so I will mention here just that everything I have highlighted in this chapter can be achieved only if the family embraces and teaches proper stewardship of the four Ts of True Wealth to every generation. The Living, Lifestyle, and Legacy analysis focuses only on your two primary financial assets: your cash flow and the assets you are already responsible for stewarding.

Even if you do a great job of stewarding your assets and cash flow in ways that protects, preserves, and passes on that stewardship, from a financial point of view, it does not mean you will become significant unless you develop a sense of people stewardship also. That is the next chapter of your story.

SECTION II

The Foundation

CHAPTER 6

Your Worth

My guess is that you instinctively thought of a dollar amount when you read that chapter title. Since I have already spent a fair amount of time discussing financial issues, that would be understandable, but it is not my intent in this case. This time, I am focusing on your service to humanity because your real worth is determined by whatever that service is.

I mentioned this concept in previous chapters, but now, I will get more specific. By now, you may have noticed I have a fondness for acronyms. I use them because it helps me (and I hope will help you) remember important concepts and topics and offers a measure of order and organization of processes. Let's see if it works.

What did the letters in IDEA represent? By the way, this is a good formula for solving problems and making decisions. Get clarity on what the real problem or goal is and the resources you have or need. Then, design a plan that identifies and tests all the possible solutions, their outcomes, and specific actions and steps needed to accomplish the option that has the highest probability of succeeding. And then, execute the action plan and constantly analyze the results to see what parts are working and change what is not working. At Family Wealth Leadership, we have identified five major areas in which you can serve and develop your passions. These will be the foundation of your personal and family significance statements. The acronym is GOALS.

When most financial advisors and financial planners use the word *goals*, they are talking about financial goals as in how much money you will need for college educations, retirement, weddings, buying a new or vacation home, and investment and liquidity goals. These are all important and necessary to quantify and adequately plan to achieve, but they are not the type of goals that produce significance, and our goal is always personal and family significance.

These are not in order of importance or priority and are not mutually exclusive. In fact, everyone will probably identify with all five. The question is how to effectively and efficiently allocate your resources to achieve these GOALS in proportions that are right for you, realizing that yours may be quite different from your spouse's and any other family member's goals.

G—Giving

This area of service relates to the social capital I mentioned previously; it involves people and causes outside your family. This is family philanthropy and social responsibility. It is helping those who are in need and the area where the greatest probability of achieving legacy and significance rests.

Holy Coach: Tell them to use their money to do good. They should be rich in good works and generous to those in need, always being ready to share with others. Every man shall give as he is able, according to the blessing of the Lord your God which He has given you. You must each decide in your heart how much to give. And don't give reluctantly or in response to pressure. "For God loves a person who gives cheerfully."

Give freely and become more wealthy; be stingy and lose everything. The generous will prosper; those who refresh others will themselves be refreshed. (1 Timothy 6:18; 2 Corinthians 9:7; Proverbs 11:24–25 NLT; Deuteronomy 16:17 NASB)

Jesus sat down near the collection box in the Temple and watched as the crowds dropped in their money. Many rich people put in large amounts. Then a poor widow came and dropped in two small coins. Jesus called his disciples to him and said, "I tell you the truth, this poor widow has given more than all the others who are making contributions. For they gave a tiny part of their surplus, but she, poor as she is, has given everything she had to live on." (Mark 12:41–44 NLT)

Giving is not a financial issue; it is a heart issue. For where your treasure is, there your heart will be also. (Matthew 6:23 NIV)

O—Own Family

You have a responsibility to serve your family, including spouses, children, parents, grandchildren, grandparents, aunts and uncles, nephews and nieces, and in-laws. When I say responsibility, I am not saying you are responsible for them but to help them become responsible human beings. In a world in which families are geographically dispersed, it is probable you may not have even met some of your cousins and relatives. My focus is predominantly on generations one, two, and three when working with families. However, if the situations call for it, other relatives and extended family may be brought into the planning process. The important question is, what are you teaching your children and grandchildren through your words and your examples?

Holy Coach: But those who won't care for their relatives, especially those in their own household, have denied the true faith. Such people are worse than unbelievers. He must manage his own family well, having children who respect and obey him. For if a man cannot manage his own household, how can he take care of God's church? (Or his business) Children are a gift from the Lord; they are a reward from him. Children born to a young man are like arrows in a warrior's hands. How joyful is the man whose quiver is full of them! He will not be put to shame when he confronts his accusers at the city gates. Grandchildren are the crowning glory of the aged; parents are the pride of their children. Tell your children about it in the years to come, and let your children tell their children. Pass the story down from generation to generation. (1 Timothy 5:8; 3:4–5; Proverbs 17:6; Psalm 127:3–5; Joel 1:3 NLT)

A—Affinity Groups

Affinity is a natural attraction, liking, or feeling of kinship with people with whom you have a close relationship. This includes friends, neighbors, coworkers, your employer, your employees if you are an employer, people at your place of worship, and people in activities in which you are involved. Here too you have a responsibility to serve. If you are an employer, do your people work for you, or do you work for them? Legally, they work for you, but how successful would your business be if your employees could see that you were working for their best interests, that you were grateful for their services, and that you did things for them to show how much you appreciated them? My guess is that their loyalty, dedication, commitment, and morale would be quite high.

Holy Coach: So he (Jesus) got up from the table, took off his robe, wrapped a towel around his waist, and poured water into a basin. Then he began to wash the disciples' feet, drying them with the towel he had around him. (John 13:4–5 NLT)

Jesus had twelve employees gathered in a room for a business dinner. He knew His role as the boss would end in the next twenty-four hours. A typical boss would expect his staff to serve him, but Jesus demonstrated His care for them by doing something completely out of the norm by reversing roles. Did it have an effect on the team's commitment and loyalty? Ten would be martyred, Judas hung himself, and the twelfth would spend his retirement years imprisoned on an island for promoting the company's mission that spread to every corner of the world and continues to impact lives today. He wrote the final book of the Bible, Revelation, while imprisoned.

If you are employed, the concept of service is obvious, but do you serve grudgingly or with joy? Do you give it your best or only enough to get by? Are you working to benefit only yourself or the people you work with and for? Interestingly, by doing the second, you achieve the first.

Holy Coach: Lazy people irritate their employers, like vinegar to the teeth or smoke in the eyes. Trustworthy messengers refresh like snow in summer. They revive the spirit of their employer. As workers who tend a fig tree are allowed to eat the fruit, so workers who protect their employer's interests will be rewarded. Two people are better off than one, for they can help each other succeed. If one person falls, the other can reach out and help. But someone who falls alone is in real trouble.

Likewise, two people lying close together can keep each other warm. But how can one be warm alone? (Proverbs 10:26, 25:13, 27:18; Ecclesiastes 4:9–11 NLT)

Your city, your community, your neighborhood has hurting people. They may be living next door to you or down the street. What kind of neighbor are you?

Holy Coach: Jesus replied with a story: "A Jewish man was traveling from Jerusalem down to Jericho, and he was attacked by bandits. They stripped him of his clothes, beat him up, and left him half dead beside the road. "By chance a priest came along. But when he saw the man lying there, he crossed to the other side of the road and passed him by. A Temple assistant walked over and looked at him lying there, but he also passed by on the other side. "Then a despised Samaritan came along, and when he saw the man, he felt compassion for him. Going over to him, the Samaritan soothed his wounds with olive oil and wine and bandaged them.

Then he put the man on his own donkey and took him to an inn, where he took care of him. The next day he handed the innkeeper two silver coins, telling him, 'Take care of this man. If his bill runs higher than this, I'll pay you the next time I'm here.' "Now which of these three would you say was a neighbor to the man who was attacked by bandits?" Jesus asked. Never abandon a friend—either yours or your father's. When disaster strikes, you won't have to ask your brother for assistance. It's better to go to a neighbor than to a brother who lives far away. Do not withhold good from those who deserve it when it's in your power to help them. If you can help your neighbor now, don't say, "Come back tomorrow, and then I'll help you." (Luke 10:30–36; Proverbs 3:27–28, 27:10 NLT)

Being a good Samaritan means caring for others and not expecting anything in return. Three men had a chance to be significant. If you had been the injured man, which of the three would you consider was significant to you? Over two thousand years later, almost everyone knows the story of the Good Samaritan. We even use it in our common language as a descriptor for a generous and kind person. Is that the legacy you would want for yourself and your family?

L—Legal Agencies

We Americans enjoy freedoms and opportunities not available to the majority of people in the world because of our unique form of government. Very few countries and societies allow individuals to legally accumulate the kind of wealth Americans have. This comes at a cost; it requires money, people, and leaders to be devoted to government at every level.

Part of our job as financial advisors is to minimize taxes for our clients, and we do that. No one likes to pay taxes, but we need to accept the fact that there is some amount that is fair if we want to continue enjoying the advantages we have in this country.

Holy Coach: Now tell us what you think about this: Is it right to pay taxes to Caesar or not?" But Jesus knew their evil motives. "You hypocrites!" he said. "Why are you trying to trap me? Here, show me the coin used for the tax." When they handed him a Roman coin, he asked, "Whose picture and title are stamped on it?"

"Caesar's," they replied. "Well, then," he said, "give to Caesar what belongs to Caesar, and give to God what belongs to God." (Matthew 22:17–21 NLT)

Without getting into politics, our government is supposed to be of the people, by the people, and for the people. That means we have a responsibility to serve our country. Since the *a* in *America* doesn't fit nicely into my acronym, I had to go with "Legal Agencies," but I am saying we all need to include service to our country as a goal. What form that takes is up to you. We say that military personnel "serve" their country, but so do police officers, firefighters, teachers, and government employees, even councilmembers, politicians, senators, members of Congress, and presidents.

Holy Coach: Everyone must submit to governing authorities. For all authority comes from God, and those in positions of authority have been placed there by God. So anyone who rebels against authority is rebelling against what God has instituted, and they will be punished. For the authorities do not strike fear in people who are doing right, but in those who are doing wrong. Would you like to live without fear of the authorities? Do what is right, and they will honor you. The authorities are God's servants, sent for your good. But if you are doing wrong, of course you should be afraid, for they have the power to punish you. They are God's servants, sent for the very purpose of punishing those who do what is wrong. So you must submit to them, not only to avoid punishment, but also to keep a clear conscience. (Romans 13:1–5 NLT)

No matter your political preferences, would you want to live in a world without some form of government? There would be chaos, violence, and civil unrest and wars; it would be the survival of the fittest. Your government needs your Time, Talent, Training, and Treasures in an employee or volunteer leadership role or as a funding source, so find ways to give back to your community, city, or country.

S—Spiritual

I am a Christian, but I want to offer wisdom to anyone who wants to live a life of joy and significance regardless of religious background or belief. The truths I have provided are true regardless of one's personal faith. Whether someone believes in God or is an atheist does not change wisdom and laws that consistently produce desired results.

Everyone has a spiritual side and I am not talking about religion or ethnicity. I am talking about that part of human beings that feels there is something greater than themselves that has a role in their lives and defines who they are. Whatever or whomever that is must be served.

In my own life, believing that a creator God has a master plan and has given me a mission, a specific role, and being a part of accomplishing that master plan gives my life meaning and purpose. You need to discover your role in a master plan; the role is the service you offer. If there is a master plan, your role is not optional, it is a requirement. If you do not fulfill that responsibility, you will never be fulfilled. I believe you have been given specific talents, skills, and abilities to accomplish your part of the bigger plan. You have been wonderfully designed; you are valuable and needed. What are you passionate about?

Passion

The five GOALS need to be based on what you feel passionate about, the things that stir your soul and move you emotionally. What causes you to express strong and intense feelings and emotions? What makes you angry, brings tears to your eyes, and saddens you, makes you smile, or makes you feel good about yourself? What would make every day satisfying, causing you to want more of those feelings? Find and pursue your passion and you will never work a day of your life.

Financial

Returning to the financial form of worth, there are three components for which goals need to be established. The lifeblood of every business and individual is cash flow. Without cash flow, nothing happens. If monies going out are equal to monies coming in, the status quo is maintained but there is no growth. More monies going out than coming in is degeneration and possibly disaster. For growth to occur, monies coming in must be greater than money going out.

About now, I am probably getting a "Duh! I know this!" from you, but then, why are so many people barely getting by and heavily in debt? It might be assumed this is a condition relegated to low- or moderate-income individuals. Not so! It is not out of the question for me to be working with a client who has a six- or seven-figure income and a negative cash flow. One reason is that they have not set goals for how they use their cash flow. Let me use a word that can send chills up the spine: *budget*. Hopefully, you are not feeling a little squeamish right now—it is not a bad word!

Budgeting is often thought of as an activity for low-income families that are barely getting by. When cash flow is tight, pennies must be pinched and anxiety runs high. As income increases and there seems to be a little margin, the pressure recedes and the need to know where every dollar is going isn't quite as important. The checking account is actually growing. Life is good.

Then something interesting happens. Various toys start showing up. Cars and homes are upgraded. The checking account, like water, seeks its original level because the expenditures magically rise to the level of the income. There is a problem, though. The bigger house brought with it higher property taxes, utility expenses, and insurance premiums, all of which increase every year. Likewise, for the two new cars and the new boat. Fortunately, the income increases again. Now the excess cash flow can be saved and invested, right? Maybe not. You get the picture.

A budget is simply goal setting for your cash flow; it is a plan. Remember, without a plan, you can wind up somewhere you do not want to be. Without a budget, you almost surely will be where you do not want to be. On the assumption that your financial objective is to be secure and comfortable, will having homes and toys and things but no savings or investments for that rainy day accomplish that? Will spending every dollar you bring in provide security? It may provide creature comforts, but will it give you emotional and spiritual comfort?

If you are fortunate enough to have more income than you could ever spend and are accumulating wealth, is a budget still necessary? I believe it is. Going back to GOALS, your goal setting should start there and carry through to your cash flow. Each one of the letters in the acronym has an impact on your finances. Again, cash flow is the lifeblood for achieving your goals. Once your major life goals are clear, you will be in a better position to allocate your cash flow effectively to achieve those goals. That allocation is a budget, the power and energy that can light up your life. Think of a budget as the instrument that turns diffused light and energy into a laser beam that gives you the power to do things you could never do if your light (money) is spread over way too many things.

The second financial component is assets. Assets are of three types: those that appreciate, those that depreciate, and those that produce income and in some instances appreciate as well. Multiple-choice question: check off which types you think are best to have. My guess is you eliminated the assets that depreciate. Here then is a mystery. Why do so many people buy more assets that depreciate or produce no income than acquire the preferred assets? They have multiple cars, motorcycles, RVs, boats, and homes. And homes need furniture, appliances, floor and wall coverings, a pool, landscaping, and air conditioning. You will argue that a home is real estate and an appreciating asset. It can be, but let me remind you of 2008. Real estate values plummeted, and the foreclosure rate skyrocketed especially where people bought vacation homes; in those areas, demand went down as fast as a rock in a pond.

Another mystery regarding their abundance is most of these depreciating assets have ongoing and increasing expenses and are purchased with debt, requiring even more cash flow. If cash flow is the lifeblood, the patient is now in danger of bleeding out. Gas prices, utility costs, taxes, insurance, and maintenance costs keep going up and up and up. Even if the real estate is appreciating, which is not certain, these asset types produce no income and, in fact, the related expenses probably wipe out any real estate appreciation. (I am referring to residences for personal use, not income- producing real estate investments.) They become a life-blood leech. I am reiterating that I am not saying these things are bad and should not be added to your balance sheet. I am saying you need to be clear as to what you want your assets to accomplish and set a goal for every major asset. Owning a home to raise your family is an honorable, noble, and legitimate goal. Owning a bigger, more expensive home to impress your friends and satisfy your ego may not be appropriate. If owning a couple of all-terrain vehicles facilitates family fun and bonding and creates valuable memories and traditions, go for it because those are good goals. If the new set of golf clubs keeps Dad on the links instead of the kid's soccer field on the weekends, that's a bad goal.

The third financial component is a four-letter word: *debt*. I do want to be clear. Unlike some advisors, I am not saying debt should be avoided at all costs, although I suggest you think of it in those terms; that is just not realistic or even possible in some cases. I am saying debt is dangerous, like playing with a supposedly tame lion; it can suddenly turn on you and eat you alive. Perhaps the better analogy is a herd of horses. They can be useful as work animals or to produce income, but they can cause a stampede that tramples you when they are out of control; remember the coffee grinder incident in the movie *City Slickers*?

You need to set goals for the type and amount of debt you are willing to take on. Reread the Family Wealth GOSPEL for the type of debt I believe can be considered; any other type should be avoided. You should use credit cards to purchase only essentials and pay them off every month. I know that is difficult today when so many purchases are Internet generated. It just means you must be more diligent in what you categorize as essential. Do not use credit cards for discretionary purchases, especially if they are emotional purchases. I do believe using credit cards that offer rewards or cash-back benefits are actually good stewardship, AS LONG AS YOU ARE NOT TEMPTED TO BUY WHAT YOU DO NOT NEED, AND ALWAYS PAY THE BALANCE OFF EVERY MONTH! Otherwise, be old-fashioned—use cash.

I include cosigning for other people's debts in this category. I am hard pressed to find any circumstance in which cosigning is a good idea due to the detriment it can have on the person doing the borrowing, your own financial situation, and the relationship you have with the borrower.

I would like to flip to the people side of the family again. The financial resources I discussed above are necessary, but they are not your most valuable resource for achieving significance. Your children and grandchildren are your most valuable asset; they are the paper on which you can write your family's story and pass it from generation to generation. Just as goals need to be established for individual financial components, each person in a family needs to have personal goals. The most important thing you can do for your children is help them discover their God-given purposes and how they can accomplish them. This will be a stepped process with children because they are evolving and changing constantly and quickly.

Think in terms of the goal-setting process I described in IDEA. Something as simple as learning to tie their shoes can be treated as a goal. I am not suggesting it should be made more complicated than it needs to be. With children, the objective is helping them ingrain a process early that can serve them well in making decisions and setting a path for their life. Starting with simple tasks can help them be clear on the right objective or problem when they face more-important issues. This requires time and questions.

The most visible or obvious circumstance is not necessarily the real problem or objective. Learning to tie shoes is not the issue; it is what happens when a person does not know how to do so. What would it do to the child's esteem if he or she was ten and the only one on the sports team who couldn't tie his or her shoes? Kids can be cruel. That may seem like a silly example, but it could just as easily be learning to read and write or add and subtract. So be clear about the objective.

Next, identify the resources needed that are in place or must be acquired. Now, explore all the possible solutions and test each to see if the desired result is achieved. If multiple steps or actions are required and must be accomplished in a predetermined sequence, develop an action plan using as much detail as is necessary. Then execute the plan.

Holy Coach: Then the Lord said to Moses, "Quit praying and get the people moving! Forward, march!" (Exodus 14:15 TLB)

Finally, administer the process. Keep doing what is working and change what isn't. Repeat the process. Do not expect perfection—it is not possible. Strive for excellence. And remember there is no one size fits all. Every child, every person, is different. It needs to be their plan, not yours. I have included Figure 6.1 that identifies subcategories under the areas I described above where you should set specific goals that can be measured. Figure 6.2 is a worksheet to help you set goals in these areas and ascertain specific steps, actions, and time frames. I will go into more detail in on this in Chapter 17.

The question is, *What are you worth?* If it is only about the numbers, your answer was probably easy and quick, but is that how you want to answer the question? You are so much more valuable than a dollar sign on a piece of paper. I know you feel that way about your children and grandchildren. Take this simple test. Please answer each question with a score from 1 to 5, with 1 being Strongly Disagree and 5 being Strongly Agree. Answering these questions truthfully will give you clarity of where you are currently in your life and what you need to work on to identify your vision and fulfill your purpose. Clarity will give you greater confidence, and confidence can propel you to achieving your ultimate vision and the purpose for which you were created. Note: For these questions, family is defined as one individual or multiple individuals related by blood or by a common vision or purpose in any manner. The scoring is on the following page.

1. I have clear values that guide my purpose and have written them down so I can integrate them into my life and share them with the people who are important to me.

2. I have a written plan for how to use my Time, Talent, Training, and Treasures to help me achieve my true purpose.

3. I consistently and openly communicate with and express appreciation for the important people in my life.

4. My family consistently discusses and deals with topics that can be difficult, uncomfortable, or confrontational and still maintain harmony.

5. Our family members have individual personal written vision and mission statements, and the family as an entity has written vision and mission statements created through involvement with all family members, and we have family consensus on the purpose of our family's wealth.

6. Our family has a system for capturing and transferring the family's history, wisdom, experiences, defining moments, and skills to future generations that increases the probability they will be successful.

7. Our family requires, much like a boot camp, that all family members participate in training to help them become financially smart and prepared to successfully manage their own and the family's wealth so the next generations will receive ever-increasing value.

8. Our younger children are encouraged to participate in our family philanthropic activities and pursuits and decisions on how to use the family's wealth for this.

9. Everyone in our family is involved in, understands, and can communicate basic financial terminology and vocabulary regarding investments, estate planning, budgeting, spending, and how to efficiently and effectively utilize money and wealth.

10. Our family has a well-defined written plan for achieving its purpose.

11. All family members are encouraged to be involved in serving and financing the needs of those less fortunate, both as a family and individually.

12. All our family members have a high degree of trust in each other and are committed to helping each other become successful and significant.

13. I am confident that the family's financial holdings are positioned to minimize losses and are earning returns aligned with our comfort for risk.

14. I am confident the tax, legal, and investment strategies we have employed will optimize the family's True Wealth of Time, Talent, Training, and Treasures.

15. I have answered the question, "How much is enough?" for myself and for each of my heirs and have communicated this to each one, and they feel good about these decisions.

16. We have a written family progression plan that defines how, when, and to whom access, management, and control of the family's True Wealth will be efficiently and effectively transferred. This includes defining each person's role and responsibility and adequately preparing them in advance to assume those roles and responsibilities. All family members have been involved in preparing this plan and have favorably adopted it.

17. All family members are encouraged to take an active role in some level of management and involvement and freely express their desires, interests, and passions for the success of the family and themselves. All family members are comfortable they can share their opinions, differences, and objections in a safe environment without fear of rejection or retribution.

18. I am sure that our family assets are protected from frivolous creditors, litigation, marital conflicts, and other who would take advantage of what we have worked so hard to achieve now and in future generations.

19. Our current plan encourages and provides mechanisms for all family members to make their own way, be responsible for their own success, make informed and intelligent decisions, add value to the family and the community by sharing their knowledge and experiences, take appropriate risks

for fair rewards, be good stewards, and become significant as defined by them.

20. We communicate well throughout our family and regularly meet as a family to discuss issues and changes. We have regularly scheduled family meetings to conduct the family's business.

Scoring

If you scored a perfect 100, I refer you to the introductory paragraph where I said it is best to answer these questions truthfully. No family is perfect, and in my experience, every family is dysfunctional somewhere. A perfect score would only be fooling yourself. Please note these scores are only approximations to give you a sense of how healthy your family is and whether help is needed.

Score of 88 or better: Your family has done some extensive planning and feels most areas of your lives are in balance. However, it would be a good idea to review your situation and have someone coach you on additional areas that can use improvement, especially when it comes to involving your children and grandchildren in building your family's legacy.

It would still be good to meet with a family wealth coach to ensure your desires and objectives are intact.

Score of 72 to 87: You have done some planning, but there are still gaps that need to be closed. Without making a conscious and concerted effort to overcome entropy, your family will remain more closely aligned with the 70 percent of families who do not effectively transition their wealth. Families in this range have improved odds of success with the least amount of work. Working with a professional family wealth coach is highly recommended.

Score of 50 to 71: You need help. You should meet with a family wealth coach to help you identify the areas that need the most focus and how best to use your Time, Talents, Training, and Treasures to achieve your desired results.

Families in this range fall solidly within the 70 percent statistic of families who fail to successfully transition their wealth and values. Those families are characterized by devastation to the family wealth by the heirs, strife and conflict in the family, and the destruction of family unity in the following generations. Shirtsleeves to shirtsleeves is almost always assured. These situations can be changed for the better by developing family leadership through effective professional coaching, planning, and implementing the changes necessary to increase the odds of a successful transition provided your family is willing to commit the time, resources, energy, and substantial work that is required.

Score under 50: You have no plan. You now understand your family is in extreme jeopardy of losing everything you have created, including your family's unity and relationships when your wealth transitions to your children and grandchildren who are completely unprepared to manage, preserve, and grow it.

You should meet immediately with a family wealth coach to prioritize the areas of focus and to build a plan that involves your entire family.

The financial industry normally defines wealth as encompassing all forms of family assets and resources, including financial, businesses, and any that appears on a balance sheet. It also includes the family name and reputation, each individual's background, experiences, education, and the intellectual and networking capacity of all family members and spouses. At Family Wealth Leadership, we encapsulate all these into our Four "Ts" of True Wealth for each individual and the family's combined Time, Talent, Training, and Treasures.

CHAPTER 7

Your Wealth

By now, you know the word *wealth* has far more significance than what is in your wallet, as Capital One wonders. Ask anybody that question and you will get the standard response: something related to finances. Because you have read this far, you now know the four Ts of True Wealth are more than financial. These can be divided into sub-categories of forms of capital. Like the word wealth, most people identify the word capital with money, but we also have human, intellectual, social, and spiritual capital. Before I discuss these in more detail, let's hear what the Holy Coach has to say about managing wealth.

The kingdom of heaven is like a man who was going to another place for a visit. Before he left, he called for his servants and told them to take care of his things while he was gone. He gave one servant five bags of gold, another servant two bags of gold, and a third servant one bag of gold, to each one as <u>much as he could handle.</u> Then he left. The servant who got five bags <u>went quickly to invest the money</u> and earned five more bags. In the same way, the servant who had two bags invested them and earned two more. But the servant who got one bag went out and dug a hole in the ground and hid the master's money.

After a long time the master came home and asked the servants what they did with his money. The servant who was given five bags of gold brought five more bags to the master and said, "Master, you trusted me to care for five bags of gold, so I used your five bags to earn five more." The master answered, "You did well. You are a good and loyal servant. Because you were loyal with small things, I will let you care for much greater things. Come and share my joy with me."

Then the servant who had been given two bags of gold came to the master and said, "Master, you gave me two bags of gold to care for, so I used your two bags to earn two more." The master answered, "You did well. You are a good and loyal servant. Because you were loyal with small things, I will let you care for much greater things. Come and share my joy with me."

Then the servant who had been given one bag of gold came to the master and said, "Master, I knew that you were a hard man. You harvest things you did not plant. You gather crops where you did not sow any seed. So I was afraid and went and hid your money in the ground. Here is your bag of gold." The master answered, "You are a wicked and lazy servant! You say you knew that I harvest things I did not plant and that I gather crops where I did not sow any seed. So you should have put my gold in the bank. Then, when I came home, I would have received my gold back with interest."

So the master told his other servants, "Take the bag of gold from that servant and give it to the servant who has ten bags of gold. Those who have much will get more, and they will have much more than they need. But those who do not have much will have everything taken away from them." Then the master said, "Throw that useless servant outside, into the darkness where people will cry and grind their teeth with pain." (Matthew 25:14–30 NCV)

When someone has been given much, much will be required in return; and when someone has been entrusted with much, even more will be required. (Luke 12:48 NLT)

There are lessons in this parable. First, and I know this is hard to accept, but it is not *your* wealth—you are merely the manager or the steward (the title I favor) of it. Second, you are put in charge of an amount you are capable of managing based on your performance managing what you have already been given. You must prove you are capable before you will be given more responsibility. This should not be a surprise; it is basically how our world works whether in business, sports, education, politics, or families. We bring our children along slowly, give them simple tasks and chores while they are young, and then allow them more freedom and responsibility when they have demonstrated good judgment and decision making with the less important activities.

Third, we are expected to improve what we have been given. We have no idea what the backgrounds of these three men were or their personalities or abilities. However, the master evidently had a good fix on their skills and abilities since the amount given to each was different. I am stretching here, but I wonder if he had helped them refine their talents and gave them the training they would need for this responsibility. How and why he chose them and determined how much to put in their trust was not arbitrary. He was evidently confident they would increase his capital or he wouldn't have given them anything. I wonder what he expected of the third guy and if his assessment was confirmed.

Fourth, notice that the master did not tell them what to do with what they had been given, nor did he hover over them to ensure they did what was expected of them: "Then he left." It is a matter of trust. This is an important concept regarding transferring wealth to the kids. Estate planning is too often an attempt to control from the grave using legal documents. There isn't and never will be volumes of papers and documents capable of controlling or changing behaviors. If children have not been taught and practiced responsibility and stewardship prior to dad and mom's passing, they will not change after their parents pass.

Fifth, the wise servants acted quickly. This ties in to my second point. It seems that the two wise servants had some skills and experience. They did not have to take an online trading class or earn an MBA; they had prepared for this day. They didn't know when it would come, but they were ready when it did. They also understood the time value of money. The sooner they could put it to work, the more they could make. They managed their time and training effectively.

Sixth, the master expected them to take risk and rewarded them for doing so. We are not told how they invested the money, but a 100 percent return in a relatively short time is pretty good. It does say, "After a long time the master came home," but even at a 10 percent annual return, it would take seven years to double according to the rule of 72 (dividing 72 by the interest rate gives the number of years for an investment to double).

For example, a 6 percent return requires 12 years to double the investment. Don't expect any investment advisor to duplicate this feat in what appears to be a much shorter time; to get such a return requires significant risk. Of course, Jesus was making a point, not recommending anyone should take imprudent risks, but He also made the point with the lazy servant that avoiding risk is wrong.

Seventh, doing the right thing in the right way produces a positive result and creates even more opportunities. The lazy servant lost out and the wise servants got more. We are not told how they were personally compensated for demonstrating good stewardship, but in our world, and I suspect in this story, either their salaries increased with the added responsibility or there was a nice end-of-the-year bonus or commission. The master said to the first two servants, "Come and share my joy with me," so he evidently cut them in on a piece of the action. More likely, it was stock ownership since Jesus started this parable with, "The kingdom of heaven is like . . ."

Eighth, money is a test. If you want to know other peoples' values, and what is important to them, look at their checkbooks and calendars. Okay, in today's world, look at their credit card statements and their smartphones. I already talked about cash flow, assets, and liabilities. If their cash flow is negative, their liabilities are high, and nonproductive assets dominate their balance sheets, what would be your assessment of their stewardship grades?

Finally, doing nothing is not acceptable. You are in this world to produce. Our subject is significance for you and your family. You cannot have value if you produce nothing. Service and production are synonymous. Manufacturing or servicing a car, a computer, a television, or any product provides what people want or need. When you are not producing, your value is declining. To my mind, this is why a "sitting on the beach" retirement is not an option. It may not be an option for some because they failed to save enough for retirement, but that is not my point here. Even if more than enough financial resources are available, the idea of being stagnant and rudderless is just not appealing to them. They must be active and challenged. When you stop producing and serving, you begin dying! I needed to share the above story of the master's treatment of his servants to set up my discussion of the four Ts of True Wealth.

Holy Coach: Wise people are rewarded with wealth, but fools only get more foolishness. (Proverbs 14:24 NCV)

I want you to have the wisdom you need to live a joyful and fulfilling life. Accumulating wealth is not that difficult, nor does it require an MBA. Anyone can become a multimillionaire if they spend less than they make, save and invest the difference in prudent investments, and start saving early and often. Save $300 monthly and earn 8 percent on it for 50, and you will have $2,300,000. I just gave you a formula, but I didn't give you wisdom. Any fool can follow these simple criteria. Wisdom comes into play by knowing how and in what to invest, but also knowing that starting and consistency are the keys to making anything happen.

Time

Holy Coach: There is a time for everything, and a season for every activity under the heavens: a time to be born and a time to die, a time to plant and a time to uproot, a time to kill and a time to heal, a time to tear down and a time to build, a time to weep and a time to laugh, a time to mourn and a time to dance, a time to scatter stones and a time to gather them, a time to embrace and a time to refrain from embracing, a time to search and a time to give up, a time to keep and a time to throw away, a time to tear and a time to mend, a time to be silent and a time to speak, a time to love and a time to hate, a time for war and a time for peace. What do workers gain from their toil? I have seen the burden God has laid on the human race. He has made everything beautiful in its time. He has also set eternity in the human heart; yet no one can fathom what God has done from beginning to end. I know that there is nothing better for people than to be happy and to do good while they live. That each of them may eat and drink, and find satisfaction in all their toil—this is the gift of God. (Ecclesiastes 3:1–13 NIV)

Would you believe me if I said there was sufficient time in your day for you to get done everything important that needs doing? My guess is you responded with, "Fat chance. You haven't seen my to-do list." I get it. My list is constantly growing, too. But let me suggest it is not a time problem but a priority and control problem. We all have the same amount of time, yet other people seem to have time for their families, for vacations, and for recreational and spiritual activities and they still get their work done. My question had a key condition: I included the word *important*. You may have heard the admonishment, "Don't major in minors." The problem is that we do not prioritize what is important to us; we are easily distracted by nonessential activities. Computers and smartphones were supposed to make us more productive. To some extent, they have, but, honestly, how much time does that alluring glow emanating from the HD screen suck out of your day? Are you the fastest draw in the office or on your block when that text alert goes off?

Another priority problem is that we allow other people to enforce their priorities on us. Sometimes, this is unavoidable, but most of the time, it's because we cannot say no. We want to please and be accepted, so we accept a task that helps someone else, and the important things we should be doing are pushed down the to-do list as other people's desires are slipped into first, second, and third place. If you do not set your own priorities, someone else will set them for you.

What are you doing that someone else can or should do? We get into this mode of believing we are the only one capable of doing something, but we stifle ingenuity, creativity, and motivation in others when we hold onto the reins too tightly. A business owner who tries to do everything and make all the decisions becomes a slave to the business and the business will not grow. This is also true in families if the patriarch is a dictator. Honestly, you are not good at everything. There are things we are doing right now that someone else could do better, and continuing to do them ourselves uses up valuable time we could use for something more important, such as spending time with our spouses and children.

This can be a major issue for business owners when the business rather than the family becomes the priority. It may be a control issue. We have all heard, "I have to work twelve hours a day, seven days a week to take care of my family." The problem is that person wakes up one day to discover there is no longer a family to take care of. Cat's in the cradle! Even when it is something you do not enjoy doing, you will not give it up because you feel you must be in control.

See if you relate to this scenario. Parent asks child to do something. Time goes by. Child hasn't done it. Parent asks child again to do something, time goes by, child hasn't done it. Parent asks child a third time to do something, time goes by, child hasn't done it. Parent gives up and does it for the child. The normal parent response at that point is, "It was easier and faster to do it myself than fight with my child." Although that is probably true, the message sent to the child is, "Just wait it out and eventually parent will do it for child." The child just moved his or her to-do list onto yours. Now you're working two to-do lists, yours and theirs. No wonder there isn't enough time in your day to get everything done.

Bringing this back to significance, it is critical to learn how to use your time efficiently and effectively to complete the tasks that bring significance. Priorities must be established and guarded jealously and intensely. Here is a short list of priorities that vie for your time: family, work, friends and relationships, self-improvement, health, spiritual enrichment, philanthropy, community service, public service, and recreation and rest. I am sure you have more you can add to this list.

I will let the Holy Coach close this section with an example of a woman who had her time-allocation priorities confused. Let me set the stage. Lazarus (yes, the same gentleman Jesus called out from his grave) was evidently not married because his two sisters, Martha and Mary, lived with him. Martha was the oldest, so running the house was her responsibility. Jesus came to town and decided to have dinner at the Lazarus household. But Jesus was not traveling alone. There were twelve guys who went everywhere with Him. Jesus was well known in Lazarus's neighborhood (that's what happens when you raise someone from the dead), and it is likely Lazarus invited a few neighbors, so this would not have been a small, intimate dinner for a few people.

As Jesus and the disciples continued on their way to Jerusalem, they came to a certain village where a woman named Martha welcomed him into her home. Her sister, Mary, sat at the Lord's feet, listening to what he taught. But Martha was distracted by the big dinner she was preparing. She came to Jesus and said, "Lord, doesn't it seem unfair to you that my sister just sits here while I do all the work? Tell her to come and help me." But the Lord said to her, "My dear Martha, you are worried and upset over all these details! There is only one thing worth being concerned about. Mary has discovered it, and it will not be taken away from her." (Luke 10:38–42 NLT)

It is so easy to become distracted by the unimportant and miss what is important if you do not guard and prioritize your time to do those things that are significant, which lead to you being significant.

Talent

The above parable is normally referred to as the parable of the talents. Two thousand years ago, a talent was a measure of weight and money. It was something of value that a person could possess and use to better their lives. I do not know how the word transitioned into a description of the innate abilities every person possesses, but that is how we use it today.

Holy Coach: God has given each of you a gift from his great variety of spiritual gifts. Use them well to serve one another. In his grace, God has given us different gifts for doing certain things well. So if God has given you the ability to prophesy, speak out with as much faith as God has given you. If your gift is serving others, serve them well. If you are a teacher, teach well. If your gift is to encourage others, be encouraging. If it is giving, give generously. If God has given you leadership ability, take the responsibility seriously. And if you have a gift for showing kindness to others, do it gladly. (1 Peter 4:10; Romans 12:6–8 NLT)

Most conversations limit the discussion to three Ts: Time, Talent, and Treasures, whereas we added the fourth, Training. This is an important differentiation. In the Holy Coach's comments, did you notice the distinction? Five times, He said, "God has given." You cannot acquire talents; they are God given. You were born with them. I love to sing. There is only one problem—I can't. When we did skits and recitals in elementary school that included singing, I was given the speaking parts. You may be a good singer or play an instrument. Perhaps you have artistic talents, can dance, are good at sports, are a genius in math or science, a good speaker or salesperson, or have entrepreneurial talents. I am five-foot, ten inches and weigh 155 pounds. I played football and basketball in high school, but there is a reason this book is not about my professional football or basketball career. I have some athletic talent, but not that much. You can refine and enhance your talents through training and practice, but you cannot achieve excellence at something you are not gifted to do. Attempting to do so is a waste of time, yet people will spend years and lifetimes in jobs, careers, and pursuits they are not equipped for and achieve mediocrity and live only adequate lives.

To be significant, you must discover and gain clarity (remember that the I in IDEA was Investigation) of the talents you were given. A flathead screwdriver is designed specifically to turn a certain type of screw. When it is used as a chisel, can opener, small crowbar, or hammer, the tip becomes rounded and chipped and the handle cracks. It becomes useless when it is used for tasks for which it was not intended or designed to accomplish. You have God-given talents intended to help you become significant—discover and develop those talents and you will be. Spend your life trying to be a hammer, a chisel, or a can opener when you were designed to be a screwdriver and you will never achieve significance.

Holy Coach: The Lord has filled Bezalel with the Spirit of <u>God</u> and <u>has given him the skill, ability, and knowledge</u> to do all kinds of work. He is able to design pieces to be made of gold, silver, and bronze, to cut stones and jewels and put them in metal, to carve wood, and to do all kinds of work. Also, <u>the Lord has given</u> Bezalel and Oholiab, the son of Ahisamach from the tribe of Dan, <u>the ability to teach others</u>. The Lord has given them the skill to do all kinds of work. They are able to cut designs in metal and stone. They can plan and sew designs in the fine linen with the blue, purple, and red thread. And they are also able to weave things. (Exodus 35:31–35 NCV)

Holy Coach: He did all this so you would never say to yourself, 'I have achieved this wealth with my own strength and energy.' Remember the Lord your God. He is the one who gives you power to be successful, in order to fulfill the covenant he confirmed to your ancestors with an oath. (Deuteronomy 8:17–18 NLT)

Not developing and using your talents or thinking they are the result of anything you have done is not wise. It is also not wise to use your talents for something they were not designed to be used for because that never works. What was the outcome for the servant who buried his talents (gold)? What he had been given was stripped away, and he was thrown into the street. Burying your talents and not using them to produce value will cause your talents to atrophy like an unused muscle. Instead of progressing positively through life, those who bury their talents or do not use them for righteous causes will be cast out of the family, their work, and society. What you can do with your family's talents is help all those in it discover theirs and promote and protect them. Here again is a short list to consider, but by no means should it be limited to these: values, character, ethics, morals, spiritual gifts, personality, good habits, unique abilities, heritage, legacy, health and well-being, discernment and diligence, and having a servant's heart.

Training

I mentioned that you can improve, enhance, and refine talent through training and practice. Practice is simply a component of training. This is why I added Training as the fourth T. Whereas Talent cannot be acquired, you can be trained and you can pass it on by training others. Of the four, this T makes all the difference in achieving significance for yourself, your children, and your family.

You cannot create more time or talents for and in your children. There are only twenty-four hours in a day, and your children's talents will be whatever they will be. The primary reason 70 percent of wealth is lost during the transition to the next generation is because children and grandchildren have not been properly trained in how to use their Time, Talents, and Treasures to become good stewards, nor have they been trained how to identify, design, develop, and implement the value they can offer the world.

Holy Coach: Train up a child in the way he should go: and when he is old, he will not depart from it. (Proverbs 22:6 KJV)

Students are not greater than their teacher. But the student who is fully trained will become like the teacher. (Luke 6:40 NLT)

Sports is probably the best and easiest example of the importance of training. Professional athletes train, and train, and train. Putting a dancer or figure skater in the same category as a sports figure, their training is intense and consistent. If it isn't, they will never reach the top of their respective disciplines. Would you pay to see a substandard performance by dancers or skaters or a losing sports team? Winning teams draw large crowds and pay their players big bucks. Athletes understand the importance of discipline, which is another word for training. When you discipline your children, you are training them to do what is right so they will be successful. Do you want children who just show up for the game of life or who have been trained and disciplined to win? I know that seems like a silly question, but if it is silly, why are they losing the wealth they inherit so rapidly and tragically? Honestly, parents are not doing a good job of training their children in the art of stewardship or giving them the practice they need with proper supervision.

Holy Coach: Fathers, do not provoke your children to anger by the way you treat them. Rather, bring them up with the discipline and instruction that comes from the Lord. (Ephesians 6:4 NLT)

You have been believers so long now that you ought to be teaching others. Solid food (i.e., wisdom) is for those who are mature, who through training have the skill to recognize the difference between right and wrong. (Hebrews 5:12, 14 NLT)

Discipline is hard for both the trainer and the trainee. Discipline requires discipline! If I am going to teach my children discipline, I must have the discipline to do so. If it is sports, I, the trainer, must be on the field, court, or ice before my trainee shows up and leave only after he or she goes home. Then I probably have homework that needs to be done to formulate a training regimen and adapt it to the individual since each student is different.

Being the trainer or coach is hard work; it requires as much dedication as that required of the athlete or performer, but all successful athletes and performers recognize and acknowledge when they are standing on the platform or stage being honored that their success was due in large part to their trainers and coaches. The hard work is worth it. The trainer doesn't get the honor—the trainee honors the trainer. The trainer achieves significance through the trainee.

Athletes and performers achieve significance by providing a service we call entertainment. We get that, yet we are falling short when it comes to preparing our children to experience a successful performance and win the game of life.

Holy Coach: You will say, "How I hated discipline! If only I had not ignored all the warnings! To learn, you must love discipline; it is stupid to hate correction. Only a fool despises a parent's discipline; whoever learns from correction is wise. (Proverbs 5:12, 12:1, 15:5 NLT)

And have you forgotten the encouraging words God spoke to you as his children? He said, "My child, don't make light of the Lord's discipline, and don't give up when he corrects you. For the Lord disciplines those he loves . . . For our earthly fathers disciplined us for a few years, doing the best they knew how. No discipline is enjoyable while it is happening—it's painful! But afterward there will be a peaceful harvest of right living for those who are trained in this way. (Hebrews 12:6, 7b, 10a, 11)

All athletes are disciplined in their training. They do it to win a prize that will fade away, but we do it for an eternal prize.

So I run with purpose in every step. I am not just shadowboxing. I discipline my body like an athlete, training it to do what it should. (1 Corinthians 9:25–27 NLT)

The most loving thing you can do for children is to discipline them and teach them to embrace discipline for the values and rewards it offers.

Although I am saying you need to train your children in stewardship, I think parents are not able to do this without help, nor should they. There is great value in introducing a professional coach into the process. This can occur at any age, but it is especially important when the children are old enough to make life-impacting decisions. I have played sports and have coached kids in sports, including my sons. What I learned, and suspect you understand, is that it was best for my sons and for me when someone else coached them.

This short list includes learning, encouraging, teaching, and demonstrating values, morals, ethics, education, wisdom, reputation, skills, tradition, experiences, hard work, serving others, interpersonal skills, alliances, networking, and family unity.

Treasures

There are two possibilities for how treasures are used: they are earned or burned. The earned is understandable; someone had to earn the treasures. Even if inherited, someone else did the earning. But, burned has two connotations. Picture yourself sitting on the floor by your cozy fireplace and one by one tossing your hard-earned $1,000 bills into the fire. Sound like a good idea? That is one type of burn.

Now imagine you buy gas so you can go on your journey. This treasure is also being burned, but do you see the difference? The first scenario gives nothing in return. Sure, there may be a little heat for a very short moment, but that warmth disappears quickly and the cold rushes back. This is the problem with using treasures for things that only satisfy pleasures. They feel good for a moment, but the feeling goes away quickly, and more dollars are required to feel good again. The fire dies out when the dollars run out! There is nothing but ashes, and your kids don't want your ashes.

The second scenario is about the journey and using your treasures to get to your desired destinations along that journey, and having a vehicle you can give to your children to help them on their journey when your journey has ended. When you use your treasures as fuel to get somewhere, you get something long lasting in return. Additionally, you can use it as fuel in a vehicle that produces more fuel. The fuel in the farmer's tractor provides a return on his investment. Taxi and delivery truck drivers, and the furniture or car hauler, make money from the fuel they buy. There are only two choices. Every dollar you spend is either moving you closer to your goals and objectives or farther away—there is no neutral! Even if you fuel your vehicle, but only run the engine while the gearshift is in neutral, you are going nowhere fast. Just like the fireplace, the fuel runs out, must be replenished, and the car becomes useless when there is no more money to buy gas.

Holy Coach: Those who are rich should take pride that God has shown them that they are spiritually poor. The rich will die like a wild flower in the grass. The sun rises with burning heat and dries up the plants. The flower falls off, and its beauty is gone. In the same way the rich will die while they are still taking care of business. Don't store treasures for yourselves here on earth where moths and rust will destroy them and thieves can break in and steal them. Wherever your treasure is, there the desires of your heart will also be. (James 1:10–11; Matthew 6:19, 21, 24 NCV and NLT)

We treasure our treasures because we think they can somehow bring certainty into our lives. Although I understand and can be susceptible myself to falling into that mental trap, I know there is truly nothing we humans can do to remove all uncertainty. History is filled with families and nations that had more wealth than anyone can imagine, yet their reigns ended, and no one remembers them except for a few paragraphs or chapters in history books.

Any certainty about jobs, careers, homes, and retirements was wiped out in the 2008 recession. Wealth that took decades to build was cut in half for many families. Yours may have been one of them. The irony is that we accumulate more wealth so we can worry less, but the more we have, the more we worry.

Another irony is people will not engage in philanthropy because they believe they will not have enough if they give it away, but they will spend vast amounts buying things they do not need. Spending $20,000 on a vacation to Europe for your family could be a good thing—the kids would love it, and family bonding is possible. Of course, there will be side trips, food, gifts, souvenirs, and buying more luggage to carry all that stuff home, which raises the cost of the vacation to maybe $25,000 or $30,000.

I'll let you answer these next questions. What if you spent that money on a trip to a poor village in Africa instead to build a small hospital or a school, dig some water wells, or deliver food and medical supplies? Would the family still have a bonding opportunity? Twenty years later, which trip would your children say had the bigger impact on them and whom they turned out be? Which souvenir would wind up in the attic or basement and which on your desk or mantel—the wooden shoes from Amsterdam or the picture of three or four smiling faces of children having a meal and maybe a lollipop?

Holy Coach: Share your food with the hungry, and give shelter to the homeless. Give clothes to those who need them, and do not hide from relatives who need your help. Feed the hungry, and help those in trouble. Then your light will shine out from the darkness, and the darkness around you will be as bright as noon. Teach those who are rich in this world not to be proud and not to trust in their money, which is so unreliable. Their trust should be in God, who richly gives us all we need for our enjoyment. Tell them to use their money to do good. They should be rich in good works and generous to those in need, always being ready to share with others. By doing this they will be storing up their treasure as a good foundation for the future so that they may experience true life. (Isaiah 58:7, 10; 1 Timothy 6:17–19 NLT)

Buying things or going on nice vacations is not inherently wrong; I am not promoting a puritanical lifestyle. My message is about significance and how to achieve it. People spend money on what they don't need instead of giving to those who are in need, including their own family in some instances, in an effort to remove uncertainty from their lives. The irony is that the closest we can ever get to certainty is by investing in people and causes that will care and provide for us when there is no more money. The only certainty we can have comes from those who love us for who we are, not what we own.

The reason I can encapsulate wealth into these four Ts is that they cover all the forms of capital. *Financial capital* is what we normally think of when we hear that word, but it is the least important form of capital. The four Ts are all necessary and important. All of them must be nurtured and given your complete attention—intention is not enough.

Human capital is simply people; nothing in this world can be accomplished without people. Again, you cannot be significant by yourself. *Intellectual capital* is essentially what I hope you are getting by reading this book, a wisdom manual that shares with you the greatest source of wisdom ever written.

Social capital is all about relationships. This is especially true where attention is critical as opposed to intention. The latter is what we tell others when we have failed to meet their expectations. Dad intended to make it to his child's soccer games but didn't. Daughter intended to call Mom on her birthday but got busy and time slipped away. Attention is what they enjoy when we have met their expectations.

Finally, there is *spiritual capital,* which forms the basis of your morals and principles. Your spirit is who you are. We can call it personality, but it is much more. It is that part that drives you, that gives you hope and optimism or sadness and depression. It is the part that visualizes opportunities and needs and causes you to take action. Your spirit is inborn, but it is shaped by your experiences and relationships. It is the source of the answers to those eternal questions, Where did I come from? Why am I here? Where am I going?

You can see how human, intellectual, social, and spiritual capital are intertwined. Every member of your family represents all four of these, and everyone is unique and necessary to a person's significance. This is why it is critical to understand each person's makeup and uniqueness so that the family's resources, the five forms of capital (in addition to the four mentioned, I'm including financial capital), can be allocated to allow each member the greatest probability of succeeding and becoming significant.

You have a spirit that must be satisfied. Only you can decide what that means for you. You already know that my spirit craves a relationship with my Creator. If I was created for a purpose, my spirit will never allow me to rest if I am not pursuing that purpose.

Are you feeling restless, unsatisfied, unworthy, unfulfilled, or unnecessary? You should not because you are extremely valuable. You have a wonderful purpose; you just need to discover what it is and what you need to do to accomplish it. If you don't fulfill your purpose, others lose the benefit they might have enjoyed had you done so. If you want to know how and why you were designed as you have been, the best way to find out is to talk to the Designer. Significance is fulfilling your purpose. Service and stewardship are how you get it!

CHAPTER 8

Values Are More Valuable Than Valuables

I have asked you about your worth and your wealth. What are your values? What do you offer the world? The word *value* has several meanings. Like wealth and worth, people usually interpret value in its financial sense. Telling me about your house, your investment portfolio, 401(k)s, cars, and possessions is a typical response.

Holy Coach: The rich think of their wealth as a strong defense; they imagine it to be a high wall of safety. In the blink of an eye wealth disappears, for it will sprout wings and fly away like an eagle. (Proverbs 18:11, 23:5 NLT)

I have used *value* numerous times in this book in the personal sense. I hope I have also encouraged you to recognize you have tremendous value when you use your talents for the right reasons and causes. Here are two of the *American Heritage Dictionary* definitions of *value*: (1) "Worth in usefulness or importance to the possessor; utility or merit"; and (2) "A principle or standard, as of behavior, that is considered important or desirable." The first definition is the personal connotation. I would modify it to include "importance to the beneficiaries" as well as to the possessor. I hope I have convinced you that your value is a factor of the "worth in usefulness or importance" you offer to the beneficiaries of the people and causes you serve.

But it is the second definition I discuss in this chapter. What principles and standards are important and desirable to you? I am not asking whether these are behaviors and character traits you think are nice and you wouldn't mind embracing. Instead, I am asking which personal values you would be willing to give up your life for rather than compromising. I am not trying to be dramatic, but if you claim a certain value or character trait as important to you but your lifestyle contradicts that value, is it really one of your values?

A related word in the definition is *principle*. You may have had an English teacher give you the secret for remembering the difference between *principle* and *principal*. The "le" at the end of the first matches the "le" in "rule"; so, a principle is a rule to be followed or obeyed, a truth or law that works every time. In physics, it would be gravity, or Newton's third law of motion that states for every action there is an equal and opposite reaction. What you sow is what you reap. You plant corn, you reap corn. In life, if you want people to be kind and respectful to you, you must treat them with respect and kindness.

Two more definitions to cover: *unifying* and *integrity*. We normally associate integrity with honesty and consistency. We think of it as someone who does what he or she says they will do. They can be trusted. These are all true, but the definition of integrity from the *American Heritage Dictionary* is the one I want for now: integrity is "steadfast adherence to a strict moral or ethical code. The state of being unimpaired; soundness. The quality or condition of being whole or undivided; completeness." Unifying is "combining into a single unit;

to make or become one; unite; to bring together so as to form a whole; and to join and act together in a common purpose or endeavor."

Let me bring these definitions together in the phrase *unifying values*. The single unit is you. The integrity is strict adherence to moral and ethical codes. Values are the moral and ethical codes. Your unifying values are the moral and ethical codes you adhere to steadfastly to achieve unity and integrity in your life. Again, they are the moral and ethical codes you will never compromise under any circumstances. Your unifying values are your rules and principles for how you will conduct your life. Your values govern what is valuable to you and how you will use your valuables to realize your values. They guide your decisions, your planning, and how you treat people. Before you plan your life, you must be clear on what is important to you. In this chapter, I help you to clarify your unifying values.

Holy Coach: A house is built by wisdom and becomes strong through good sense. Through knowledge its rooms are filled with all sorts of precious riches and valuables. The wise are mightier than the strong, and those with knowledge grow stronger and stronger. Wisdom is more valuable than gold and crystal. It cannot be purchased with jewels mounted in fine gold. A good reputation is more valuable than costly perfume. And the day you die is better than the day you are born. (Proverbs 24:3–5; Job 28:17; Ecclesiastes 7:1 NLT)

I have included a list of values in Figure 8.1, but this is not an exhaustive list, so feel free to add other values that are important to you if they are not on the list. The intent is not that you personally try to identify with every one of these. Rather, select five or ten by writing them down. Then reduce the list again to your top three values.

You will not be eliminating the others permanently, only temporarily, so you can work with a few at a time.

There is no right number. You can attempt to prioritize them, but I do not think that is necessary or even possible. For example, commitment and honesty may be two of your unifying values. It would be difficult to rank one over the other or suggest that one is more important than the other. Your five or ten top values will probably be different from your spouse's, and that too is okay. This is not an exercise in conformity but in discovery. In this case, it is all about you. Identifying your values will be relatively easy because you will intuitively know them. You will be able to relate to many of the values on the list, so the hard part is narrowing them down to a few that you can develop actions around. It is important that you be honest and objective. You are looking to discover who you are or want to become, not a fictional you.

Figure 8.2 is a worksheet we use to help people process their values as the first step of developing their personal significance statements. The following text explains each section of the worksheet, and I then offer an example using my own worksheet in Figure 8.3.

In the first section, list the three top values you identified from Figure 8.1. I use trust as the example. The short action phrase could be, *"I will always honor my promises and follow through on what I say I will do."* There are two reasons for putting this in writing. First, any time you write something, your brain absorbs it in a much stronger way. You can review as often as you wish, and it will become part of your behavior.

Second, I encourage you to have an accountability partner/mentor with whom you share your worksheet. Throughout this book, I encourage you to utilize a coach for your family. In our coaching, we maintain this worksheet and review it either individually or possibly during family meetings. This is not the same as the mentor arrangement, which should be between two individuals who can be honest and critical in a positive context. The point is that everyone should be trying to help each other be successful and significant according to their personal unifying values.

The next paragraph is a brief description of the anticipated benefits to you and others if you are steadfast in this value. *"When I demonstrate my trustworthiness, I feel good about myself, and other people will be able to rely on me and will trust me with greater and more important responsibilities that will, in turn, help me grow and become a better person."*

The next section is where you apply the GOALS. I have each of the letters listed on the worksheet in the order I personally believe is most important, but the order is less important than making sure all five areas are addressed. Even though I have listed them independently, you may choose to aggregate them. For brevity, I do the latter. The first exercise is to document how achieving this value in your life will look in three years. I use three years because that is long enough to develop behaviors while incorporating sufficient urgency to get started; any longer could allow you to procrastinate getting started, and procrastination is a killer of significance (see Chapter 3).

The second part is to tie this into allocating your four Ts of True Wealth. *"When I am trustworthy, my spouse will be confident of my love and devotion; my children will know that everything I do is for their benefit even if it doesn't seem that way to them at that moment. My country and state will never find deceit in my tax returns. My friends and peers will entrust me with their friendship because they know I am reliable. I will faithfully be serving at my church and at least two charities that work with underprivileged and disabled children."* In this paragraph, I was able to address Giving, Own Family, Affinity Groups, Legal Agencies, and Spiritual.

I have only used one unifying value for this example, but you can combine values in these statements. If commitment is another of your values, you could modify the above by saying something like, *"My spouse and children will trust me because they will know I am committed to their security and betterment, which I will demonstrate by ensuring my actions are consistent with my promises to them."* Applying the four Ts can encompass all your values rather than being specific to each value. I have included this, however, in each of the GOALS because it is important to be specific in each of these areas.

Again, you can consolidate all five areas of service into one paragraph or complete one paragraph for each service, which is my preference. For brevity, I am providing only one example here, in this case for family.

"I will have a date night with my spouse every Friday and a special weekend away for our anniversary. I will attend all my children's athletic and recital events. I will also spend one day each month with each child, one on one, doing whatever they want to do. I will be home every evening by 6:00 p.m. so we can have dinners together. We will go on two family vacations every year. I have athletic abilities and musical talent, so I will spend time teaching my children how to play sports and, if they are inclined, how to play the guitar. A portion of our income will be used to encourage them to be involved in organized or individual sports, and we will pay for trainers or musical instructions if they demonstrate their commitment and they have the talent to become expert in their chosen endeavors. We will also commit to providing $25,000 per year for four years for their college educations but expect them to make up any difference through scholarships and working. We prefer they not incur debt to acquire their undergraduate degrees." Do you see how this incorporated commitments to using time, talent, training, and treasures?

Now you can deal with the dangers, opportunities, and strengths that will allow you to accomplish your unifying values. Dangers are anything that would or could be an obstacle to implementing your values in your life. If the value is trust, a danger might be a situation at work or in your business that would require you to compromise your honesty. Or it could be promising to do or deliver something you are incapable of doing. Likewise, it is not unusual for work to infringe on family time and activities. If this is true, you will need to have an honest and hard discussion with yourself on which is the higher priority.

Opportunities are different from strengths in that they are more external situations whereas strengths are more internal. Strengths include all five forms of capital and the four Ts of True Wealth available to you. Having a strong and close family, a supportive spouse, and a job or a business that allows you the needed time to spend with family, take vacations, help in your community, volunteer in worthy causes, and having the financial resources and training to carry through on your promises are examples of strengths. Opportunities could include going to another employer or having a new client who can replace the employer or client who is asking you to compromise your values.

In the family setting, an opportunity might be hiring an extra person so you can free up time at work to spend with your family. That extra person could be an employee at work or the landscape maintenance person, the pool cleaner, and domestic help so everyone in the family can be together at the same time. One caution, though. Do not hire help around the house so your children do not have to complete their assigned tasks as part of their responsibility to the family. Cleaning their own rooms, helping with household chores, and mowing the lawn and raking the cuttings and leaves are all character builders that teach responsibility and the value of work.

The final steps are developing specific actions you can take immediately and over time to deal with the dangers, opportunities, and strengths you just identified so you can fulfill your unifying values. Immediate actions are those you can implement in the next ninety days. Staying with our value trust example, you can show up at your kids' sports activities this weekend before the game starts, stay until the game ends, and leave the cell phone in the car. Every night next week, you can be home to sit down with the entire family for dinner. At work, you can find ways to do your work better and keep your promises to your boss or employees.

Intermediate actions are those you will implement over a longer period. If the action is finding a new job or new client, that will take time, but you must make it an objective. If this switch is necessary to honor your promise to your spouse and children, set a specific deadline for getting it done and share your plan with them. When it happens, their trust in you will be reinforced.

Likewise, you can share your plan for improving trust at work with your employer or employees. The TV show *Undercover Boss* provides a great example of this. After disguising himself or herself and working on the frontline with various employees, a boss reveals his or her real position. The bosses discover while undercover how valuable their employees are as well as the problems to be fixed within the company. Then they make commitments on what they are going to fix and when they will be fixed. The three or four employees highlighted in the show receive commitments for cash gifts, promotions, family vacations, education, and other benefits.

The show's producers follow up a few months later to see the results of the changes and generosity. You can imagine the positive impact on employee morale and trust when they experience firsthand management honoring their promises. The opportunity was going undercover to learn the truth about the company's commitment to its greatest resource. The strengths were the willingness to be vulnerable, to hear the truth, to commit to the changes, and to follow through on their commitments, and they had the resources and capabilities to fulfill their promises. That is not a bad formula for families needing to improve trust.

This process is first completed for the patriarch and matriarch; then it can be completed for each child. The process is repeated for the family unit. A family meeting is held to create a family mission (significance) statement, but before the significance statement can be drafted, the family must identify its unifying values just as you did for yourself.

Since there will be input from many individuals, the list of values could be relatively extensive. The family will need to negotiate the five to ten unifying values its members determine best represent the entire family. There must be consensus; majority rule is not possible because those who do not agree with the entire list will not buy into the objectives the family will ultimately develop.

When this exercise is completed for yourself, your individual family members, and the entire family, you are ready to create your personal mission (significance) statement and your family's significance statement. The personal statements are done only by the subject individual with the help of a coach. The family significance statement is crafted by the entire family under the guidance of a coach.

The coach is even more important to include in the family setting because there will be different objectives and perspectives on the mission and purpose for keeping the family assets aggregated rather than dividing and dumping them on all the heirs. Consensus will avoid division in the ranks. As I said previously, this does not mean everyone gets everything he or she wants or will be 100 percent satisfied with the outcome. It will be a negotiation and compromise, but the objective is the greater good of the whole family, not its individual members. By achieving the greater good for the whole, the greater good for the pieces is also achieved.

Later, when the family entity is making decisions about specific investments, business opportunities, or rules related to providing family funds for education, buying homes, or funding individual pursuits, a majority vote can be used, but consensus is necessary when establishing the family enterprise's purpose and objectives.

Figure 8.3 is an example of my personal unifying values worksheet for your reference and aid in helping you document your own unifying values.

CHAPTER 9

Your Mission

Now that you have an understanding and have documented your highest values in life for you personally and for your family unit, you can create three very important paragraphs: a vision statement, a values statement, and a mission (significance) statement. Again, you should have personal statements for every family member and a separate statement for your family. I discuss in a later chapter why we like families to have a foundation and a family holding company, but for now, understand that each of these entities will have these three statements. They will be different for each entity because they have different objectives. One is a nonprofit and the other a for-profit. If these two entities are utilized, their combined statements will become the statements for the entire family. Even if the holding company is not formed, the family unit will still need these three statements plus separate statements for the foundation if it is created. The value, vision, and mission statements for the family require all family members to participate, and there should be consensus in order to have buy-in by everyone impacted by the family assets.

As with the values worksheet, we work through the significance statement worksheet first and provide a personal worksheet as an example. Please understand that my personal examples are just that—they are only to help you develop your own. Yours should be in your own words, not mine, and centered on your passions.

A vision statement is a brief paragraph describing what you would like to see happen by achieving your significance. If you had the power to make the world a better place, what would that better world look like?

The value statement is a short paragraph defining the value the world would experience through your significance. A simple example of a vision statement would be, "My vision is that every child in America will not go to bed hungry." The value statement might be, "When every child has enough to eat, disease and illnesses will decline and we will have a healthier and stronger generation prepared to improve society."

The mission statement, also relatively brief, describes how you will use your four Ts of True Wealth to accomplish your vision. The vision, value, and mission statements are the what, why, and how (and can include the when and where), respectively. All three statements should be of a length that they can be easily memorized and shared with others. Specific words and steps or actions to accomplish the mission can be defined and explained in a separate paragraph or piece of paper that is not part of the formal mission statement. The mission statement describes your purpose in life in a way that anyone hearing it will understand what you are passionate about accomplishing while you inhabit this planet.

Figure 9.1 is the format we use at Family Wealth Leadership to craft personal mission (significance) statements. The questions are self-explanatory, so I will not go into great detail about them. The primary point in answering these questions is to be specific. As I say in the first question, "world peace" is not an acceptable answer because what would that mean? A dictator would define it as complete submission to his or her rule. Our forebears felt world peace had its best chance through personal responsibility and limited government interference. A second problem with this kind of ambiguity is this objective is impossible if peace is interpreted as everyone and every nation loving each other. Ain't going to happen. So, as you answer these questions, keep it real. Dare to dream and imagine in big ways, but what you put on paper must be doable or you won't do it.

The second question goes to the heart of this exercise. What would significance look like for you? In one sense, the question is premature since you have not had a chance to complete this worksheet yet, but I put it there so you get into the habit of thinking about what significance means to you in every life decision. You need time for fun, entertainment, and relaxation, but even these activities can be carried out in ways that move you toward significance. An example would be becoming a Big Brother or Big Sister. You could have an extremely positive impact on a child and have a good time. Answering this question at this point may be difficult. I have learned that most people do not know what will give their lives meaning, so do not worry if this is a struggle—just give it your best shot.

The next three questions are designed to help you become aware of your heart. These are the emotional you. Passion emanates from your emotions.

Holy Coach: Wherever your treasure is, there the desires of your heart will also be. (Matthew 6:21 NLT)

I have used this quote several times because it applies to every area of life. In this case, it is saying you will use your Treasures—and I will add your Time, Talent, and Training—to engage in those activities that stir your heart. I said earlier that you can know what is important to others by looking at their credit card statements and smartphone calendars. Where they allocate their four Ts reveals the state of their hearts. What we are hoping to do is reverse this by understanding your emotions first so the resources will be properly allocated to what will help you become significant.

The form indicates three topics can be identified, but you can list as many as you wish. At this point, you do not want to limit your choices or predetermine which passions are most important to you. In fact, more is better. I have used three different emotions so a pattern may become evident. If several issues appear in all three emotions, that may be a passion you want to pursue. You will have several passions; it certainly could be more than three. However, by the time you draft your three statements, narrow the selections to one or two or combine several passions into one. Trying to do too many things will dilute your energy and resources. You want to be laser focused.

I provide six questions to help you define where you can make a difference based on what satisfies your heart. These should be answered in context with your answers to the heart questions. For example, if your mad, sad, and glad answers were about animal cruelty, one possible answer for the first fill-in is, "I care about animals that are mistreated, abused, and abandoned." Again, you are not limited to only three; you should list as many as you wish.

Then the whittling occurs by answering the remaining four questions in this section. These should be answered for all the issues and passions you have identified up to this point. The purpose of these four questions is to help you narrow the field; they help you understand where you can have the greatest impact. At that point, you can start eliminating a few if you have a long list from the previous section.

Now you will tie your passions and reasons into your GOALS. These are short statements, probably one sentence each, about how you will create significance through service to people and causes in each of the five categories. You will notice that I have subcategories for affinity groups since it encompasses a wide assortment of people. Using my own example under the category of friends, I wrote, "Foster important friendships with a few close friends, and be there for them in every circumstance." I share this to demonstrate that the message should be clear without requiring a detailed explanation. Your statement should be short enough to be easily remembered and spoken so when you share it with friends, they will know they are important to you.

Next, you will work on your vision statement. Using the above and your responses from the "My Life Values and Vision" worksheet, write a relatively short paragraph that describes your vision that aligns with what you believe your purpose is for being on this planet. Your vision statement is a consolidation of everything you've written in the previous sections. Hopefully, your work to this point has given you enough information that you have clarity on your passions. Your purpose is to accomplish your passions, so your vision statement is your prediction of what could result from your success in doing so. This is my personal vision statement. "My vision is that every client family, and family member, through fulfilling their individual and joint purposes, will achieve significance by being a cohesive force that makes the world a better place for others and themselves."

Your value statement describes the benefits other people or causes will experience when you are successful in fulfilling your purpose. This is the same exercise you completed for each of your unifying values, but now, you are consolidating all your work on both worksheets into a short paragraph of how lives could change as a result of what you do. Here is my value statement. "Everyone wants to be significant, but significance can only be attained by fulfilling the purpose for which you were created. A fulfilled life is a life lived with, and on, purpose." The clients, the families, and the family members I am fortunate enough to work with will be leading lives of significance because I was able to provide them the wisdom they needed to discover their life purpose and carry it out. Making it personal, if your family were my client, my purpose is helping you achieve your purpose. My success depends on your success. I will be significant when you are significant.

You are now ready to draft your personal significance statement. Based on all the above, write a relatively short paragraph that describes your mission in life. Please note this is not to be specific about your work or career, your family, or your personal pursuit to satisfy your wants and needs but about your life and what you believe, and others would agree, would make you a significant person in their lives.

Here is my personal significance statement: "I will use my time, talent, training, and treasures to help people, especially families, live a more significant, purposeful, fulfilling, and joyful life by successfully utilizing their time, talents, training, and treasures in biblical service and stewardship to benefit God, others, and themselves."

Figure 9.2 is the expanded version from my worksheet. I include on the worksheet how I will execute my mission statement. Although this is technically not part of the mission statement (remember, you want to keep it short so you can easily quote it to someone else and they will easily grasp and understand it), adding the "how" is important for you so you know what to do and will act immediately and consistently.

I also include a description of what my significance would look like. This is critical—it is the target you are shooting at. Whether you are shooting a gun, arrows, or darts, you can hit a blank wall all day, but so what? Hang a target on the wall and you then have a way to gauge your success. The movie *American Sniper* highlights my point. This Navy SEAL must take out a target 1,000 yards away, an almost impossible shot. He must adjust his sights and aim to allow for gravity, wind, and even the density of the air due to humidity and heat. If he is off only a millimeter in his calculations, at 1,000 yards, he will miss the target by several yards. Now it is your turn. Find a quiet place and have fun.

Our objective at Family Wealth Leadership is to transform a loose-knit, divided, oftentimes dysfunctional group of individuals with personal and diverse agendas into an efficient and effective team focused on a common and shared purpose that encourages all team members to prosper and be significant. This will be accomplished only if the family adopts a business mentality and operates like a for-profit enterprise. Think of your family like the J.C. Penney, J.P. Morgan, Walton (Walmart), and Disney families. Would these names be familiar today if the founders had merely divided their wealth among their heirs who then went their separate ways? Are the heirs wealthier now than if their predecessors had received wealth individually and most likely spent it?

These are obviously hypothetical questions, but since we know the 70 percent statistic is in play (70 percent of wealth is lost in the transition between generations), we can assume the heirs in these families, although not all may admit it, are happy that their family operated like a business. As publicly owned companies now, I am sure they all have vision, value, and mission statements. And so should your family. This effort requires a day, or maybe a weekend, away from the clutter and noise of busy lives for the entire family to gather in a neutral location for a family "business" meeting. However, it is a good idea to include time for family fun and bonding. That said, there is a danger that what is intended to be a business meeting can deteriorate into a family vacation. Remember, the objective is to develop a business attitude and disciplines. An agenda should be established and strictly adhered to.

Public companies often take their employees away for a couple of days for management meetings to plan and educate, but they also allow time for entertainment and social events. That is a good template for a family meeting. The purpose of this meeting is to create the family vision, value, and significance statements. The process is the same. The worksheet can also be used for the family exercise. Start with identifying the values, develop a clear vision of where the family is going, and draft the family mission statement. This will take time and a lot of discussion and negotiations. Everyone must be heard and nothing is ruled out at first. Only after everyone has voiced his or her thoughts, opinions, and preferences can negotiations begin. As I have said before, this will be the difficult part and not everyone will get everything he or she wants, but consensus, not majority rule, is essential to achieve 100 percent buy-in. The following is an example of how a family mission statement might look.

"Our family is committed to strengthening our family bonds and relationships through regular family meetings, family enhancement events, and involvement in community outreach and fun as a way to strengthen those bonds. We intend to grow the family assets and prepare the next generation by providing for the family's **education**, growth, and security." I bolded the word *education* as an example of defining important words that further clarify the overall mission statement.

Specific words in the mission statement were defined so everyone could be clear as to the intent. This is an important step to achieving trust and communication in the family. As I have previously mentioned, the telephone game demonstrates how easily what one person says and another person hears can change. As the mission statement passes through multiple generations and societal changes, you can imagine how words can take on different meanings and the mission become bastardized and confused. I encourage you to take the time to define.

Education is defined to mean financial support for any family member attending an accredited institution offering academic or vocational training, to include payment for room, board, tuition, travel, and all related expenses for the normal completion of the course, degree, or certificate of completion within the standard time frame for such degree, except that delays caused by the institution's unavailability of classes shall not be calculated in the time requirements. Annual progress reports will be required to qualify for support.

Additional definitions for community outreach, growth, and security would also be appropriate. A definition for family may also be important. Does *family* exclude in-laws? What if a child is adopted or there are stepchildren?

Going back to the word *education*, at Family Wealth Leadership, we take it a step further by encouraging the family to establish committees for major activities. The education committee can create specific criteria and measurements for a person to receive funding and continue receiving it. They may be required to have a certain grade point average in high school to receive initial funding and maintain, for example, a 3.0 GPA while in college to receive continued funding. There could be a requirement to attend junior college before moving on to a four-year school. Will advanced degrees be funded, and if so, how?

Committees to help family members buy their first homes or buy or start businesses can also be in place. We also encourage a family enhancement committee responsible for creating and managing family events to satisfy the "fun" objective in the family mission statement. One advantage of keeping the family wealth and family members together is the opportunity to be creative. Make killing two birds with one stone fun. If this sounds like an overwhelming task, it can be. Again, your family will be best served by having a coach at the meeting to guide the activities and arbitrate any difficult issues or discussions that could keep the family from making progress.

You may find it difficult to complete this worksheet, but I can assure you that doing so can be life changing. This will be the first time some have ever thought seriously and methodically about their purpose much less transcribed it to paper. It will take time and careful thought. I suggest that your first draft be done alone and somewhere that is quiet so you will not be interrupted and will avoid input from anyone else. Once you have completed it, you can have it reviewed, but the reviewer should be someone who is a positive person and will encourage your efforts. The last thing you want is someone telling you what you cannot do or be. This too is where an objective coach can be valuable.

Lloyd Reeb, author of *Success to Significance* and spokesperson for the Halftime Institute, tells the story of a business executive he counseled about creating his personal mission statement.[1] The executive had no idea what he was passionate about or his true purpose. His work had consumed his time and energies, and now he wanted something more for his life. Since he couldn't come up with anything, Lloyd suggested he make notes for one week of what he was reading, watching, and listening to in the paper, on television, and the radio. At the end of the week,

---

[1] Reeb shared this story at a Halftime Summit.

he told Lloyd he still had no idea what his purpose was. Everything he read, watched, and heard was about sports.

How would you have counseled him? Sometimes, our passions are so familiar that we don't recognize them as passions. With Lloyd's help, the executive finally realized he had the talent and training to start a ministry to help inner city kids get involved in sports and develop facilities where they could gather with adult supervision and find volunteers who would coach and train them. Today, it is one of the largest and most successful organizations in his city at getting kids off the street and turning them into responsible citizens. Not bad for a guy who had no clue as to his purpose in life.

CHAPTER 10

Your Next Step

Previous chapters set the stage for this chapter. Some of it may seem redundant, but I will be hitting details and specifics I skipped in those previous allusions.

Ownership

What do you own? Right now, you may be mentally sorting through your safe deposit box or filing cabinet looking for the pink slip (it's pink in California) for your cars, the deed for your house, and your bank and investment company statements to show me the evidence of what you own. The truth is that you own nothing; it is all on loan. I say this for two reasons. Many of the things that issue a certificate of ownership you probably purchased with financing or a lease. If the car in your garage is on a lease, it is not yours. Or you borrowed from the bank or finance company to buy the car or your home and the title is in your name, so you own it. Not exactly! Stop making the payments and see who owns it. A lot of homeowners unfortunately learned that truth in 2008 and 2009. You will say, "Yes, you have a point, but when I make that last payment, it will be all mine." Maybe, but most people don't make last payments, especially on thirty-year mortgages; they sell or trade in and buy something more expensive with new financing. Even if you own your home free and clear, skip a few years of paying the property taxes and see who really owns your house. The roofer falls off the roof and brings a lawsuit against you for his injuries. The only value you have is the equity in the home, which must be sold to pay the damages the judge awarded the roofer. You just lost the house and became a renter in a property someone else owns.

But then you might say, "I paid cash for this or that, so I own it." Wrong again! Depending on our estate tax laws at the time of your death, the size of your estate, and the level of planning you have done, the federal and state governments will take up to 60 percent, so your heirs will get only 40 to 50 percent of what you thought you owned.

Some states do not have estate or gift taxes, so the estate taxes could be less. But who now owns even the 40 or 50 percent that passed to your heirs? Not you! You're dead. Sorry to be morbid, but that's the fact. You own nothing because you cannot take it with you. You have never seen a hearse pulling a U-Haul trailer.

Someone once said that life was like the game of monopoly. You go around the board buying property and trying to accumulate as much money as you can, and maybe you even win. But when the game is over, all the pieces, the properties, and the money goes back in the box.

Holy Coach: The earth is the Lord's, and everything in it. The world and all its people belong to him." Yet true godliness with contentment is itself great wealth. <u>After all, we brought nothing with us when we came into the world, and we can't take anything with us when we leave it</u>. So if we have enough food and clothing, let us be content. The world and all its people belong to him. (Psalm 24:1; 1 Corinthians 10:26; 1 Timothy 6:6–8 NLT)

If you can grasp this fact of your lack of ownership of anything, it can change your life. Owning things does not make us important—they just keep us awake at night worrying that we will lose them.

Many years ago, I was in a car accident. Everyone was safe, but my car was damaged. You would naturally assume I was quite upset with the condition of my vehicle, but I wasn't because it wasn't my car—it was a loaner from the shop that was servicing my car. Police report in hand, I turned their car back in, picked up my unblemished car, and drove off with a smile on my face. I wasn't happy about the accident, but my point is that we do not worry about what we do not own and we constantly worry about what we do own. We live in a world that believes ownership of things brings happiness when in fact it creates stress and discontent that robs us of happiness.

Stewardship

If we own nothing, what is our role when it comes to the valuable things in life? And what is valuable? Let me answer the second question first. What is valuable is your time, talent, training, and treasures, and that carries over into the forms of capital I have already given you. The answer to the first question is that we are to be good stewards.

Holy Coach: Moreover, it is required in stewards that a man be found faithful. (1 Corinthians 4:2 KJV)

Stewards do not own what they manage; instead, they protect, preserve, and increase it as though they were the owner. Remember the parable of the talents. The two servants who doubled what the owner gave them were rewarded with more. Not so much for the third guy! Steward is equivalent to being a good servant, and a good servant provides good service. The two good stewards achieved significance when their master bestowed it on them because their service added value to the master. Reminds me of that formula: Service + Stewardship = Significance.

I talked about stewarding children in Chapter 1, but I want to cover a few more important points here, and I offered this bit of wisdom a couple of times, but I want to draw your attention specifically to the phrase "heritage from the Lord."

Holy Coach: Children are a heritage from the Lord, offspring a reward from Him. (Psalm 127:3 NIV)

I realize this may be difficult to accept, but your children do not belong to you. They were given to you to steward until they are able to steward themselves responsibly. This is by far your greatest role and responsibility in life. If you desire that your family will be significant, it starts with properly stewarding your children.

Holy Coach: Train up a child in the way he should go, and when he is old he will not depart from it. (Proverbs 22:6 NKJV)

The key words here are "in the way he should go." Notice that it doesn't say in the way you think he should go or the way you want him to go. Some parents try to relive their lives through their children by creating a mini me; this can look like the father who brings a child into the business intent on having that child take over when dad retires or dies. The problem is this is not necessarily the way he or she should go. Trying to make others into what they are not designed to be will make them good for nothing.

Another typical situation is the mother who always wanted to be a model, actress, dancer, etc., and pushes her daughter in one of those directions, or the dad who is trying to live out his football or baseball fantasy through his son, but the son wants to be a scientist or computer technician. What they should be doing is helping their children identify and increase their talents. This is not easy; it may be disappointing for parents, but the parents can get help from others who can be objective and realistic.

Coaches and advisors may be able to see that no matter how much dad wants it to be, the boy is not going to the NFL nor is the daughter going to Hollywood or Broadway. Having a coach allows children to express rather than suppress their passions if they think their parents would be disappointed and may even reject the idea when their desires do not match their parents' desires for them. It is not unrealistic to think that a child who wants to go to a trade school instead of the parents' alma mater could wind up less favored than the child who complies.

Being a good steward means improving what you have been put in charge of managing. Whether it is finances, tasks, assets, people, time, projects, equipment, or children, your stewardship responsibility is to improve what you have been given for its intended purpose. Your children are your most important gift and your most important responsibility. Your children are the real answer to the question, What is valuable?

The other reason properly stewarding your children is important is because they will carry on your legacy and perpetuate your family's significance. If they have not been properly stewarded, there will be no legacy and thus no significance. If your children have not been groomed to achieve their individual significance, they will be unable to carry on the family's significance. This has consequences that go far beyond your family. My work is so important to me because I believe our society is in great danger from the destruction of the traditional family unit. If we want our world to be a better place for our great-grandchildren, we need strong, responsible, unified families to pave the way and be good examples for others to follow. Your most important job as a parent is being the best steward you can be of your family. I am not overstating it when I say the world's future is riding on how well you do your job.

Competitive Spirit

If you are like most parents, your children have been involved in organized sports. In addition to the exercise, social lessons, discipline, learning about authority, following directions, and learning teamwork, your children learn to compete. Sports are a wonderful metaphor for life—one big, ongoing competition. As much as we would like it to get easier for ourselves and our children as we and they get older, that just is not reality.

In ages past, humanity competed with the environment. The hunters were in competition with whatever they hunted. Whoever was victorious dined on the loser. The farmer fought floods and droughts. Nations waged war against their neighbors and still do. Today, they compete for oil or nuclear resources. Children compete for admission to the best schools and then for those few jobs that will have more applicants than openings, and then they compete for promotions, titles, and raises.

Too often, I work with families in which the parents try to shelter their children from competition. They use their wealth to buy an advantage, grease the wheels, eliminate failures, provide destructive support, and minimize the struggles that accompany competition. One classic statement we hear from parents is, "Our children shouldn't have to work while going to college or work two jobs to afford an apartment the first time they leave the nest. We will give them the money for the rent. We will buy them new cars and give them credit cards." You have heard and maybe have said, "I don't want my children to work as hard as I had to work," or, "I don't want them to struggle the way we had to struggle." Why not?

Holy Coach: Dear brothers and sisters, when troubles of any kind come your way, consider it an opportunity for great joy. For you know that when your faith is tested, your endurance has a chance to grow. So let it grow, for when your endurance is fully developed, you will be perfect and complete, needing nothing. (James 1:2–4 NLT)

Every successful person I've met says, "It was difficult getting to this point in my life, and there were times I didn't know if I would make it, but I wouldn't change a thing because I learned so much more from my struggles and failures than I ever learned from my successes." I am willing to bet you have said or thought something very similar. The worst stewardship you can do of your children would be to remove competition from their lives. If they have not learned to compete, they will not survive. Here's an example. Your daughter has demonstrated some athletic ability and an interest in tennis. You get her lessons, and she plays in a few tournaments and wins. She moves up a level and continues to win because she has some natural talent. The next level has a higher caliber of players and the competition is getting tougher, so she isn't winning quite as easily as before. She will have to spend more time practicing and less time socializing. She opts for the social events, and winning continues to decline. You hate to see her lose, and you don't want her to be depressed, so you move her down to a level where the competition is not as intense.

Let's assume she had made it to the professional ranks and is losing. The victor receives the silver plate and $25,000 and the loser nothing. You don't want her ego bruised, and you certainly don't want Sally to look bad to her and your friends, so you buy her a trophy and give her an amount equal to the winner's purse. The next tournament and the next, the same result. How long will it take her to figure out she doesn't need to practice or work that hard because she is still getting paid just to show up?

You may think this is a ridiculous example, but similar scenarios happen all the time. A son's business is failing because he isn't giving it the attention it needs, but he doesn't need to become a better operator as long as someone else is paying the bills because a failure would blemish the family name. Imagine a daughter brought into a family business to fill a role she is not qualified to fill and paid a salary greater than someone else would receive.

You get the picture. Here are the big questions. What is the impact on such sons and daughters? What lessons did they learn? Was their esteem enhanced legitimately? What did the parents do for their offspring's dignity and future? Would allowing them to compete and fail or win on their own possibly produced better sons and daughters?

Holy Coach: Discipline your children, and they will give you peace; they will bring you the delights you desire. Whoever spares the rod hates their children, but the one who loves their children is careful to discipline them. (Proverbs 29:17, 13:24 NIV)

Stewarding your children includes instilling in them the value of work and the personal dignity it will provide them. I mentioned before that wealth can easily dis-incentivize children when it comes to working. If money flows freely, why work? When dad and mom are paying for everything, the choice is easy. Get a job or go to the beach or the mall, and go in the car the parents provided. Not a hard decision.

I have heard the argument that parents would rather their children not work while they are in college so they will have more time to study. I am sure there are a few kids for whom that might work, but since I can still remember my college days, albeit a long time ago, all I can say is, Yeah, right! We value what we legitimately earn. Remember, every time you give, you take something away.

Holy Coach: And when we ate another person's food, we always paid for it. We worked very hard night and day so we would not be an expense to any of you. We had the right to ask you to help us, but we worked to take care of ourselves so we would be an example for you to follow. When we were with you, we gave you this rule: "Anyone who refuses to work should not eat. (2 Thessalonians 3:8–10 NCV)

Lazy people want much but get little, but those who work hard will prosper. (Proverbs 13:4 NLT)

Setting the Example

You may have heard the phrase, "It's caught, not taught." The idea is children learn better by following the example you set as opposed to being told what to do.

Holy Coach: In the same way, encourage the young men to live wisely. And <u>you yourself must be an example to them</u> by **doing** good works of every kind. <u>Let everything **you do** reflect the integrity and seriousness of your teaching</u>. **Teach** the truth so that your teaching can't be criticized. **Care** for the flock (children) that God has entrusted to you. **Watch over** (your children) willingly, not grudgingly . . . Don't lord it over the (children) assigned to your care, but <u>lead them by your own good example</u>. (Titus 2:6–8a; 1 Peter 5:2–3 NLT)

Leading works better than pushing. You cannot push a string uphill, but you can pull it.

Teaching through words, written and spoken, is necessary, but you remember those famous words you heard growing up and probably used on your children, "Do as I say, not as I do!" Do you walk the talk?

The reason walking the talk is so important is any inconsistency creates distrust, and lack of trust is a relationship killer. It is also a truth killer. If you say one thing but do the opposite, how is a child to know which is true and right? If your statements and actions are consistent, that sends a powerful message. If inconsistent, the message will be even more powerful but in a negative way. The example reinforces the statement. The example, not the words, changes behavior. Children imitate their parents. The little guy pretends he is shaving with dad in the morning. The little girl puts on mom's high heels. They are following the examples set for them. The apple doesn't fall far from the tree; children are a reflection of their parents.

Another benefit is that examples build your own integrity and empathy, and teaching by example is a lot easier and less stressful for everyone. Parents can easily fall into the trap of nagging their children. How successful has that been? How do you respond to nagging? That is the same result you will have if you use that technique on your children. I am having a cliché fest, but actions do speak louder than words.

Holy Coach: And now a word to you parents. Don't keep on scolding and <u>nagging</u> your children, making them angry and resentful. Rather, bring them up with the loving discipline the Lord himself approves, with <u>suggestions and godly advice</u>. (Ephesians 6:4 MSG)

And set the right example for them by following your own suggestions and advice!

Talking to Your Sons and Daughters

After saying actions are critical, I do not want to insinuate that talking to your children is not also critical, but talking and nagging are not the same. Talking is a two-way street. When you say something, you need to wait for a response. In some families, especially if the patriarch or matriarch is a strong personality and very controlling, the talking sounds more like commands than conversation. Children want to be heard. Listening is a way to show them they have value. It is a teaching opportunity to share values and purpose. If the objective is to train up children in the way they should go, how will you know what the "should" is if you are not listening to what they are trying to tell you?

Holy Coach: My dear brothers and sisters, always be willing to listen and slow to speak. Do not become angry easily, because anger will not help you live the right kind of life God wants. (James 1:19–20 NCV)

If you listen to your children, they will learn to listen to you. Quality listening is a learned skill developed through conversation. This is especially true in helping children develop their communication skills with adults. In their early years, the parents, grandparents, aunts, and uncles were the primary adults. Every one of these persons should be engaging the children in active communications so they will develop good speaking and listening skills.

Instead of always sending children to another room or outside to play while the adults talk, find ways to include the children in some part of the adult discussions. You want them to learn they can be valuable contributors to the family structure. Think about the values and wisdom they will catch as the family discusses purpose, successes, trials, tribulations, and the importance of spiritual, ethical, and moral qualities. Think about what you would learn about your children as they voice thoughts and ask questions. What wisdom would they learn from participating in the group conversation instead of playing on the computer or in the street?

Holy Coach: Wise children take their parents' advice, but whoever makes fun of wisdom won't listen to correction. (Proverbs 13:1 NCV)

You may learn something by talking to your children. Do you know what your children are learning in school, from their friends, or from other adults? Society, culture, and their friends can be bigger influences on children than their family environment can be. Are these third-party sources teaching your children your values or theirs? Which do you want them to have?

Holy Coach: Moral dropouts won't listen to their elders; welcoming correction is a mark of good sense. Listen to good advice if you want to live well, an honored guest among wise men and women. (Proverbs 15:5, 31 MSG)

Although the Holy Coach directs this to "listening to their elders," the word *children* can be inserted. Maybe that good advice will originate from your children. As adults, we lose connection to the innovations and creativity of each new generation. My grandchildren know more about computers and the Internet than I do, and I am reasonably informed and knowledgeable about both. More important, their generation has a new language and way of communicating: they use symbols and words that didn't exist ten years ago. We need to be listening to our children or we will fall farther behind the new generations and will be unable to communicate with them.

Today, we are in danger of forfeiting the ability to listen and communicate well because of our digital culture. The greatest contributor to the destruction of families is the breakdown in trust and communications. The responsibility is on the adults in the family, and they must be purposeful and innovative in creating opportunities and situations for active discussion both in the family and one on one. It will not happen if left to chance, and the children will not be the initiators.

I watched a father and his two children in another booth at a restaurant. The entire time they were there, the father had little to no interaction with his children. He read his paper while they played on their digital devices. What a missed opportunity! What is happening at your dinner table? Is there any valuable communication taking place, or is the only thing talking the television?

Trust and communications are essentially conjoined twins in that they share vital organs. If there is no communication, trust will not exist. They cannot be separated or both will die. Trust depends on knowing what to expect from and about someone else. I can trust you because I know who you are, what you stand for, and what you will and will not do. The same is true if you trust me. How do we know these things about each other? We know because we talk and carefully listen to each other. How will you know if you can trust your children? How will they know they can trust you? Talk to each other often and for extended periods—no one or two-word conversations in a three-minute dialog. Go somewhere that it is impossible to find a cellular or Wi-Fi connection.

There is a commercial in which a group of guys drives from location to location, with one getting on top of the truck, holding up his cell phone, and reporting, "Not here!" Back in the truck; they drive to the next location and the next, saying, "Not here!" About the fifth try, deep in the woods in a canyon and again holding up the phone, his response is, "This is it! No cell phone connection!" They set up their tents. That is where you need to make camp with your children.

Attention, <u>Not</u> Intention

A good example of how to listen and communicate is to give the other person your complete and full attention. We are all guilty of hearing but not listening. We hear the words but our attention is somewhere else. The message being sent never makes it past the eardrum to the brain. Honestly, intention is useless unless it is accompanied by attention.

How do you show your spouse and your children that you love them? You give them your attention, and love is attention. If you are not giving your family your attention, you must have an honest conversation with yourself whether you are giving them the love they deserve and need from you. Maybe a better idea is to ask your family members if they are getting the love and attention they want and need from you. Another useless word, like *intention*, is *try*. We use these words to make ourselves feel better, but they don't make anyone else feel better if the attention is lacking. You can try to be a better father or mother, son or daughter, or friend, but until you actually are one, it does not have much value for anyone else. You can intend to have a family vacation or day outing, but it will not accomplish anything until it happens.

What is accomplished if attention is lacking is resentment and destruction of trust. When dad says to his child he intended to make it to the soccer game and doesn't, or the daughter tells mom, "I tried to see you on your birthday, but something came up and I couldn't make it"; the inattention devalues and cancels out the "intention" and "trying." The child learns dad cannot be trusted to follow through on his "intentions." When mom hears the daughter say she will "try" to visit this weekend, mom knows not to get her hopes up. If a family never achieves significance, it is usually not because of a lack of trying or intention, it is because they were unwilling to give it the "attention" it needed. I suggest you strike these words from your vocabulary.

It's About Time, Not Money

One of biggest problems I see in families, especially families of wealth, is parents who think money buys love and respect. I talked about this in the subject of toxic giving. Parents are mystified when their children have no respect or interest in the family or what the parents want. "We gave our children everything, the best that money could buy, and they still don't want to spend time with us." Why should they if you gave them things as a substitute for time with them?

Your children want you, not your money or what it can buy. It is easier and faster to write a check, but relationships require time and attention, not dollars and intention. You can see how all these qualities are intertwined. It is impossible to talk about one without discussing the others. A large net worth will never make a family significant. Estate planning attorneys and financial advisors can draft the best legal documents possible and create wonderful financial plans, but the family will never reach significance if the focus is only on the money, which is what most financial and estate plans do. The human side of the plan is minimized or ignored.

Create Opportunities to Succeed and Fail

If you have encouraged your children to compete, they will have failures and successes. In baseball, batting .300 is considered successful, but that means the batter failed 70 percent of the time. A good basketball player hits maybe 40 to 50 percent of his shots, a 50 to 60 percent failure rate. Those seem like dismal statistics. Who wants to have someone on the team that fails 50 to 70 percent every time they shoot a basket or swing a bat? Obviously, there are a lot of people since owners pay athletes millions and fans buy tickets or pay for cable sports channels to watch them.

One man lost his job and ran for his state legislature and lost. Then he started a business, which failed, so he again ran for office and was elected to his state legislature. Shortly after being reelected, he had a nervous breakdown. He got a law degree and went into partnership with another attorney. He ran for speaker of his state legislature and was defeated. His first law partnership was dissolved, so he went into a new partnership. He threw his hat in the ring to be nominated to Congress and was defeated. He went on to lose re-nomination for his legislative seat, he was rejected for a position as a land officer, defeated for the U.S. Senate, defeated for selection as a vice presidential nominee, and defeated in another run for the U.S. Senate.

Good grief! Did this man do anything, right? Oh yeah! Maybe it was the part where he was elected president of the United States in 1860 and guided the country through the worst internal war it would ever face, a civil war that would have torn this country apart, but he succeeded in holding the union together? Or was it the part where slavery was abolished and all people, no matter their race or skin color, were freed to pursue their dreams and destinies? I don't think anyone would put Abraham Lincoln in the failure bucket!

The only failures are those who do nothing or do not learn from their experiences. If you do not provide opportunities for your children to succeed or fail, you will be the failure, not them. When you taught your children to walk, how many times did they fall? When they fell, did you tell them not to get up because they would fall again, or did you encourage them to try again? They didn't know they could walk until you created opportunities for them to stand up and take a step. You lifted them to their feet while your spouse kneeled a short distance away to catch the little tykes when their wobbly legs collapsed.

Your role as their parent has not changed now that they are older. Help your children step out in life by giving them the opportunities to skin a few knees and challenge them to explore where they have never gone before, places where they will not know what they will find until they get there. Your favorite question should be, "What did you learn from that experience?" Undesirable results are not failures; they are successful steps in learning a better way.

Stewardship is absolutely required of your four Ts of True Wealth for yourself and your children and grandchildren. It is likely that no one has ever talked to them about this concept of stewardship. I applaud you if you are the exception, but unfortunately, many more parents have not taught or been models of good stewardship. Even if you have done a good job of teaching them financial stewardship, you might not have taught them stewardship of their time, talents, and training. If you don't help them or arrange help for them, it will not happen. But to teach them, your own house must be in order, so the following is for your benefit as well as theirs.

CHAPTER 11

Optimizing Your Wealth

In this chapter, I get more specific and offer tools on how you can clarify and optimize your four Ts of True Wealth. If you would like copies of any forms, worksheets, or information included in this chapter, you can email me at kkolson@familywealthleadership.com. You can also visit our website at www.familywealthleadership.com.

Time

Start by completing the little worksheet I have included as Figure 11.1, "Allocating Time to Personal Goals." Many of the exhibits are in Excel or Word format. If you would like to have me forward them in these formats so you can complete them on your computer, I am happy to do so.

Note that the middle column is where you enter the percentages of the amount of time you would like to spend in a one-year period. I suggest you enter all the percentages for each objective <u>without trying to calculate the math the first time</u>. After making all your desired entries, add up the column. It is not unusual to exceed 100 percent the first time. I think that is worthwhile because it highlights how easily we can misjudge how much time we have.

Adjust specific percentages to bring you to 100 percent. The two columns to the right will give you the equivalent hours per year and the average hours per week. These are ballpark figures; it will not be possible for you to spend exactly these amounts of time every week, but that is not necessary. Nor will you hit these numbers perfectly over the year. The objective is not perfection but awareness of your time so you can order your life and time more purposely to accomplish your highest priorities.

I have also provided Figure 11.2, as an example of a time tracking log you may want to use. This will require some discipline, but you will find it enlightening because most people do not know how they spend their time and, more importantly, how much time they spend on unnecessary, unimportant, and nonproductive activities.

Earlier, I said you might be surprised to know you have enough time to accomplish the important things in your life. You will if you eliminate the nonessentials, but you must identify them first. The example reflects my personal tracking of how I was spending time at work, so the activities are work related. You will need to change them to the activities that fill your days.

The first schedule is a daily tracking sheet. Whatever you are doing at that moment you enter in the left column, then enter your start and stop times. The next day, you use a new worksheet. I tracked my time for one calendar quarter. You may not need to go that long, but you should at least go for one month to get a more accurate representation since every day and every week can vary significantly.

The second page is the summary of all the individual days' tracking results for one week. If you use our Excel spreadsheets, the calculations will be automatic. If you prefer another format, by all means use whatever works for you. The objective is awareness, not exactness.

Finally, compare your tracking hours to the hours calculated on the "Allocating Time to Personal Goals" worksheet. Do the hours match up reasonably close? If not, you now know where you will need to make adjustments in daily, weekly, and yearly activities.

Of your four Ts, time is the most valuable. We all get twenty-four hours a day year in and year out. Significant people steward their time fiercely and judiciously to eliminate waste so they have more time for activities that bring them success.

My guess is this exercise produced some revelations. If you make the necessary changes and teach your children how to effectively steward their time and lives, you will have taken a major step toward significance.

Talent

Rick Warren uses of the acronym SHAPE in his book *Purpose Driven Life* as a tool for helping others discover their God-given purposes. The first four letters fall under the talent T: The S is a person's spiritual gifts. The H is heart gifts. The word I have been using is *passion*; your passions reflect what is in your heart. The A stands for your abilities, including your physical and mental abilities. While I treat abilities as talents, it is fair to say they can overlap into the training T. The skills of a surgeon, dancer, scientist, teacher, and so on are a combination of talent and training. Training, which I cover next, is the resource we use to develop and enhance our talents. That is why I believe it is important to understand the differentiation. Training can be acquired whereas talent cannot.

The P is personality, and it falls solidly in the talent category, but you can acquire skills and techniques that can improve your social graces and attributes. Happiness and joy are choices, and you can learn strategies and tactics to overcome sadness and depression. The E is about your experiences and they can occur only in training, which I cover shortly.

So how do we steward our talents and help others be good stewards of theirs? Again, we apply IDEA. First, you must discover what talents you have. To some degree, this will be obvious, but you may have talents you didn't realize you had. It's very possible you are unaware of some of your children's talents. There are several types of testing you can use to uncover your family's SHAPE. One is offered at Saddleback Church's website, www.saddleback.com. Two sources we use are Strengths Finders at www.strengthsfinders.com and Kolby at www.kolby.com. Other tests can give insight into a person's aptitude or personality and be helpful. We favor the two we use because they help determine how people may interact in a team situation, which is our definition of a family.

I'll share my top five strengths as an example. They are in order of greatest to less great. Mine are Maximizer, Relator, Responsibility, Belief, and Individualization. My Kolbe results, again from most prevalent to less prevalent, are Fact Finder, Follow Through, Quick Start, and Implementer. My "Natural Advantage" as a result of those four traits is strategic planner, which obviously aligns with my profession; I am doing what I was designed to do.

For me to have the most success, I should surround myself with people who have different talents. If everyone is the same, everything is done the same way and there is no innovation or creativity. Diversity in talents, abilities, and personalities produces significance. How all these are defined and interpreted is not important for this discussion; what is important is assembling an effective team of family members possessing different talents and aligning those talents with the required roles. Testing can help assign the right people to the roles in which they will be successful in performing in the family team. Drawing on my real estate background, developing an office building or shopping center required an architect, various engineers, a general contractor, landscapers, electricians, and so on. Leasing the building required marketing, legal, and leasing agents. If everyone had the same talents, skills, and abilities, the building would not be built. The quarterback may be the most important player on a football team, but a team of all quarterbacks would lose every game. Individuals will achieve significance only when they know how and why they are shaped as they are and deploy those talents the way they were designed to be used.

The next step is designing and developing a plan for improving and maximizing your talents and helping your children do the same. Executing the plan through programs and strategies are the action steps that fine-tune the talents; practice and dry runs hone those talents. They must be used or they will wither on the vine. Administering your talents means using them for the purpose they were designed to achieve. Still, there will be adjustments requiring more training and education and practice. Families achieve significance when everyone on the family team is achieving significance.

Training

The primary question when it comes to stewardship is to make sure you and your children have access to the right training. This is why being clear on your purpose is important. Many people earn college degrees in majors they never use. Training includes education, vocational training, experiences, mentoring, reading, and involvement in activities that require practicing, drills, and implementing the lessons learned. Training should be designed around individual aptitudes, personalities, and passions. All parents want their children to have college degrees, but that may not be right for all children. For some, work experience or vocational school may be better at least until they can commit to the time and effort required to earn a degree.

Those who do not put in the time and hard work will not value the training. It is also a good idea if the individual must contribute something to their training. One reason we prefer to aggregate the family wealth under the control of the entire family is to ensure assets are available to help all in the family access the training they need to be successful and significant. But we also want rules in place to qualify for assistance, and one of those rules should be that 100 percent financing is not available. Using college as the example, the beneficiary may have to work part time or get a scholarship or grant, and family funds can make up the difference. We want them personally invested in their future so they will value the training but also so they will retain a sense of dignity. Your stewardship responsibility is to help your children identify their talents and shape, and then design their training to bring out their talents and fulfill their purpose.

Treasures

I saved the big one for last. Stewardship of your treasures is a concept that is easy to understand, but difficult to implement. I offer Holy Coach wisdom and emphasize that the question everyone wants to avoid must be constantly at the forefront, How much is enough?

Holy Coach: I collected great sums of silver and gold, the treasure of many kings and provinces. I hired wonderful singers, both men and women, and had many beautiful concubines. I had everything a man could desire! So I became greater than all who had lived in Jerusalem before me, and my wisdom never failed me. Anything I wanted, I would take. I denied myself no pleasure. I even found great pleasure in hard work, a reward for all my labors. But as I looked at everything I had worked so hard to accomplish, it was all so meaningless—like chasing the wind. There was nothing really worthwhile anywhere. I observed yet another example of something meaningless under the sun.

This is the case of a man who is all alone, without a child or a brother, yet who works hard to gain as much wealth as he can. But then he asks himself, "Who am I working for? Why am I giving up so much pleasure now?" It is all so meaningless and depressing. Those who love money will never have enough. How meaningless to think that wealth brings true happiness! The more you have, the more people come to help you spend it. So what good is wealth—except perhaps to watch it slip through your fingers! (Ecclesiastes 2:8–11, 4:8, 5:10–11 NLT)

The man without an heir posed an appropriate question. Why are you working so hard to accumulate more and more just to give to your heirs so they don't have to work hard? This is an unpleasant analogy, but why would anyone give more and more drugs or alcohol to an addict or alcoholic? In many ways, the outcome is the same—it does harm and injures the recipient.

The lesson from this story is wealth accumulation, in and of itself, should never be the primary goal or end all. You should use wealth as a springboard and fuel, combined with your Time, Talent, and Training to achieve significance. Manage and control Treasures carefully and wisely. The following topics cover the whats, whys, and hows of doing so.

Budgeting

Figure 11.3 is the cash flow worksheet we use when coaching clients. However, a better alternative is to utilize a software program such as Quicken; it isn't that expensive, and it is a great tool for budgeting and tracking your income and expenses and producing a multitude of financial reports. It is easy to use; it just requires some of your time to update.

Another alternative is a web-based program called Mint. I am not endorsing either of these, but you should have some way of capturing the data and producing useful reports so you will know your financial status at all times. If you prefer using an Excel spreadsheet, that can work, but an advantage of software programs is that they can automatically download data from bank and investment accounts, credit card companies, and some utility companies so you do not need to make manual entries. That's time stewardship!

I also suggest you consider utilizing the services of a bookkeeper if you cannot or do not want to keep your accounting records current. The small price you pay to be on top of your finances is well worth it.

Holy Coach: Don't brag about tomorrow; you don't know what may happen then. The wise see danger ahead and avoid it, but fools keep going and get into trouble. They do not know what the future holds, and no one can tell them what will happen. No one can control the wind or stop his own death ... I also saw something else here on earth: The fastest runner does not always win the race, the strongest soldier does not always win the battle, the wisest does not always have food, the smartest does not always become wealthy, and the talented one does not always receive praise. Time and chance happen to everyone. No one knows what will happen next. (Proverbs 27:1, 12; Ecclesiastes 8:7–8, 9:11–12 NCV)

You may think it strange to be talking about presumption in a section about budgeting. I offer that wisdom here because not maintaining a budget is presuming everything will remain as it is today. The income will keep coming, interest rates will stay low, there will not be any emergencies, and your taxes will not change. Budgeting is a key factor for finding out how much is enough. If you do not have enough margin in your cash flow to be funding your cash reserve, retirement, and savings goals, you are most certainly presuming on the future and will most likely be unpleasantly surprised.

Giving

When you involve your children and family in generous giving to others, you give to your own children and family. I cannot stress this point enough. It is a rule, a principle, a law! The more you give, the more you get if you give for the right reasons. The formula will work every time you give without expecting anything in return. If your giving is based on getting something for yourself, it doesn't work.

Holy Coach: But generous people plan to do what is generous, and they stand firm in their generosity. (Isaiah 32:8 NLT)

Now I have problem. My editor wants me to include examples of how giving helps people and families. My quandary is how do I choose two or three stories from the hundreds I could share? Well, here goes.

Bob, a successful engineer by training, went on a ten-day mission trip to Africa. As the group traveled from one village to the next, his heart was broken by the number of people who could barely walk, some literally crawling on the ground or having to be carried by someone else. When he returned to his home in America, he put his talent and training to work. He designed a wheelchair composed of a plastic lawn chair, rubber bicycle wheels, and a footpad that can be easily assembled with a wrench and screwdriver.

Calling on friends and colleagues in the shipping and transportation industry, and individuals familiar with the politics and bureaucracies of foreign governments, he investigated and developed a delivery system. The final hurdle was raising funds to buy the materials and pay for the shipping, and assembling the chairs once they arrive in country. That was solved by using American volunteers and individuals and business owners who contributed to his cause. His Time, Talent, Training, and Treasures created the Free Wheelchair Ministry that has given, and continues to give, mobility to hundreds of thousands of people throughout the world at a cost of about $50 per chair, which includes the materials and shipping. Additionally, families and individuals make trips to villages in far-away counties to transport the chairs to remote areas, assemble them, lift a person off the ground into a chair, and see the smile and wonder in those faces. Not only did Bob's family benefit, but all those volunteer families and business owners benefited from dedicating their Time, Talent, Training, and Treasures.

Here is one of many success stories from the Halftime library. Cliff is an executive for a major homebuilder. His wife Rose's professional background includes restaurant operations and marketing at Coca Cola. Their significance would be found in building homes for the poor in impoverished areas in foreign countries. Their philanthropy took on the name HopeBuilders with the objective of securing land

and building small homes to replace the shanties. Within two years they mustered together about one thousand volunteers to raise funds and, similarly to Habitat for Humanity in the United States, they built homes on other shores.

Their investigations, designs and developments, soon uncovered another need. These shanty towns composed of structures made of tin, wood pallets, plywood, cardboard, and dirt floors were still home for these people. They did not want to move away from friends and family to a development in another town, even if the new house was better than what they currently occupied. Tapestry Homes was created to replace the pallets and tin with solid walls and a wood floor. They liken it unto the TV show, Extreme Makeover, just not that extreme. Again, the many families that get a new house is a wonderful outcome, but I know the many families and individual volunteers who travel across oceans or to other continents to spend a week or two in the heat, with hammer and saw, and living among the people in these deplorable conditions, come home changed forever.

Earlier I mentioned the Samueli Foundation as one example in my backyard of Orange County, California. Rather than me relaying their story, let me share the exact words of the Samueli family taken from their website at www.samueli.org.

Dr. Henry Samueli co-founded Broadcom Corporation in 1991 and currently serves as Chief Technical Officer of Broadcom Limited (Broadcom Corporation was acquired by Avago Technologies Limited in 2016 and renamed Broadcom Limited). Broadcom Ltd. is a global leader in providing semiconductor solutions for wired and wireless communications.

Susan Samueli, a native of Los Angeles, received her B.A. in Mathematics from UC Berkeley. She worked with IBM Corporation until 1985, after which she devoted her time to raising her children and working in the alternative health care field. Subsequently, she received a Ph.D. in nutrition from the American Holistic College of Nutrition in 1993 and a Diploma of Homeopathy from the British Institute of Homeopathy in 1994.

A Message From the Family:

For us, giving back was never a question. It began with our parents who set the example by living modestly while giving back generously to the community. Further, philanthropy has always been an important part of the Jewish culture in which we were raised and now raise our children.

We firmly believe, that as members of the community, we all have an opportunity and an obligation to give back in whatever way we can. Therefore, when the time was right, the decision was not "if" we should start a foundation, but "how" we should do it.

The philosophy behind our foundation is the belief that our grants should help to improve the quality of life for all. Our strategy has been one of thoughtful investment; we are pro-active in seeking out agencies that exemplify qualities of creativity, sustainability and entrepreneurial vision. We provide funding as an investment in the ideas of an agency and its leadership, and we fully expect a return on that investment in the form of positive results toward our goal of a vibrant, healthy and well-balanced community.

The work of our foundation represents the bridge from our family to our community, from the past to the future and from our passions to our convictions. Since we began, we have been gratified to see the impact our efforts have made thus far.

We are thankful for our grantees and their steadfast enthusiasm and dedication, and we are excited for what the future holds.

Henry and Susan

Debt Management

Since I talked about this in Chapter 6, I prefer to let the Holy Coach do the talking this time.

Others said, "We've had to mortgage our fields, our vineyards, and our homes in order to get some grain because of this famine." Others said, "We've had to borrow money to pay the king's taxes on our fields and vineyards. We have the same flesh and blood as our relatives. Our children are just like theirs. Yet, we have to force our sons and daughters to become slaves. Some of our daughters have already become slaves. But we can't do anything else when our fields and vineyards belong to others." (Nehemiah 5:3–5 GW)

A word not used much anymore is *indentured*. Here is the *American Heritage* definition: "A contract binding one party into the service of another for a specified term." From the Law Library of Congress, "before the Civil War, slaves and indentured servants were considered personal property, and they or their descendants could be sold or inherited like any other property, human chattel was governed largely by laws of individual states." Throughout history, including slavery in America, the word indentured was combined with *slave*. An indentured slave owed money to his or her master and was under contract to work off the debt for however long it took. This was not optional. It was law and the master or possibly a court set the terms of the indenture; it was not negotiable. Although today's laws are more liberal, one should consider every debt transaction with an indentured slave mentality.

Holy Coach: When you are on the way to court with your adversary, settle your differences quickly. Otherwise, your accuser may hand you over to the judge, who will hand you over to an officer, and you will be thrown into prison. And if that happens, you surely won't be free again until you have paid the last penny. Just as the rich rule the poor, so the borrower is servant to the lender. (Matthew 5:25–26 NLT)

It's poor judgment to guarantee another person's debt or put up security for a friend. Don't agree to guarantee another person's debt or put up security for someone else. If you can't pay it, even your bed will be snatched from under you. My child, if you have put up security for a friend's debt or agreed to guarantee the debt of a stranger—if you have trapped yourself by your agreement and are caught by what you said—follow my advice and save yourself, for you have placed yourself at your friend's mercy. Now swallow your pride; go and beg to have your name erased. Don't put it off; do it now! Don't rest until you do. Save yourself like a gazelle escaping from a hunter, like a bird fleeing from a net. Owe nothing to anyone—except for your obligation to love one another. If you love your neighbor, you will fulfill the requirements of God's law. (Proverbs 17:18, 22:7, 26–27, 6:1–5; Romans 13:8 NLT)

Debt is neither good nor bad, but it can be dangerous. Think of it like red wine. I have heard it said that the medical profession suggests one glass a day can be good for your heart. A bottle a day could be, or could lead, to addiction and dependency. I have discussed this in other sections of this book, but this is important and needs to be restated.

The first question is whether using debt is buying something NECESSARY! Borrowing to purchase a home or car can be good debt. However, using debt to buy a home or car that is much greater than you need can put your life and wealth in jeopardy. There are exceptions, but most bankruptcy filings are not the result of people losing employment. They occur because the employment income cannot keep pace with the spending.

Clients often ask whether they should pay off their mortgage. The answer depends on a lot of variables. Currently (2017), we have the benefit of historically low mortgage rates. Buying a home versus renting may be a good financial decision right now. If the rate is 8% or greater, maybe not.

Another question, which I hinted at above, is what other options are available that might be more financially sound? Using a car as the example, is it better to lease or buy using a car loan. It depends!

Finally, how disciplined are you? Credit cards are a good example for this question. I will use myself as the example. I have three prominent cards I carry. One is for Costco (mainly for fuel and automotive and some business expenses), one for business expenses, and one for personal purchases. The common denominators in all three are there are no subscriptions fees, they all pay rewards of percentage refunds varying from 1% to 5%, and I never, never, carry a balance so I never have an interest charge of 20% or more. As a result, my credit cards actually provide a couple thousand dollars of income annually.

The point is, if you can use debt to create income, such as building a profitable business, buying rental income, or investing in a bond that pays a higher rate than the rate on the debt, and that income can be relatively secure and consistent, then that *could be* good debt.

Saving and Investing

Without savings and investing, there is no future, no significance, and no legacy. Investments take many forms and cross over all the four Ts of True Wealth. Treasures are obvious; stocks, bonds, real estate, business ownership, general and limited partnerships, and private equity transactions are examples.

Holy Coach: Money that comes easily disappears quickly, but money that is gathered little by little will grow. The wise man saves for the future, but the foolish man spends whatever he gets. Settle in any city you wish and live off the land. Harvest the grapes and summer fruits and olives and store them away. Get ready for the siege! Store up water! Strengthen the forts! Prepare many bricks for repairing your walls! Go into the pits to trample the clay, and pack it in the molds! (Proverbs 13:11 NCV; Proverbs 21:20; Jeremiah 40:10b; Nahum 3:14 TLB)

Your Time, Talent, and Training are resources too that should be invested, not wasted. Everyone views a college education as a good investment that can produce favorable, lifelong rewards. That education requires an investment of all four Ts of True Wealth. But, there is also the investment of Time, Talent, Training, and Treasures in acquiring the knowledge and fulfilling the requirements needed to qualify for college entry. Every parent will confirm that all four Ts were utilized by them and their children to get that degree. Another example was the three stories I shared about giving that involved each person's Time, Talent, Training, and Treasures. True Wealth is for investing, not hoarding or squandering.

Asset Protection

Another term normally associated with a person's financial assets and how to make them untouchable by creditors or those seeking legal compensation from you for your acts of negligence, fraud, or avoidance of responsibility. However, it is also possible that your assets can be exposed to lawsuits and creditors even if you have done nothing wrong. For example, you may be involved as a general partner in a venture operated by someone else or others whom you thought were ethical and honest. You were invited into the partnership not because of expertise but because you could provide capital or loan guarantees. The partnership raises additional capital from limited partners. Due to fraud, mismanagement, and bad decisions by the other general partners, the venture has to file for bankruptcy and all the limited partners lose their investments. Guess who the attorneys for the class-action lawsuit will come after? You and your assets.

Two more typical situations are business owners and owning investment properties. In the first, the business owners are required to sign personal loan guarantees. If the business fails, all their assets are at risk. Even if the business is succeeding, if a partner gets divorced or files personal bankruptcy, your interest and other assets could be in jeopardy. Let's assume you own a twenty-unit apartment building and a tenant trips on the stairs and is severely disabled or a painter's ladder falls on someone. Every asset you own could be lost when the court awards the plaintiff a multimillion dollar settlement.

This is too big a subject and the types of solutions too extensive and complex to discuss here, but the right solutions must be customized to the individuals and the situations. Significance, as I have been explaining it, is impossible if there are no financial assets to fund the process. A family with few assets can still be significant in many ways and may still be able to utilize their Time, Talent, and Training to impact the world in wonderful ways, but Treasures can multiply the impact. I want to help families with substantial treasures understand how to maximize the good the family can do by using its treasures as a multiplier rather than a destroyer of the family's purpose.

It is important that asset protection strategies are implemented to achieve that purpose.

Holy Coach: Later, that same servant found another servant who owed him a few dollars. The servant grabbed him around the neck and said, "Pay me the money you owe me!" The other servant fell on his knees and begged him, "Be patient with me, and I will pay you everything I owe." But the first servant refused to be patient. He threw the other servant into prison until he could pay everything he owed. When the other servants saw what had happened, they were very sorry. So they went and told their master all that had happened. Then the master called his servant in and said, "You evil servant! Because you begged me to forget what you owed, I told you that you did not have to pay anything. You should have showed mercy to that other servant, just as I showed mercy to you." The master was very angry and put the servant in prison to be punished until he could pay everything he owed. (Matthew 18:28–34 NCV)

Let me be very clear about my definition of asset protection versus a common practice that I am not endorsing. The latter includes strategies to avoid a person's legitimate obligations and possibly tax evasion. In some cases, these efforts could be illegal and fraudulent, and the only significance achieved will be the media coverage of that person's arrest, trial, and imprisonment. That will not build a strong and unified family.

Protecting Your Family

Whereas the previous section addressed protecting Treasures, this section is about protecting the Time, Talent, and Training components of your family's wealth.

Holy Coach: Some of them were saying, "We have many sons and daughters in our families. To eat and stay alive, we need grain." Others were saying, "We are borrowing money against our fields, vineyards, and homes to get grain because there is not much food." And still others were saying, "We are borrowing money to pay the king's tax on our fields and vineyards. We are just like our fellow Jews, and our sons are like their sons. But we have to sell our sons and daughters as slaves. Some of our daughters have already been sold. But there is nothing we can do, because our fields and vineyards already belong to other people." (Nehemiah 5:2–5 NCV)

This book is not about specific financial products, and I am not promoting any products we utilize for this purpose, but I must discuss the use of insurance as a tool for protecting your family. For most people, the word *insurance* prompts a love/hate emotion. Consider the insurance on your car or house. You will be happy if you never have an accident or fire, but you hate making payments on something that essentially gives you a zero return. However, if you do have an accident or damage to your home and the insurance company covers it, you will be pleased that you made those payments.

Although you may emotionally hate making the payments, intellectually, you know it is the smart thing to do. A car and a house are replaceable treasures, so even though we may not like the idea, we readily accept the need for it. Yet when we get into a discussion about insurance on people, who are not replaceable, then insurance resistance is activated. Life, health, disability, and long-term care insurance is meant for people, not things. How will the talent and training values be accomplished if those creating and managing the family wealth are not able or available to do so? Insurance is the only way to protect your family until sufficient accumulated assets and income exist to sustain your family and keep it growing. My objective is to simply help you understand that insurance is a tool that can help your family achieve significance when used properly. Insurance has two primary functions: to create an adequate immediate estate to meet all knowable and unforeseen circumstances until sufficient assets are available to eliminate the need for the insurance and to make liquid assets available when needed so as to avoid being forced to sell illiquid assets at below-market values in an emergency.

Life insurance is often promoted as an investment to help fund retirement. Although there are valid situations where life insurance could be a good investment solution, I suggest caution in making that decision without having a clear understanding of the costs, the return on investment, the tax implications, and whether there are better alternatives. There are many and varied types of insurance products with new offerings being originated constantly from a multitude of companies. Any insurance program should be designed around each individual's and the family's needs, objectives, and financial circumstances. If there is no actual and traditional need for what life insurance is intended to do, buying it solely as an investment is usually not your best alternative.

My prayer for you is that by learning and applying the wisdom shared in this book, you will one day be able to say,

Holy Coach: I have no greater joy than to <u>hear</u> that my children are walking in the truth. (3 John 1:4 NIV)

SECTION III
Taking Action

CHAPTER 12

Preparing for the Transfer

At some point, everything you have will go to someone else. The questions are to whom, when, how, how much, and for how many generations. That includes not only your financial assets but also your family's reputation, heritage, and value to humanity. How all these are addressed determines whether significance will or will not be achieved. This chapter discusses those issues.

Holy Coach: I hated all the things I had worked for here on earth, because I must leave them to someone who will live after me. Someone else will control everything for which I worked so hard here on earth, and I don't know if he will be wise or foolish. This is also useless. (Ecclesiastes 2:18 NCV)

Financial Preparation

It's all about taxes, cash flow, and control. When we start the estate planning process with clients, they want to pass wealth to their children and grandchildren, minimize gift and estate taxes, keep as much cash flow for themselves as they can, and certainly not give up control over anything. The problem is these three objectives are conflicting. We can minimize taxes, but we may have to forfeit some cash flow and give up some or all control to do so. Proper and effective estate planning walks the fine line between these three while acknowledging in this case that you cannot have your cake and eat it too.

Gift and estate taxes are computed and paid based on the size of the estate at the second death of a married couple. In theory, it is possible to drive those taxes to almost zero by reducing the size of your estate to a dollar amount the taxing authorities allow to pass without tax.

Holy Coach: "Here, show me the coin used for the tax." When they handed him a Roman coin, he asked, "Whose picture and title are stamped on it?" "Caesar's," they replied. "Well, then," he said, "give to Caesar what belongs to Caesar, and give to God what belongs to God." (Matthew 22:19–21 NLT)

One way to minimize gift and estate taxes, which we include in our clients' estate planning, is incorporating philanthropy, so giving to religious organizations can be an excellent choice.

Holy Coach: Pay your taxes, too, for these same reasons. For government workers need to be paid. They are serving God in what they do. Give to everyone what you owe them: Pay your taxes and government fees to those who collect them, and give respect and honor to those who are in authority. (Romans 13:6–7 NLT)

Of course, moving assets out of your estate means you potentially lose control over them and the cash flow they could provide. Estate planning is extremely complex, which is why financial, tax, and legal counsel should be involved, and they should be working as a team, not disconnected and uncoordinated individuals, to achieve what is in the best interest of the family as a whole, and not focus only on the patriarch and matriarch, assuming the parents care about their family's legacy. Unfortunately, not all do.

Holy Coach: I want to tell you this: While those who will inherit their fathers' property are still children, they are no different from slaves. It does not matter that the children own everything. While they are children, they must obey those who are chosen to care for them. <u>But when the children reach the age set by their fathers, they are free</u>. Wealth inherited quickly in the beginning will do you no good in the end. Good people leave their wealth to their grandchildren, but a sinner's wealth is stored up for good people. (Galatians 4:1–2; Proverbs 20:21, 13:22 NCV)

Just as cash flow was important and necessary to build your net worth, the process now reverses: the assets must produce the income required to maintain your lifestyle. For my purposes here, I combine cash flow with growth of assets even though they are technically different. Cash flow is normally considered to be actual cash distributed to investors from an investment. Examples are interest on bonds and loans, dividends on stocks, and net income from real estate—investors can reinvest the cash or spend it. Growth is the appreciation of an investment due strictly to market and economic activities. Think about your home, with a constantly changing value until you sell it at a gain or loss. Any stock you own can go up or down in value; you realize the gain or loss when you sell it and pay taxes on the gain or possibly take a tax credit on the loss. But, until then, it is an unrealized gain or loss. If you buy 100 shares of stock at $100 per share today, and in a year you still own the 100 shares, but they have a market value of $110, the $10 is your appreciation or growth. However, it works in both directions. If your 100 shares are worth $90 then you had negative growth. We call that risk. Every investment has a degree of risk. If your investments become profitable, you can sell them and invest the proceeds or use them to pay living expenses or purchase other things.

Before transferring assets out of your estate to children, charities, or anyone or anything, you need to analyze how many assets you must retain to be certain your needs will be met. There are two choices. You can keep sufficient assets so there is no depletion of your principal, or you can calculate a conservative amount of assets needed that will not be depleted until you die. For example, if you need $5 of income and want to retain all the principal until you die, you need to earn a secure 5 percent return on each $100 of principal invested. If you plan on drawing on the principal, you would need to retain approximately $71 of assets instead of $100 and could transfer the extra $29 to whomever while you are still alive. It's been said that the perfect estate plan is when the check to the mortuary bounces, not that we recommend that strategy!

If you are a business owner, a lot of thought, planning, and working with a coordinated team of advisors is extremely important. The choices are many, but you can hold on to the business, sell it, or transfer it. If you hold on to it or transfer it to family, you may still need to be involved in managing it. Selling it can convert an illiquid asset to cash, which must be invested, or a program with the new ownership that pays out over some period that can provide cash flow. It also creates significant risk since you would lose control over the asset producing the income and you have no idea if the new ownership can keep the business successful enough to continue making the payments to you.

Holy Coach: He called them together, along with the workers in related trades, and said: "You know, my friends, that we receive a good income from this business." (Acts 19:25 NIV)

Deciding what to do with a privately owned business, how and when to do it, and why is one of the most difficult and complex transactions a family will experience. Most of the time, it will be an unpleasant experience that causes severe and irreversible damage to the family. Again, detailed and complex planning with a family coach and strong team of advisors is necessary. Here are the statistics: "In a 2013 survey conducted by the Exit Planning Institute, 78 percent of business owners have no formal transition team, 83 percent have no written transition plan, and 49 percent have done no planning at all."[1] Also, 70 percent are out of business after the first transfer and only 3 percent are still in business by the third transfer. Those statistics are for outside-the-family transfers. If the business stays in the family, the numbers will be worse when family infighting, greed, and competition are involved because the potential source of conflicts and disputes (the business) and all the complexities of operating a business are ever-present, unlike a third-party sale that replaces all that complexity with something simple like cash or liquid investments. Or for a little more spice and fire, we can make it a blended family of unrelated individuals with divergent agendas and wants.

---

[1] Exit Planning Institute website (www.exit-planning-institute.org); 2013 conference, State of Business Owner's Readiness Survey.

Another factor and reason to engage a coach well before an actual transaction occurs is to prepare the business owner for what will be a life-changing event. I've mentioned the halftime concept several times. Well, the business owner who doesn't have a job on Monday and suddenly realizes it is going to be like that from then on is in halftime and probably not liking it. If you are a business owner, your whole life, identity, and personal value are probably tied to the business. Now who are you? What is your purpose? Where are you supposed to go? What are you supposed to do? When you've been the captain of the ship most of your life and find yourself without a ship, all the wealth you have will be unimportant if you have not identified your purpose for your remaining years.

Business owners are driven, purposeful, get-it-done types. Sitting on the beach, playing golf every day, or even traveling may be fun for three or six months, but then, boredom and depression can set in. Another Exit Planning Institute statistic:

About 80 percent of former business owners regret selling (or transferring) their companies less than a year after the sale (transfer). What accounts for this seller's remorse? The main reason is lack of preparation on the part of the business owner.[2]

Let me interpret that statement for clarity. The lack of preparation in the financial sense is certainly a big factor regarding their remorse. Typically, business owners have higher opinions of their business's values than the true values. They haven't factored in the capital gains taxes that will take a good portion of the sales proceeds, leaving a net amount much less than anticipated or possibly needed to sustain their desired lifestyle.

[2] Exit Planning Institute website (www.exit-planning-institute.org): 2013 Conference, State of Business Owner's Readiness Survey.

They haven't figured out if they can live off that amount once the business income is gone. As the above statistics prove, he or she has not done the proper planning and preparation to achieve the highest value. But the bigger lack of preparation is in the absence of any planning for the personal and emotional void that will exist if he or she is unable to fill that void with a purpose and activities that fulfill and excite their spirits. The Holy Coach has offered this wisdom several times, but it bears repeating,

Those who love money will never have enough. How meaningless to think that wealth brings true happiness! The more you have, the more people come to help you spend it. So what good is wealth—except perhaps to watch it slip through your fingers! (Ecclesiastes 5:10–11 NLT)

The ex-business owner with a lot of wealth but no purpose is like a Rolls Royce with a full tank of gas but nowhere to go. You can wake up every morning, walk out to the garage, and sit behind the wheel, but if you have nowhere to go, what's the point? You could take it out for a few scenic drives, but that gets you nowhere. Business owners who have not properly planned for their second half will have a difficult time guiding their families to significance. If they cannot identify their personal missions, how will they, as their family's leader, be able to help their family create their family mission statements? Better to own a SUV or pickup that can be used to help other people and causes than a Rolls Royce in the garage.

Once there is clarity on what to do with the business, and then what the business owner will do when there is no business to go to, the third big issue is control. People associate ownership and control as essentially the same. Questions for you: Is it more important to own the field growing wheat or corn or the right to as much of the harvest as you need to feed your family? Do you need to own the water well if you have the legal right to as much of the water it offers for your survival? If someone gives you a guaranteed right to live in a home rent free for as long as you wish, does it bother you that the title is not in your name?

Ownership and control of an asset are not as important as ownership and control of what the asset produces or provides. This is a critical concept to accept when it comes to effective estate planning and transferring assets out of your estate to minimize gift and estate taxes. The most important benefit of any asset is not the asset itself but the cash flow it generates. That provision can be income, growth, or a reduction in expenses and expenditures that would use up your cash flow. Not having to pay rent or a mortgage payment is an example of the latter. Good estate planning can transfer assets to others while you are alive, allowing you to keep the cash flow and minimize the transfer taxes. To some extent, you can have your cake and eat it too.

All good stuff, but here is an even bigger reason to start the transfer while you are alive. Your objective is family and individual significance.

Train up a child in the way he should go, and when he is old he will not depart from it. (Proverbs 22:6 NKJV)

If you start the transfer while you are still around to also provide the training and teach your children your values and lessons, they will be better able to carry on the family heritage and legacy. There is that formula again: Service + Stewardship = Significance. By passing control to your children while you are alive, you will assess their abilities and provide them the help they need to become who they were created to be. This transfer can be controlled and monitored so it happens in ways that produce the best outcomes. Waiting to transfer assets at your death does just the opposite. In exercise or weight training, a person starts with lighter weights and gradually increases the weight as the muscle grows stronger. It is also a good idea to have a trainer or coach.

Gold bricks are wonderful assets I am sure you would love to have if I had some to give you. Assuming I have about ten tons of gold bricks I could hand to you, would you prefer I hand them over one every month or pull up in a dump truck and crush you under them? Same bricks, different results. In the periodic transfer scenario, if I see you are not using each brick wisely and responsibly, I can stop or slow down the distribution and get you the training and experience you need. When I am satisfied you are ready, I can restart the distribution and even increase it.

As I become more comfortable, I can even increase the distributions to two bricks, then three, and so on. Passing control while you are able to control the transfer and outcome is much more preferable to leaving it to chance after your death. Wealth improperly transferred to children unprepared to steward it properly can be hazardous to your family's health!

Holy Coach: The rich are always trying to control your lives. They are the ones who take you to court. (James 2:6b NCV)

Too many parents hide their net worth from their children rather than including them in their estate planning and implementing a training program while alive to monitor and control the process. It is impossible to control from the grave with legal documents if you have not prepared your children with the stewardship qualities they will need to achieve significance. This is especially true if you own a business.

Suppose you own a nice car you no longer need because you have other vehicles. You can sell it, but you don't need the cash, or you could donate it to charity. You have three or four children and several grandchildren of driving age. How do you think they would feel if you sold it or gave it away without first asking them if they would like to have it? What if your car could have provided an upgrade for one of the children's cars that needed expensive repairs? It could have been transportation for a grandchild starting college who needed a car because he or she was planning to stay at home and drive to school rather than live on campus to save costs. It is your car, and you have the right to do whatever you please with it, but why not talk it over with the rest of the family before taking an action that cannot be undone?

That is a simple example of what happens to privately held businesses. The patriarch and matriarch sell the business before finding out if any or all their children would like to keep it in the family. It's your business to do with as you please. Even when children are involved in the business, it can be sold without children ever having the opportunity to participate in the decision. Obsession over retaining control while you are still alive will achieve a self-filling prophecy that your family will very likely wind up in a court battle after your death. Although the business is not legally owned by your children prior to a sale, they may have assumed they would be the owners one day. Think about the negative consequences it could have for your family when they learn their expectations are gone forever.

I've hinted at it previously, but this is perhaps the biggest stumbling block to a family's significance. This works in two directions: fighting for future control and for control while parents are still alive. The children want control, but the parents don't want to give it up. Some of the children want control over specific assets without sharing control with their siblings. When control rests in the hands of more than one person, different agendas and opinions will potentially create disagreements and conflicts and sometimes lead to court battles. It is not unthinkable that parents and children will be on opposing sides of a court confrontation.

Control is such a monumental issue and source of chaos and disputes that it must be addressed early while expectations can be managed. Families fail to reach significance because trust and communication are nonexistent. That creates a very wide gap in expectations, and that is when wars start. I gave you my simple car example already—that was an unmanaged expectation. Compare that to two children who each expect to take over leadership of the family business. The conversation did not take place before the parents' deaths. One gets the control through the estate, or worse, neither gets it because the CEO position is filled by a nonfamily company executive. Definitely a formula for disaster! Planning and preparation with a coach is critical and should occur long before dad and mom are no longer with us.

Giving Gifts While Alive

Holy Coach: Even though you are bad, you know how to give good gifts to your children. How much more your heavenly Father will give good things to those who ask him! (Matthew 7:11 NCV)

Implied in those words is that these gifts are given while the giver and the receiver are alive. As a parent, you will continue to give your children and grandchildren gifts. Some are tangible and expensive whereas others are intangible such as sharing time and wisdom with them. Some are very valuable, others not so much. Some are good, some not so good. We have all received things we did not want or cannot use. Every gift sends a message and creates consequences not only between the giver and the recipient but also for other family members and friends. It can say "I love you," but to someone else in the family, it could say, "I always loved her more than you." A gift can take the form of one person doing something that the other person is supposed to do. The first person thinks he or she is doing a nice thing, but the second person feels he or she is not responsible. Gifts can also diminish a person's appreciation of value. Once the Christmas wrap is in the trash, that toy or gift you paid a fortune for is played with or used for about two days then relegated to the closet. As the gifts get bigger and more expensive—cars, homes, financial support, undeserved positions in the family business—greater caution must be exercised as to your purpose and messaging. It is about managing expectations. Unmet expectations are the result of poor communications, which leads to breakdowns in trust in the family. Those in turn produce that 70 percent failure rate in generational wealth transfers and no possibility for significance.

The following are ten questions you should ask yourself *before* giving a gift of any size, especially financial gifts. Not only should you ask yourself these questions, you should also ask them of an objective third party. This is another area in which having a coach can help you avoid potential problems especially regarding the reactions and expectations of other family members not involved in the gift (see number 9). It may even be beneficial to go through these questions with the intended recipient to see how he or she answers them.

1. What is the worst thing that can happen (laziness, irresponsibility, dependency, entitlement, instant gratification, disincentive, etc.)?

2. How serious would it be?

3. How likely is it to occur?

4. What is the best thing that could happen?

5. How good would it be?

6. How likely is it to occur?

7. What will it teach the recipient? Stewardship or irresponsibility, the value of earning it yourself, dignity, or dependence?

8. Who else needs to be part of the decision?

9. Who besides the recipient will be impacted?

10. What would Jesus do, and will it please God?

I realize number 10 may not be a concern for some readers, but I ask that you not automatically dismiss it. Whatever your personal beliefs are, the answer to this question is still important. In effect, the question is asking how would someone who has perfect knowledge of right and wrong, knows the results of doing each before it happens, knows intimately the persons involved and how they will react emotionally and relationally, and always makes the right choices advise you before making the gift. Wouldn't you want input from the wisest source that exists? Even if you do not believe in God, try to imagine how someone with His attributes would answer question ten.

If the answers to these questions confirm a gift is in order, the next question is how much, assuming it would be some form of financial gift. This question should be answered *after* the ten questions have been answered. You may have an amount in mind prior to going through this drill, but that could change after doing so. It could be more or less than originally anticipated, or it could be zero if the answers indicate there could be more harm than benefit to all involved, especially the beneficiary of the potential gift.

When should this gift be made? In my gold brick story, we looked at two major time frames: while the givers (the parents) were alive and after their passing.

Holy Coach: Wealth inherited quickly in the beginning will do you no good in the end. (Proverbs 20:21 NCV)

This question of *when* subdivides those two major periods into more specific times. Does the gift start at a certain age and continue for a specific amount of time? Are there conditions or criteria for receiving the gift? Helping fund a child's education is a good example; such a gift starts when the child starts college and ends upon graduation.

However, it could end sooner if grades are not maintained or the child drops out.

The same question applies after death. It is normal for trusts to include a mechanism whereby the recipients receive their inheritances in steps rather than immediately. For example, a third is distributed at age twenty-five, the next third at age forty, and the final third at age fifty-five.

Distribution could be built around specific events, purposes, or performance. Marriage or birth of grandchildren might be such events. Starting a business or buying a home could be a funding purpose. Getting a job, accomplishing certain tasks, or being involved in charitable activities could be performances that trigger disbursement. The options are many and varied but, remember, attempting to control someone from the grave is difficult, the outcomes unpredictable, it could create resentment on the part of the person being controlled, and it could leave the door open for legal challenges.

Other determinates for when a gift should be made include tax implications and the age, maturity, demonstrated responsibility, experience, wisdom, discernment, and the intelligence of the recipient. Too much responsibility too soon can do more harm than good. Is there a need or only a want? If the gift allows people to take advantage of an opportunity that could help them become successful and that opportunity could vanish if not acted upon immediately, that might be cause for an immediate gift. But if gifts would allow recipients to procrastinate or put off doing what they should be doing, it may be better to wait and provide the gift after certain performance criteria are met. For example, helping fund education for the fall semester could be conditioned on grade point averages the previous year. Helping a child buy a vehicle or home could happen after a child saves an agreed-upon portion of the down payment or has the income to afford all or most of the monthly payments. As you can see, there are no simple answers; these decisions require communication, negotiation, and planning. Although we often give from the heart, without careful and objective thought, the timing of the gift, and the gift itself may not be advisable.

Holy Coach: The human heart is the most deceitful of all things. (Jeremiah 17:9a NLT)

What are you trying to accomplish with the gift? This may seem obvious. You are trying to show someone you care about him or her, to do something nice for someone, and/or because it makes you feel good about yourself. Those are all valid reasons, but they are too general. For example, giving to a charity has a specific purpose and possible outcome depending on the type of charity and its mission. Perhaps it feeds the hungry, protects the abused and disadvantaged, improves the environment, or finds homes for abandoned animals. In the same way, giving to your children should be done with a specific objective in mind. I'm not talking about special day gifts for Christmas, birthdays, and anniversaries; I am thinking about gifts to children and grandchildren for things they should buy for themselves or for their children.

There are exceptions when this type of gift may be in order. However, there is a tendency, especially in families of wealth for which cost is not a consideration, to give money and things with little thought to the effect it might have on the receiver and other family members, especially when it comes to grandparents and grandchildren. Unfortunately, it can be a case of trying to buy love or seeking to feel good about one's self because the giver is insecure or has low self-esteem. That kind of giving leads to the toxic giving discussed in Chapter 1. Always filter every gift through the ten questions before making the gift.

I have talked about some of the significant tax implications connected to the timing of gifts to heirs. Part of an estate transfer strategy is to reduce the estate to a size that can potentially avoid or minimize gift and estate taxes. That is possible only if the transfer starts while dad and mom are alive. Philanthropy also plays a role. This can be very complicated; it requires careful and intricate planning with a team that includes the accountant, attorney, financial advisor, all family members, and the coach.

The objective of all gifts to your heirs and family, especially younger children, should be to teach, educate, and train them to be responsible and productive people. Every gift should prepare them to be good stewards of the four Ts of True Wealth and to develop a service mentality for GOALS. The objective is to have a team that will successfully manage the family foundation and family holding company to accomplish the most good possible and pass the family values to future generations. They must be trained in how to manage and operate a business that will grow, be profitable, and increase the value from which they will all derive benefit for themselves and their families. Gifts that discourage this kind of personal growth and development are toxic gifts.

The Second Death

The preceding sections focused on transferring wealth prior to death. I now shift to what you must consider regarding transferring wealth after the second death (assuming it is a married couple). The first thing to understand is that all the ten questions are as applicable to the passing of your estate after your death as they are regarding gifting while you are alive.

As you lay out your desires for what you want your estate to accomplish after you are gone, every decision and instruction should be filtered through these ten questions. This is even more important because you will not be around to monitor what is happening to your family and it will be irreversible.

Holy Coach: Good people leave an inheritance to their grandchildren, but the sinner's wealth passes to the godly. (Proverbs 13:22 NLT)

I will explain what happens if no estate planning has been done compared to using the basic documents of typical estate plans and what each accomplishes. If you die without wills and trusts, your estate must go through probate; your state will assign your personal estate to a court- appointed judge who will review your family situation and distribute your assets according to federal and state laws. It will usually be evenly distributed to your children, but if a child has predeceased you and there are grandchildren by that child, it gets more complicated. It can get more difficult when illiquid assets such as real estate and businesses are involved. The primary consideration is your desires for how you wanted to pass your estate will be unknown to the judge, so he or she will do whatever he or she decides is best for everyone— whether or not it actually will be. As such, the actual distribution could take a long time and be an arduous process.

Another negative is it will all be a matter of public record. Everyone will have access to your personal and financial records; someone could write a book or article about your family and estate. Another concern is the taxes must be paid within nine months of the death. If there is insufficient cash to do so, illiquid assets must be sold to raise the cash. Confusion, disagreements, and the possibility that assets will be sold below market value are real possibilities.

The better alternative and the minimum estate planning you should do is to create wills and trusts and associated documents such as powers of attorney and health care directives. A will is simply a written document that explains where you want your assets to go and defines health care issues and guardianship of minor children, for example. The companion document is a revocable (means it can be changed by you prior to death) living trust. It describes in greater detail what you declared in your will. There are three parties to a trust: the grantor (you), the beneficiaries (those who will receive your estate), and a trustee or trustees. While you and your spouse are alive, you will act as co-trustees of your living trust. When one dies, the survivor becomes the sole trustee. When the survivor dies, whomever you have designated as trustee(s) will take control of the estate and must carry out all the duties exactly as you described them in your legal documents.

Since this is not a book on the intricacies of estate planning, suffice it to say that at the first death, the living trust automatically divides into two, maybe three trusts. One remains revocable, meaning it can be changed at any time by the grantor, and the remaining trust(s) become irrevocable and cannot be changed. Having wills and trusts avoids probate and keeps your personal and financial records confidential. No one has the right or ability to research your estate, and it will also be executed faster. The trustee is legally obligated to carry out the instructions in the trust as soon as possible. No judge is involved to slow it down. The biggest advantage and reason for having a trust is the potential to save substantial estate and gift taxes that would significantly deplete the amount of inheritance to your family.

Today, the law allows the husband to transfer $5.4 million without being taxed, and the wife the same amount. For the following discussion, I am rounding down to a combined $10 million since this amount is always subject to change. Anything over that is taxed at rates as high as 60 percent if your state levies estate taxes. Please understand that trusts *do not* eliminate or minimize income taxes; they impact only estate taxes (I am using "estate tax" as a combining term to include gift taxes, which can be taxed differently). Dying without wills and trusts will maximize your estate taxes and minimize the amount your family receives. Having a trust will reduce estate taxes and increase the amount your family receives. If the total estate remains under $10 million, there may be zero estate taxes. However, for estates larger than that, there will still be estate taxes on the amount over $10 million. Note of caution! While current law uses the $10 million number, this could change significantly every time we have national elections. Conservatives normally want to reduce taxes and liberals usually try to raise them. The range over the last twenty years for the estate tax credit has ranged from $600,000 to the current $10 million. If Congress lowers the credit, everyone whose estate is greater than the reduced amount (current allowance is $10.8 million combined for husband and wife) will pay more estate taxes depending on the level and quality of estate planning he or she does.

Holy Coach: God gives some people great wealth and honor and everything they could ever want, but then he doesn't give them the chance to enjoy these things. They die, and someone else, even a stranger, ends up enjoying their wealth! This is meaningless—a sickening tragedy. (Ecclesiastes 6:2 NLT)

That "someone else" is too often the government, which we prefer not receive anything.

As we work with client families and society in general, we see a wide range of knowledge, sophistication, experience, and common sense when it comes to young adults' and children's ability to manage money and investments. Unfortunately, it usually is not a pretty picture. The estimates are that a wealth transfer in excess of $40 trillion will be passing to a generation that does not possess the skills, knowledge, experience, and values to steward this wealth productively and wisely. Most cannot distinguish a stock from a bond, a mutual fund from a savings account, or an investment in commodities from a real estate investment. They understand how to use credit cards but not how to pay them off. The idea of spending less than they earn and saving and giving to charity eludes them.

Holy Coach: There is another serious problem I have seen under the sun. Hoarding riches harms the saver. Money is put into risky investments that turn sour, and everything is lost. In the end, there is nothing left to pass on to one's children. (Ecclesiastes 5:13–14 NLT)

Invest what you have in several different businesses, because you don't know what disasters might happen. (Ecclesiastes 11:2 NCV)

253

The plans of hard-working people earn a profit, but those who act too quickly become poor. (Proverbs 21:5 NCV)

It is no wonder fortunes are lost and families destroyed. You wouldn't get on an airplane whose pilot had not gone through extensive training and years of real experience, nor would you put your life in the hands of a physician who hadn't graduated from medical school and did not have years in practice. Yet that is exactly what will be happening in this massive transfer of wealth about to occur. A pilot and a doctor spend years under the watchful eyes of trained professionals before they are turned loose to fly a plane or practice medicine.

Preparing and teaching children and grandchildren should start early and continue over many years while adults are present to guide and instruct them. Assuming they will somehow acquire these skills and knowledge after dad and mom are gone is insanity. The final point under financial preparation is involvement in, teaching about, and modeling philanthropy. With good planning and proper structuring, significant estate taxes can be eliminated, control over the use and investing of the funds can be maintained, cash flow can be made available, many people and causes can be helped, and children and grandchildren can learn important lessons, values, compassion, charity, and love. A family not involved in philanthropy will most probably not survive financially beyond the third generation. It is almost impossible to be a significant family whose children have significance if philanthropy is not embraced and actualized. It is not a matter of requiring large dollar amounts but a matter of attitude and heart.

Philanthropy can be conducted in relatively small amounts through donor-advised funds and charitable remainder or lead trusts or in larger amounts through a family foundation. And that doesn't mean treasures are the only form of charity. Sometimes, the best thing you can do for the charities or causes you want to support and for your own family is to donate your Time, Talents, and Training. Volunteers are always needed; very few charities can survive even if they have the finances if they have no volunteers. If they must pay people, maybe 60¢ of every dollar actually funds that need. Using volunteers instead could raise that to 85¢ of every dollar. More important, as I've continually stressed, involving children and grandchildren in boots-on-the-ground volunteerism can be life changing.

Preparing People

I want to share with you what I know to be the one source of true wisdom, not what the world and people make up as a substitute. To fulfill that objective, I have offered proverbs and Scripture.

Holy Coach: Their purpose is to teach people wisdom and discipline, to help them understand the insights of the wise. Their purpose is to teach people to live disciplined and successful lives, to help them do what is right, just, and fair. These proverbs will give insight to the simple, knowledge and discernment to the young. Let the wise listen to these proverbs and become even wiser. Let those with understanding receive guidance by exploring the meaning in these proverbs and parables, the words of the wise and their riddles. Fear of the Lord is the foundation of true knowledge, but fools despise wisdom and discipline. (Proverbs 1:2–7 NLT)

Preparing the next generation to be responsible stewards is much more difficult and challenging than dealing with your finances, yet it is much more important and rewarding. It is possible to plan and manage finances without the aid of financial professionals, and many successful businesspeople have. Some individuals enjoy managing their own investments. With today's software programs and spreadsheets, almost anyone can do projections and financial modeling.

But dealing with people and people issues is completely different. It is difficult for two or three individuals who are on different sides of an issue to find a workable solution. Emotions, history, and I daresay greed make resolution almost impossible. Along that same line, objectivity will be hard to find. I mentioned how important the ability to truly listen is. Individuals with different agendas concentrate on their own wants and needs, not really listening to what the other person needs. And the message received is not always the message the sender intended. Communications is not an activity for which going it alone is the wisest option.

As always, IDEA is the formula we use, so the first step is interviewing everyone involved to investigate each person's past, present, and future—the past to uncover issues and events that may be affecting family relationships, the present to find out where they are and what they need to make their life better now, and the future to discover where they want to go and what a significant life would look like for them, their families, the entire family, and the roles they can play in achieving that significance. With that information, we can have a family meeting and begin to draft the family significance statement and the role each person could play. We develop a plan for achieving the family mission that comprises objectives and strategies to help all involved enhance their talents, get whatever training they need, and learn how to free up their time so it can be used for education and training they require, getting the experience they need, and refining their talents.

It is always our objective to create a family foundation and family holding company, which I discuss in more detail in the next chapter. Whether these are formal entities depends on the size, desires, net worth, and family makeup. For my example, I will assume these are formal entities. A holding company needs a president, a financial officer, marketing, and one or more deal makers to name a few roles. A foundation needs a director, a fundraiser if it is open to public donations, someone to research the causes and purposes it will support, and someone to organize events and trips so family members will get boots-on-the-ground experience.

As with any good business, job descriptions, qualifications, and performance standards need to be established and clearly communicated to everyone. Remember, the holding company is a for-profit enterprise that needs quality management and personnel. Favoritism toward family members must be resisted especially if nonqualified persons are in unsuitable roles; it will hurt them and the company and damage the family's integrity. Resentment and jealousy will not be far away if the perception exists that some people get a pass on poor performance or compensated more than they deserve. Standards of performance must be adhered too stringently. Filling these important roles requires an objective assessment of each person's qualifications, education, experience, and personality. That doesn't mean someone should be automatically eliminated for a particular position or role. Businesses have formal training programs. My first job out of college was in banking. I came in as a trainee and was assigned to a branch where I worked as a teller, in new accounts, as a safe deposit clerk, and a host of other entry-level positions. These had nothing to do with becoming a loan officer, but they provided education and experience I needed.

I attended classes to learn how to make all kinds of consumer loans and was assigned to a branch where I made loans under the watchful eyes of a manager and assistant manager. Once I proved myself competent at that level, it was on to more classes on financing businesses. I "graduated" to handling bigger and bigger loans. In short, I went through a rigorous training and learning process. Accounts receivable, equipment financing, and secured and unsecured lines of credit were part of the curriculum, then a new assignment to a branch that financed businesses. I initially got the little guys, then the bigger, more complex businesses as I gained experience. I relayed this information not because you needed to know my history, but because it is a good example. I eventually became the vice president of a major office's real estate department.

This is the kind of training and work experience family holding companies and foundations can provide for every generation. I was given the training and experience I needed. It allowed me to "practice" at each level where I couldn't do too much damage if I made mistakes, and eventually become the vice president of a major office's real estate department. There should be a formal, even written, program for family members to get the training and experience they need and the requirements for taking on more responsibility and more important roles.

Another advantage to using these two primary entities in a family is that they can create learning opportunities for every generation that might not be available without them. In everyday life and work environments, how often does a person have the opportunity to be involved in the inner workings of a foundation or learn how to analyze buying or selling businesses, buildings, or apartment complexes and then negotiating the transaction? Where does one get the help and skills necessary to start a business? These are the opportunities a family can offer that normally cannot be acquired anywhere else. In the safe environment of a family, a child or grandchild might communicate a vision and new idea that outsiders would criticize and discourage. The family can prepare a child to explore, experiment, and fail or succeed and then encourage and assist in new ventures.

Finally, preparing future generations requires mentorship. A family is in the unique position to offer positive encouragement and honest criticism out of love and concern for its members. When they come of age, everyone in the family should have a mentor and be a mentor. Mentoring is different from coaching or friendship. A mentor can be a friend or family member or someone outside the family, but the mentor and the person being mentored do not have to hang out together or even be geographically close. Mentoring can be done over the telephone, the Internet, Skype, email, or a WebEx. Mentoring has a specific purpose, agenda, and action plan.

Mentors are accountability partners who help those being mentored set specific goals and objectives and connect regularly to see if progress is being made and what adjustments are necessary. The mentor also offers accolades and maybe some type of rewards when successes are achieved. They should establish regular meeting dates and adhere to them religiously.

So there it is: how to prepare the financial and the people side of the family. I hope I was successful in demonstrating why both tracks are needed and why it is necessary that both tracks be laid simultaneously in order to build strong, committed, responsible people and a unified family; the tools to do that are in the financial side of the family. Trying to do either one without the other will prove unsuccessful and neither will survive. Shirtsleeves to shirtsleeves in three generations will be the result if both sides are not coordinated.

CHAPTER 13

Backbone Required

I want to emphasize two important facts. First, there is a huge void in the financial industry when it comes to what I would consider real and beneficial financial planning. Anyone can run financial projections for savings goals and retirement and tell you how to invest and what to include in your wills and trusts. Although those efforts may prove successful, those advisors will have done nothing to overcome entropy and the deterioration of the family.

Likewise, the therapy industry may help a family progress to healthier relationships, but that will not necessarily allow the family to avoid conflicts when it comes to passing wealth to the next generation. As wealth increases and the estate becomes more complex, the therapy will most likely fail the family's possibility for significance because the money track was never coordinated with the people track.

The second fact is that railroad ties are needed to hold everything together and provide a firm foundation. A coach with the resources to deal with the people and money tracks simultaneously can help a family develop structures that give it reasons to come together and help it avoid wrecks. In this chapter, I address the need and types of solid structures we use.

Is some form of structure that important? Most families today are disconnected and geographically dispersed. They may get together on holidays, birthdays, and anniversaries, but that can be hit or miss. Married sons and daughters have in-laws and usually children to squire around to activities and such, so they have to share their time between two families, not just the family they were born into. And they have children to raise, busy weekends with the children's activities, their neighbors and friends, and work. Without a specific reason to spend time with their parents and siblings, it will not happen even if everyone is only a few miles apart. If your children are out of the home and raising their own families, you know what I mean.

Our objective is family and individual significance. To accomplish this, we need to turn the individual family members into a team with a shared mission and purpose and a well-defined game plan for achieving that mission, and everyone must clearly understand and accept their roles and responsibilities as a member of the team. Athletic teams have a structure. In fact, the team is the structure. There is no team if there is no reason for its members to assemble.

Our bodies require many specialized organs to keep us alive. We need hearts, brains, stomachs, kidneys, intestines, muscles, and livers to name a few. If we could somehow assemble on a table and connect all our vital organs and keep them functioning, would we have a viable human? Oh, there are a couple of key components missing. A skeleton and skin. Without those two, we would be a low-budget science fiction movie at the Saturday matinee called *The Blob*! The skin holds everything together and protects the organs from external hazards, and the skeleton provides a foundation on which many of the body parts are anchored and serves as a delivery mechanism for our cardiovascular and nervous systems.

Think of the vital organs as the people side of the family. They are what makes and keeps the family alive. The skeleton and skin are the structures that unite everything and give it a foundation and the ability to accomplish what our bodies were meant to accomplish. Without these two structures, our bodies have no mobility, no strength, no protection from all the challenges and dangers the world will throw at us. Having the right structures allows the family to move forward and achieve its purpose. American Heritage Dictionary says backbone is, "The main support or major sustaining factor. Strength of character; determination." Families need a backbone!

Family Foundation

At Family Wealth Leadership, we believe every family should be involved in philanthropy because it is the best tool for bringing families together without competing for the family's wealth. I have already mentioned all the positive benefits philanthropy can have on your children and grandchildren. I consider *foundation* as synonymous with philanthropy and not necessarily the actual entity. If a true foundation is what the family wants and is financially justifiable, that will be what we create. For other families, something less complicated such as a donor-advised fund may be the better choice. Additionally, we explore utilizing other giving strategies such as charitable remainder and lead trusts or gift annuities, for example.

Foundations can be private or public depending on the objective. We can also combine strategies. A charitable remainder or lead trust can designate the family foundation as its beneficiary, or a donor-advised fund can be established for younger children that they can manage to gain experience in giving. This way, they will have the training and skills necessary to get involved in managing the family foundation when they are ready.

We prefer to set up an actual foundation if the family can afford it. It will be required to keep very accurate financial records and file tax returns annually to retain its nonprofit status. There are also varying rules on family members acting as directors and employees of the foundation, especially if the family elects a pubic foundation format. Public foundations also have more stringent rules on the sources of fundraising, requiring that a certain percentage of donations come from outside the family.

There are many ways to fund a foundation while you are alive or after your passing. I cannot go into all the options, but the obvious sources are cash, investments, qualified plan resources, real estate, and business interests. In a private foundation, all the money comes from the family. The patriarch and matriarch are usually the primary donors, but other family members can also contribute; the benefits to them are tax deductions and family involvement.

Using a donor-advised fund can leverage giving by avoiding the costs, time, and effort of setting up a philanthropic entity. If a public foundation is chosen, then nonfamily donors can—in fact, must—be donors. The reason we prefer a legitimate foundation over something like a donor-advised fund, as you hopefully detected from my description, is the formality of a business structure. Although a foundation is a nonprofit entity, it must be operated just like a for-profit company. That requires rules, discipline, management abilities, relationship skills, marketing expertise if third-party donors are involved, legal and compliance requirements, reporting responsibility to donors, and financial acumen. And it teaches people and relationship skills as well as researching, decision making, and negotiating skills. A foundation is an incredible university for developing significant children and grandchildren while you are around to guide them and monitor their progress.

Finally, there will be no arguments about who gets what and how much because no one has a right to any of the foundation's funds. Family members can serve in management and staff positions and receive market compensation for carrying out their duties, but they cannot be overpaid. Other things we like about utilizing a true foundation that has all family members involved is that the format facilitates the older family members to be mentors and examples for younger members of what it means and the benefits to themselves and the family to serve others who are less fortunate. It also teaches the younger members how to develop a selfless attitude and lifestyle. The children can learn, experience, and catch philanthropy from their parents and adults rather than only hearing about it. They can engage in boots-on-the-ground giving of their Time, Talents, and Training as well as giving Treasures. One important point to note: you cannot and should not force anyone to be involved—all must do it of their own volition—or it will not stick. And everyone should have the right to raise the causes they care about and have the foundation consider those causes as long as they align with the mission and criteria the foundation has established.

It is not unusual for children who at first are not interested in the foundation to change their minds when they realize they could have some influence and votes in directing foundation funds to their preferences.

Operating a foundation is an excellent tool for uniting a family, achieving significance, and leaving a legacy. One reason we all recognize the names Getty, Rockefeller, and Kennedy is because their names are on buildings, museums, and causes funded by their foundations.

We usually want to establish the foundation before forming other family entities because there will be more interest and involvement and less dissention and disagreement. Most of the time, the children are enthusiastic about the opportunity to be involved and do good deeds for their communities, so a foundation can be a stepping stone to creating the structure, which I address shortly. All the factors needed to set up and operate a profitable business can be learned through experiencing, establishing, and operating the nonprofit entity. The family foundation serves as the model. The exercise of creating the foundation's value, vision, and mission statements will provide a template when the family is ready to move on to the for-profit enterprise.

Family Holding Company

Let me explain why we believe a holding company is such a valuable tool for uniting a family and achieving significance, especially in partnership with the family foundation. Families with uncomplicated balance sheets, modest assets, and one or two children can get by with basic estate planning documents of wills and trusts that use—as we put it—the divide-and-dump method for estate distributions. If there are three children, each gets a third and they go their separate ways. However, in wealthy families, one or two children will manage their inheritance reasonably well but the others will spend it down quickly on toys, bigger houses, entertainment, and travel. Shirtsleeves to shirtsleeves in three generations!

As estates gets larger and more complicated, the probability of family feuds increases and are often never settled. Although some relatively small distributions can be made to the kids and grandkids, greater benefit can be achieved by retaining the assets in an entity that can meet the family's needs for the next hundred years. It could leverage everyone's Time, Talents, Training, and Treasures in ways that will continually increase the value of the entity while also favorably impacting the community and allowing the family to achieve significance.

Whereas the foundation deals with the philanthropic side of the family, the family holding company addresses the business side. I am not speaking about a family business. Whether there is a family-owned business is not the point, although that is often the case since we work with business owners. I am saying our objective is to get the family members to think of themselves as a for-profit business managed by the family rather than a loose-knit, informal group of individuals.

When you think about it, a family, especially a high net worth family, has all the components of a business. We call it Family Incorporated. Running an effective and efficient family is the same as running a business—the family enterprise. Like any business, six critical elements must be in place to be successful: sales and marketing; production; distribution; administration and operations; finance, accounting, and tax; and human resources.

The following are examples of some of the objectives that must be achieved if the enterprise is to prosper and fulfill its purpose. The Family Enterprise must

1. have a viable and clear purpose and mission,

2. add value to the world,

3. have a well-defined and well-designed plan,

4. execute the plan effectively and timely,

5. constantly strive to improve operations,

6. seek new opportunities and be able to adapt to changing situations,

7. analyze the risks and rewards and make informed decisions,

8. employ, educate, and train qualified personnel,

9. empower individuals to take action and be decisive,

10. encourage social responsibility,

11. be profitable and increase the value of the enterprise,

12. be ongoing, and

13. provide for an orderly and timely succession to qualified leaders who can carry on the mission.

Our role as the family's advisor and coach is to apply sound business succession techniques and strategies to the family as the wealth transitions to the next generation. I am always amazed that successful businesspeople essentially leave their business skills at the office and never apply their wisdom and experience to their families when they walk through their front door in the evening.

I was doing a presentation to a university donor group. I called it Lessons from a Lemonade Stand. The setup is your children come home from school with the mission of raising funds to buy books. You have choices at that point: write a check, send them out door to door to solicit donations, or teach them lessons—help them start a business, a lemonade stand, with your guidance and advice but requiring them to do the planning and work. This is the outline I used.

Start with investigation (what we need to think about). The word *investigation* is very important. The goal is to ask open-ended, thought-provoking questions so the children can come to their own conclusions. Try not to tell them what to do or give them answers; help them identify the options and consequences.

Location

- Set up in front of the house or down the street

- Go door-to-door

Design

- Card table with a tablecloth?

- An actual stand to be constructed?

Materials

- Can we use cardboard, wood, or plastic boxes?

- Do we have scrap wood we can use?

- Do we need to go to the home supply for material with Dad?

Supplies

- What ingredients go into lemonade?

- What kind of containers do we need?

- How will it be kept cold?

- Do we need to make a trip to the grocery store with mom?

- Where and how do we store the supplies, or do we need to buy fresh every day?

Days/Hours of Operation

- Open for business for one day. If so, what day will it be?

- Open for business for one day each week for two hours for three weeks?

- Open for business five days a week for one week?

- Open for business five days a week for three weeks?

Pricing

- How much will people pay for a glass of lemonade?

- How big is the glass?

- How about buy two and get the third free?

Costs

- What can we afford to pay for building materials?

- What can we afford to pay for supplies?

- What quality do we want to buy?

Roles and Responsibilities

- Who is doing the building?

- Who is making the product?

- Who is staffing the booth and when?

- Who is working on marketing and advertising?

Marketing

- Advertising

- Signage

- Direct marketing

Financing

- Use own funds

- Borrow

- Raise equity

Plan

- Expected sales volume

- Cost of goods sold

- Cost of materials

- Operating expenses

- Type of capital

- Cost of capital

- Repayment of capital

- Cash flow

- Giving back

Implement (make it a family project)

- Identify roles

- Buy materials

- Buy supplies

- Build the store

- Spread the word

Manage

- Operations

  i. Sales

  ii. accounting

  iii. Manufacturing

- Closing Down

  i. Facilities

  ii. Assets

  iii. Capital

  iv. Profits

What did the children learn by

- Giving them money (entitlement)

- Giving them opportunity

- Starting and running a business

- Planning

- Finance

- Teamwork

- Sharing and giving

- Debt management

- Investing

- Independence

- Other?

Never Forget

- To take advantage of every learning opportunity and understand everything is a learning opportunity

- To take advantage of every opportunity to spend quality time with your children

- That your primary role as a parent is to teach your children and be their best example

- That it requires attention, not intention

- That it will be harder but more rewarding

- That your children's future depends on what you do today

Here is a real-life lemonade stand story.

When you first meet 11-year-old Blake Britton, you'd think he is just an average kid. He loves dogs, baseball, and books. But when you talk with him, you hear him speak with a real passion for God. His faith is so strong that, while some kids are busy collecting toys, Blake is busy giving them up so he can give generously to others and to the church.

Blake has been part of the Saddleback family as long as he can remember and learned about giving and tithing to the church at a young age. When Saddleback began the Daring Faith campaign, a 10-week series during which our church was challenged to take big steps of faith, Saddleback Kids also went through the series. And during Daring Faith, Blake felt God challenge him to give in a bigger way than ever before. Blake had given money toward two of his friends' mission trips in the past, but this was something new. Even though he is just 11 years old, Blake wanted to stretch his faith.

But how could a boy his age, with no allowance, give anything? Blake's father suggested a lemonade stand, so he set up a stand at a local busy intersection and people came from every direction to buy his drinks. His customers not only seemed to like the taste of his lemonade but also the vision behind it. Blake earned many times more than he had hoped for from his generous neighbors. He was so excited; he didn't want to give up selling lemonade that day. His dad even had to drag him away so that he would have some lunch.

He was still feeling very happy about the successful lemonade stand when the next opportunity came along. Kids Small Groups (KSG) had a garage sale to finance a mission trip for the youth and Blake wanted to take an even bigger step of faith. "If I give just my Legos to the sale, then I still wouldn't make much money," he said, "so I decided to donate my bike to the garage sale as well. It gives me more pleasure to give and change people's lives than to spend money on myself for things I don't need!"

Blake collected the money from the garage sale—more money than he'd ever had before in his young life—and brought it to Saddleback during a weekend service. When the time came for Blake to place all the money into the offering basket, there was a short moment when he thought, *Wow, that is a lot of money!* But he didn't question his decision and gladly gave the money to God. "It felt really good," he recalls.

In the future Blake wants to keep raising the bar and give more and more. He is also hoping to be a leader at KSG one day and to go on his first PEACE trip next year. He has already started recycling bottles to raise money for the trip. This will be one of his biggest steps of faith yet, but he has decided to trust God instead of letting fearful thoughts distract him from his goal.[1]

A Lemonade Stand or a Family Holding Company

The only difference between the stand and a holding company is the size of the undertaking and age of our entrepreneurs. I would be a lot more comfortable turning over the family business to children who had experienced running a successful lemonade stand. Someone like Blake. How about you?

The type of entity for the holding company can take a variety of forms, depending on a family's desires and needs and tax situation. A family limited partnership or limited liability company is the entity most often used, but various types of trusts can also be appropriate. Most trusts have automatic termination dates of one hundred years, and we prefer to have the holding company go on in perpetuity, so if the trust format is selected, we would probably use a dynasty trust that has no termination provision. Other reasons for creating a new entity are to avoid estate taxes and protect assets. Strategies for both objectives are many, so detailing them is beyond the scope of this writing. It is possible that multiple entities can be used to achieve the desired asset protection. We prefer the term *family holding company* over *family bank* because the holding company, by definition, owns other entities, and the more levels of ownership we can create, the less chance someone will bring a legal action.

The objective is to limit asset exposure to only one or two assets the entity owns. For example, a family owns an apartment building, an industrial building, and a small office building. If dad and mom

[1] Saddleback Church website, www.saddleback.com/stories.

carry title to all three in their names or in a living trust, all three assets could be attacked in a legal settlement in addition to investment and bank accounts. Even if we create a family holding company that holds title to all three real estate assets, if someone is injured in the industrial building, he or she could go after all three assets, and everything else dad and mom own in the holding company. However, they could hold title to all three real estate properties in one LLC and other assets in a trust or separate LLC or limited partnership that functions as the holding company.

An even better option is to hold each real estate asset in its own LLC or limited partnership so only that asset is exposed. The holding company will be the managing member if you use an LLC or the managing partner in the limited partnership and own a 1 percent interest. It can then own the remaining 99 percent as a limited partner, thus reducing the holding company's exposure to only the 1 percent. You can also have other family members own limited partnership interests. As usual, this level of planning can be complicated, so the entire planning team needs to be involved.

These are some of the financial reasons for utilizing the philanthropic and holding company structures. The greater benefits are what they can do to unite a family; educate, train, and prepare the next generation; and help them become a significant legacy family. They create a structure and purpose for holding the family together; without structure, the family will likely fall apart. The second benefit is discipline. I already discussed in detail the need, reason, and benefits of discipline, the most important factor between a winning or losing season for any team. Another prime example is the military. A country with an undisciplined military is a country already in, or on its way to, captivity or ruin. The third benefit is rules. Businesses, governments, organizations, professional teams, societies, and many more must have rules that everyone understands and plays by, otherwise there will be chaos, violence, and anarchy.

A fourth benefit of structures is they are a platform for education and training. What better place for a young person to get real world, hands-on experience than in the loving, caring environment of family and friends? Today, we have many "educated" students trying to enter the workforce with only book learning handed down from professors who have never held a corporate job or operated a business.

Even more detrimental to your children's growth and future is that they may not be able to get the work they want. College graduates often have a difficult time getting hired for good jobs because they have no work experience on their résumés. This can be especially true in families where the children never had to work or held a job with an employer. Working in the family holding company or foundation can be a good solution. It is better to teach someone to fish than to give him or her a fish. A job in one of the family enterprises should not be a gift; it should be a boot camp. Likewise, mentoring is a fifth benefit. Surrounding individuals with people who have knowledge, experience, and scars from fighting daily battles to survive and prosper are invaluable regarding the efficient and effective transfer of Time, Talents, and Training, plus being a good steward of Treasures.

Number six is experience, and seven is personal development—the opportunity to become a well-rounded individual, doing what you were created to do in an environment that needs your talents and skills so you can achieve significance. Our objective is always to help the family and every family member become significant in terms of what that means for them. Having solid structures that give them a platform to experiment and try different things and allow them to succeed or fail in a safe environment provides a lab they could not find anywhere else.

The eighth benefit is learning teamwork. Decisions in our two primary structures should be made by consensus, not majority vote. That does not mean there will not be disagreements and conflicts—there will be—but it means everyone must negotiate and compromise until a satisfactory solution is reached. Compassion, empathy, and respect for different points of view, opinions, and needs must be weighed and measured. No one will get everything he or she wants, but the goal is always to do what is best for the family not just for today but for future generations. That may require individuals to put their personal wants on the shelf for the betterment of the team.

Trust and communication are the ninth benefits. I've focused on this numerous times already because these two factors are the primary reasons families self-destruct. Even in the best of families, and I am sure your family falls into that category, there will still be a substantial lack of trust resulting from bygone events that have not been openly and honesty discussed or resolved. Our nature is to avoid conflicts. Exploders blow their tops when things don't go their way. These gladiators leave bodies strewn all over the arena bleeding from words unsheathed and swung like a two-edged sword. On the other hand, imploders hold it all in while it eats away at their souls; they can carry grudges and resentment for a lifetime.

The reason families never resolve these issues is because they have no reason or structure to solve them. When holidays are the only time families are together, they are not going to get into unpleasant conversations around historical events that broke trust and destroyed communications between them; they think it is better to let sleeping dogs lie. Having structures that require family meetings and gaining consensus on decisions most assuredly will raise past violations of trusts and hurts that have never been resolved. I am not suggesting that having a platform for bringing out these issues is a panacea for solving them, but at least they can be an opportunity to do so in a more unemotional and rational environment with other family members who can provide objectivity and wisdom. And having a coach should be on the top of your list for helping to rebuild trust and communications.

I hope I have ingrained in you the formula for achieving significance, so repeat after me: "Service plus Stewardship equals Significance." This is the tenth benefit a family can experience by weaving holding company and foundation structures into their fabric. Certainly, people can learn service to others through their work and jobs, through volunteerism, and through stewardship by owning things. But when I present this concept to people and other advisors, I follow it up with three questions. First, regarding the four Ts of True Wealth, I ask if they had to give up one, would they give up their Time, Talents, Training, or Treasures? I tell them that whatever they give up is *not* gone forever, that they just have to start from zero and reacquire it.

Now it is your turn. Which of the four Ts would you give up? Not so easy? Actually, it is easy for some people, but most people will struggle a little with the decision until they think it through. When they finally make the decision, it will be the Treasures because they realize as long as they can effectively use their Time, Talents, and Training, they will always be able to reacquire Treasures. Isn't that how you got everything you have now?

The second question is, if that is true, why does everyone—advisors and clients alike—always put the focus on the treasures and ignore the other three? Third question: As a society, are we doing an above-average, average, or below-average job of passing the skills and experience our children need in the areas of Time, Talents, and Training? Legally, the Treasures have to pass, but legacies and significance are achieved only when a family does a good job of transferring its wisdom for developing and using its Time, Talents, and Training. The answer is always below average. There are two primary reasons for this deficiency: lack of an effective structure and purpose and the inability to deal with family dynamics on their own.

Holy Coach: "They are like a man building a house, who dug down deep and laid the foundation on rock. When a flood came, the torrent struck that house but could not shake it, because it was well built. But the one who hears my words and does not put them into practice is like a man who built a house on the ground without a foundation. The moment the torrent struck that house, it collapsed and its destruction was complete." Plans fail for lack of counsel, but with many advisers they succeed. (Luke 6:48–49; Proverbs 15:22 NIV)

Treasures do not need a structure to pass to the next generation, but without that skeleton and skin I talked about, the vital organs—Time, Talents, and Training—cannot survive.

Number eleven is financial and investment wisdom. Many children move into adulthood with a bare—at best—understanding of how to balance a checkbook much less judiciously manage investments and debt and make wise financial decisions. Sure, they may take business classes and get an undergraduate or graduate degree in business, but that doesn't mean they have any real-world experience. How many young adults get to be involved in running an enterprise or at least acquainted with the inner workings of operating a successful business? Working for a corporation at any level right out of school is not going to give them that knowledge and wisdom. If they are good and lucky, they may move up the ranks quickly, but quickly could be years. What an incredible opportunity it can be for them to gain firsthand experience through the family holding company and family foundation.

Both structures must invest their capital to get an adequate return to carry out the entity's mission. Stocks, bonds, mutual funds, real estate, private equity transactions, and other financial instruments start to have meaning for them and teach them the concepts of risk and reward and the importance of doing due diligence before acting.

That raises the twelfth benefit: learning to do extensive research to make wise decisions. First, they can learn by example, training, and mentoring and then be given small amounts so they can practice without fear of making catastrophic mistakes. As they get better, they can be given more responsibility.

A benefit I could treat separately because it is so important but I include here is *accountability*. If you were like me in school, you dreaded the words *research paper*. Why does the word *research* create such angst and trepidation? No one likes doing research because it is a lot of work. You and I procrastinated and then downed coffee while we frantically pounded a typewriter all night, finishing with fifteen minutes to spare to brush our teeth and get to class. Without accountability, we are all tempted to put off till tomorrow what we should be doing today. Unfortunately, parents do not always demonstrate the accountability their children need. In a structured environment with clear rules and objectives, and other people who can be more critical and discerning than the child's parents can be, accountability can lead to success. And children often accept positive criticism and accountability more favorably from someone else.

Thirteen is optimization, which means we want everyone in the family to be the best he or she can be. If this is accomplished, the family will be optimized and significant. Optimization occurs when all the other benefits I have discussed are realized.

Fourteen is maybe the best benefit: family enrichment. When your children were young and at home, the family was together for holidays, vacations, day and weekend excursions, sports, meals around the table, playing games and wrestling in the living room, going to church or synagogue, visiting grandparents, aunts, uncles, and cousins, and just enjoying being together. Did I bring back some memories?

But then the children move out, get married, and maybe move away. They begin making their own memories in their nuclear families, not the extended family. But operating and managing a family holding company and family foundation can bring families together again for common purposes. It can also provide the funds and activities that can build relationships, especially when the nonblood relatives come into the family. As I've mentioned numerous times, education, businesses, home purchases, mission trips, business meetings, and family vacations and outings can be funded. Bonding occurs when people work together as a team, make difficult decisions, work through troubled family relationships, build trust and communications, and deal with tragedy. Without these structures in place, family enhancements will not happen.

Family enhancement incorporates the fifteenth benefit: knowledge sharing. Again, I can be brief because this benefit is obvious. I have also shared the Holy Coach's viewpoint several times about plans succeeding with many counselors, so suffice it to say that the more wise and caring counselors people gather around them, the more likely they will be to achieve the optimization mentioned previously and become significant. Significant family members make a significant family!

Profit

I have emphasized that the family holding company is a for-profit enterprise. That is benefit sixteen. I want to focus on the word *holding* again. My previous comments were about investments. Holding companies are formed specifically to hold interests in other companies and businesses. Often, it does not produce a product or service of its own but through the entities in which it invests. This time, let us discus how our structures hold together the family members and the family wealth. If the wealth is originally, as is the case with most estate plans, distributed to family members scattered around the country and maybe even the globe, the wealth will likely be lost. Shirtsleeves to shirtsleeves. By holding everything together, you have the opportunity to use the five types of capital to generate profits that benefit every family member.

Benefit seventeen is the beneficiary of benefit sixteen: growth and increased value from profits. Every business's objective should be increased value by generating profits; profits and positive cash flow are the sources of growth and increased value. By keeping the financial and human resources together, you increase the viability and probability of constantly growing these resources and increasing an enterprise's value that in turn benefits everyone in the family and community.

Finally, benefit eighteen is about the business owner's second half. It's called life after business. I covered this in Chapter 12. When business owners sell or transfer businesses that have been their purposes in life for many years, their remaining years can become dismal and depressing. When they have nothing to look forward to, many business owners stop looking forward. The family holding company and family foundation can be surrogates for the businesses they left. They don't have to get out of business completely; they transfer their skills and wisdom to new enterprises. The original family businesses can be retained in holding companies and foundations. This format allows leadership of the original business to transfer to the children while business owners still supervise and guide the transfers and operations through the holding companies and foundations they manage.

There can be many more benefits, but I think you will agree that by having the right structures in place, your family will have much better opportunities and many more benefits than if it did not have them.

Structures, of themselves, are cold and dead. Some major cities, like Detroit and Chicago, now have entire areas of vacant and dilapidated buildings. They lack people and purpose. Uniting the people with the purposes of the structures I have described will not happen accidently or of their own volition. If I asked you to state your family's value, vision, and mission statements, my assumption is you would say you don't have these. That would be normal since few families have them because they have not developed the necessary structures. A family without a structure is just a group of individuals each doing his or her own thing going in separate directions, uncoordinated, chaotic, but all trying to get a piece of the wealth without regard to the impact it will have on others. In that scenario, who needs value, vision, and mission statements? It is like crocodiles fighting over a water buffalo. Most animals learn quickly it is safer to crowd together with the young animals in the center when threatened by a predator. The herd is their structure. For humans, the family holding company and family foundation can provide a strong fortress to protect themselves including the young ones from dangers and predators as they mature and learn to fend for themselves.

Finally, a brief word on funding these structures. There is no right or wrong way—there are many ways. Setting up the right structures for your family requires careful thought and planning, a coach, and financial and legal advisors. Obviously, the initial funds will come from the patriarch and matriarch, but all family members can be invited to invest or contribute, the latter more likely, in the foundation. When the holding company invests in other businesses, real estate, and private equity, everyone has the ability to deposit into or lend the holding company money or invest directly in the investments he or she likes.

A healthy, productive, and purposeful body includes all the vital organs needed to survive. But those organs cannot carry out their purposes without the skeleton and skin to hold it all together and give it the strength it needs to stand tall, move forward, twist and turn when needed, work, think and dream and reason, communicate, play, love, cry and grieve, serve and steward, and protect those vital organs. Think of the holding company as the skeleton and the foundation as your family's skin. Without them, your family will not survive.

CHAPTER 14

Building the Team

What differentiates the Lakers, Clippers, or the Celtics from five guys on each side of a neighborhood pickup game? What is the difference between a family composed of two dozen members who fade into history as each generation passes away and families that make history and futures that enshrine their family names and change the world? I gave you part of the answer in the previous chapter: having the right structures in place. The structures fall into the financial track category of my railroad analogy. Now I will concentrate on the people track.

We must first decide who is on the team. Unlike professional sports teams or business teams, families do not have the option of picking and choosing who will and will not be on the team—that decision was made through births and weddings. But individuals still have some latitude on who and when someone is formally added to the team, and each person has the right to choose whether he or she wants to be on the team. Although it can be assumed every family member will be on the team, that should not be automatic.

Going back to our investigation phase, everyone needs to be interviewed to determine if he or she wants to participate, and other family members need to feel that they can voice their thoughts and concerns about individual family members' contributions without reprisal to ensure the well-being of the team. The when and how are as important as the who. For example, at what ages should persons be given certain responsibilities or the right to vote on issues? Will there be education and experience requirements? The how focuses on specific roles each person can and should fill. Individuals learn differently, respond to responsibility differently, and have different time, talents, training, treasures, skills, abilities, needs, desires, and goals that must be coordinated and intermingled with everyone else's. Building a family team can be more difficult than building a professional or business team, but it is significantly more valuable, rewarding, and long lasting.

Holy Coach: Just as there are many parts to our bodies, so it is with Christ's body. We are all parts of it, and it takes every one of us to make it complete, for we each have different work to do. <u>So we belong to each other, and each needs all the others</u>. God has given each of us the ability to do certain things well. If your gift is that of serving others, serve them well. If you are a teacher, do a good job of teaching. If you are a preacher, see to it that your sermons are strong and helpful. If God has given you money, be generous in helping others with it. If God has given you administrative ability and put you in charge of the work of others, take the responsibility seriously.

Those who offer comfort to the sorrowing should do so with Christian cheer. Don't just pretend that you love others: really love them. Hate what is wrong. Stand on the side of the good. Love each other with brotherly affection and take delight in honoring each other. Never be lazy in your work, but serve the Lord enthusiastically. When others are happy, be happy with them. If they are sad, share their sorrow. Work happily together. Don't try to act big. Don't try to get into the good graces of important people, but enjoy the company of ordinary folks. And don't think you know it all! Never pay back evil for evil. Do things in such a way that everyone can see you are honest clear through. Don't quarrel with anyone. Be at peace with everyone, just as much as possible. (Romans 12: 5–6a, 7–11, 15–18 TLB)

Those words apply especially to families that want to achieve significance. I have constantly stressed that trust and communications are the major problems that lead to families self-destructing. Comparing families to professional, business, and military teams accentuates this point. Winning teams differ from losing teams even when the losing teams may have more skilled players, more confidence and trust in each other, and better ability to communicate and anticipate the actions and reactions of each member in certain situations. The receiver catches the pass because the quarterback knows where the receiver will be when he throws the football. The same is true in other sports, and the soldiers on the ground know where and when to attack because their communications with and trust in their air, armor, and artillery support is excellent.

Holy Coach: Then the other administrators and high officers began searching for some fault in the way Daniel was handling government affairs, but they couldn't find anything to criticize or condemn. He was faithful, always responsible, and <u>completely trustworthy</u>. Here's the lesson: Use your worldly resources to benefit others and make friends. Then, when your earthly possessions are gone, they will welcome you to an eternal home. If you are faithful in little things, you will be faithful in large ones. <u>But if you are dishonest in little things, you won't be honest with greater responsibilities</u>. And if you are untrustworthy about worldly wealth, who will trust you with the true riches of heaven? <u>And if you are not faithful with other people's things, why should you be trusted with things of your own?</u> No one can serve two masters. For you will hate one and love the other; you will be devoted to one and despise the other. You cannot serve both God and money. (Daniel 6:4; Luke 16:9:13 NLT)

I use six words to define trust, and all of these must exist in relationships. If even one is missing, trust will be broken or will not be established. If it is a new relationship, it might appear that all are present because one of the participants is a good actor, but the deficiency will be exposed eventually, at which time the relationship will deteriorate and crumble.

The first character attribute is *reliability*. Simply, this means you always do what you promise to do. Some synonyms are dependability, responsibility, and trustworthiness. To build and maintain trust, everyone in the relationship must be counted on to perform every time. That does not mean perfection but consistent performance no matter what obstacles might get in the way as long as the person has some control over those obstacles. This leads to the next attribute: *competency*. Competency means you make only those promises you know you can deliver on. Don't let your mouth write a check your body cannot cash. That is the point of competency. Politicians violate this one all the time, which is why most people view them as untrustworthy. We do it too when we say something to impress other people knowing there is no way we can carry it out. We also do it to win favors or take advantage of others to get what we want, hoping we will be long gone before they find out we cannot deliver on our promises. In effect, it is lying, and lies always destroy trust.

When you say you will do something, do you mean it? Are you sincere? *Sincerity* is the third character attribute. I hope you see how connected these attributes are. Sincerity is different from competence, although they may seem to have similarities. You may have ability to perform as you promised but you didn't mean it. You can be sincere in thinking you will or want to complete a task you promised to do but cannot because you are not capable of doing it. The opposite is that you have the capability, said you would do something, but never intended to do it. You were insincere! Again, it is a lie.

Whom do you care about most, yourself or the other person? We trust individuals whom we believe care more about us than themselves. This is the attribute of *loyalty*. Soldiers give up their lives because they are loyal to their country, leadership, and fellow soldiers. Good parents sacrifice for their children. Teammates can rely on each other because they are loyal to the team and teammates, and fans are said to be loyal because they go to all the games, rain or shine, near or far.

Since my focus is family significance, my definition of loyalty is "being committed to the betterment of the entire family." That means putting everyone else's needs over your own. Loyalty often requires a person to sacrifice something to help someone else. It could be your Time, Talents, Training, or Treasures. In the movie *It's a Wonderful Life*, George must take over operating his deceased father's savings and loan. He planned to go to college, but that gets put on hold. His chosen career as an architect will never happen since he must head the bank so his younger brother can go to the university.

His loyalty to his family, brother, and community was more important than what he wanted. Loyalty is not easy, but one thing George had was the trust of everyone in his community and family so that the entire community, including the bank examiner, raises enough money to replace bank funds confiscated by the movie's villain and keep George from going to prison for something he didn't do.

"Did you hear what Bob said about Jim's wife?" "Did I mention that my brother has a problem with?" The fifth character attribute is *confidentiality*. Can you be trusted not to share individual and family information that would do harm if shared? This can occur in or outside the family. Reread the section on gossip in Chapter 1. If ever there has been a relationship killer, it is gossip. Suppose you tell me something you want me—and only me—to know about you; you have the right to assume it will remain confidential. Then, if I am the only person you told this information but you hear it repeated from someone else, that would probably be the last thing you ever told me. In fact, it would probably end our friendship.

The *American Heritage Dictionary* has this definition for confidentiality: "Containing information, the unauthorized disclosure of which poses a threat to national security." Let's change "national security" to "relationships." If you cannot be trusted to keep your mouth shut, you will never be trusted in anything. When you tell someone something he or she knows is gossip about another person, what thought goes through the mind of the person hearing it from you? You already know the answer because it is exactly what would go through your mind if you were the recipient of the gossip. If others are willing to divulge private information about somebody else, what are they telling other people about me? Big trust killer!

Finally, there is one word that brings these attributes together: *care*. Care is the attribute of protecting and lifting others up even when it means they must stand on your shoulders. Care is making other people's needs, especially within your family, a priority over your own needs. The sales world uses the phrase, "People don't care what you know until they know that you care." That works in every relationship!

Team Development

What roles are required to develop and operate the family holding company and family foundation? These are real operating entities that have legal structures and file tax returns. They must be operated professionally by professionals. Just because management will comprise predominantly family members does not mean anyone should be given slack in carrying out their tasks. Because it is family, more may be required of them than would be of a nonfamily person. The coach's child always has to work harder to avoid accusations of favoritism.

It is also important to remember that not all the necessary roles will be full-time positions. Most family members filling these roles have their own professions and careers and their own family obligations that require their time and attention. In Chapter 13, I likened the family enterprise to any business by itemizing thirteen major functions necessary to build a successful company.

1. Have a viable and clear purpose and mission

2. Add value to the world

3. Have a well-defined and well-designed plan

4. Execute the plan effectively and timely

5. Constantly try to improve operations

6 Seek new opportunities and be able to adapt to changing situations

7. Analyze the risk and rewards and make informed decisions

8. Employ, educate, and train qualified personnel

9. Empower individuals to take action and be decisive

10. Encourage social responsibility

11. Be profitable and increase the value of the enterprise

12. Be ongoing

13. Provide for an orderly and timely succession to qualified leaders who can carry on the mission

People must be slotted into all those functions. Some functions may be outsourced to advisors and companies better suited to getting the job done, but someone in the family will still need to be the liaison and family representative who ensures the services are delivered timely, cost effectively, and of the expected quality. Finally, these roles should be used to gain training and experience for more important future roles in the family company or for their development in whatever careers they choose. Their roles should be enjoyable and sought after.

Holy Coach: God wants all people to eat and drink and be happy in their work, which are gifts from God. (Ecclesiastes 3:13 NCV)

The roles should also teach the value of work and encourage self-sufficiency, especially if the individual needs other work or a career to survive because you want to avoid attitudes of entitlement and a "trust fund baby" mentality.

Holy Coach: Go watch the ants, you lazy person. Watch what they do and be wise. Ants have no commander, no leader or ruler, but they store up food in the summer and gather their supplies at harvest. Plant your seed in the morning and keep busy all afternoon, for you don't know if profit will come from one activity or another—or maybe both. Lazy people don't even cook the game they catch, but the diligent make use of everything they find. How long will you lie there, you lazy person? When will you get up from sleeping? You sleep a little; you take a nap. You fold your hands and lie down to rest. So you will be as poor as if you had been robbed; you will have as little as if you had been held up. Those who gather crops on time are wise, but those who sleep through the harvest are a disgrace. Those who work hard make a profit, but those who only talk will be poor. A hard worker has plenty of food, but a person who chases fantasies ends up in poverty. (Proverbs 6:6–11, 10:5, 14:23 NCV; Proverbs 28:19, 12:27; Ecclesiastes 11:6 NLT)

I share this wisdom to make the point that roles must be aligned with the time, talents, and training of the people who fill those roles and that a primary objective of doing so is to develop a strong work ethic and sense of achievement and self-worth in all family members. Too many traditional estate plans—that is, the divide-and-dump methodology—do the opposite by encouraging laziness and a sense of entitlement in the recipients.

Team Assignments

Now that you have identified the needed roles, who will fill them? In the work world, job candidates submit résumés, participate in interviews, take tests, and could undergo trial periods before they know for sure the job is theirs. I am not recommending that process be used to fill family roles, but there are some techniques that have application.

The first question is: How many family members want and can qualify for each role? In the family holding company, there will be a CEO, CFO, and possibly a COO. There could be a lot of competition for the CEO position as well as the other two. There should be written job descriptions so everyone knows the criteria and requirements of each position and that there is a standard to which they can be compared to see if they qualify.

Then there must be a review process and determination of how the decision will be made. In the beginning years, dad and mom may be the only people making those decisions, but as new generations take over, a more formal process might be better. How will the family decide on the new CEO? There are no right or wrong answers, but the process needs to be clear and fair and, most of all, beneficial for the growth and continuance of the enterprise.

Does the family have the right talent, training, and experience internally, or will its members need to look externally? Looking externally for the family foundation may be the better option, especially if it is a public rather than a private foundation. Heading a public foundation requires much greater skill and experience—in fundraising, compliance, time, and due diligence—than the family might have. Family members will still make up the board and make the big decisions, but a trained executive director could be considered. This is also true regarding legal, financial, and tax issues.

I hinted at this above: The big question is who will quarterback the team after the patriarch and matriarch are gone. It must be someone who buys into and is 100 percent committed to carrying on the family mission and vision. This person also needs to be an excellent communicator and team builder. It is critical that he or she has the temperament, patience, empathy, and skills to address the family dynamics and conflicts.

The last thing the family needs is an autocratic leader filling the CEO/quarterback position. This should not be a role gained by default or automatically. You will probably want the decision to be made by a family board, and again, consensus, not majority vote, is the goal so everyone is committed to following the leader. If consensus is not achieved, there could be dissension and desertion in the ranks.

I have made a point several times that consensus is the ideal the family should strive to achieve. That is especially true in selecting a leader, but it may not be possible for every decision the family must make or activities they must undertake. If disagreement exists and there seems to be no way to break the stalemate, the decision defaults to the leader just as it would in any corporation or organization. This is why selecting the right leader is so important. He or she must have the knowledge, wisdom, experience, and courage to make difficult and possibly unpopular choices.

It is also possible that there could be competition for this important key role in the family. For this reason, the day the new family CEO is installed, the family should already be grooming his or her replacement. There are at least three reasons for this. First, it is just good business practice. Most business owners do a poor job of succession planning. For some reason, they think they will lead their companies forever, somehow exempting themselves from termination by death. By starting to groom leaders early, the who is clear and everyone can support the decision and help that person be prepared when the time arrives.

Second, it will give the family the time to observe and assess whether that person is progressing satisfactorily, what training and experience he or she needs, or whether someone else should be considered in case that person is not living up to the standards.

The third reason is having a contingency plan in place if the existing leader is not performing in the best interest of the family or cannot hold the position due to disability or death.

Good leaders are not born but trained. Sure, some people seem to have inherent leadership talents, personalities, and abilities, but there has never been a good leader who didn't have education, training, and hands-on experience in dealing with real world problems and failures and was able to turn them into successes.

I have emphasized this advantage several times, but the family holding company and family foundation are two of the best training grounds anyone could have. Many jobs and careers do not develop leaders or teach the values of service and stewardship. These are honorable and quality jobs, but a graphic artist, computer programmer, plumber, or electrician working for someone else and not supervising people is not learning leadership or decision making. Not everyone in a family wants to be or should be in a leadership position, but all can still participate in family decisions. Also, they may not want to lead, but they love implementing and getting things done. They can be the worker ants that make the colony function and thrive.

The important thing in a significant family is helping every family member achieve significance as defined by them, not by someone else. In Hollywood and on Broadway, the saying is, "There are no small parts." The stars, bit players, writers, camera crew, stunt people, stand-ins, and makeup artists are all critical to the success of a movie or show. In families too, there are no small parts.

Holy Coach: Direct your children onto the right path, and when they are older, they will not leave it. (Proverbs 22:6 NLT)

That's what good leaders do!

CHAPTER 15

Priorities

A basic precept of effective time management is identifying and setting priorities, yet I find this can be difficult for many people, so they don't do it. Simple in concept but difficult to implement! We have all probably said to someone or someone has said to us, "Your problem is that you don't have your priorities straight."

So, what's the problem? I think people get their priorities confused because they cannot separate their emotions from what is good for them. They have difficulty differentiating the important from the unimportant. People will make the things they want to do more important than the things they need and should do. A simple example in today's world that I suspect we have all succumbed to is the Internet. I know I can easily become ensnared. We go online to research information for something important only to be distracted by an advertisement or headline that takes us down a rabbit hole of unimportance to another rabbit hole and another. You know how hard it is to not answer a ringing telephone, and cell phones have made that task even more difficult. Now we have to contend with emails screaming for our attention, most of which are unimportant.

Before establishing priorities, whether individually or for the family entities, the values, vision, and mission statements should be in place. If these statements have not been completed, any objectives you list may not align with the individual's or family's mission. It doesn't make sense to work on prioritizing objectives that technically are irrelevant. It can be helpful to work on the individual mission statements before undertaking the family mission statement. It will be impossible to incorporate everyone's objectives, but there will be a much better chance of including many of the individual objectives if all have done their homework and come to the conference table with a clear understanding of what their individual objectives are, why they are important, and the priority in which they can hopefully be achieved.

In this chapter, I offer tools for getting family, personal, career, business, and financial priorities straight. Every activity in life, every decision, every person is vying for your Time, Talent, Training, and Treasures. Time is the obvious example as it is limited. How will you allocate your time to your spouse, your children, your work or business, to rest and relaxation, health, and to intellectual growth? Increasing in one area means taking away from other areas. Without setting priorities, some people literally work themselves to death, or divorce, or estrangement from their children. For treasures, buying toys, making poor investments, succumbing to an addiction, and trying to solve relational problems by throwing money at them can leave the family financially devastated, retirement impossible, irresponsible children, and nothing to pass to the next generation. I believe there is nothing more important in life than knowing what is most important in life for you, and making sure you are allocating your resource to those priorities.

Holy Coach: He is ready to separate the chaff from the wheat with his winnowing fork. Then he will clean up the threshing area, gathering the wheat into his barn but burning the chaff[1] with never-ending fire. (Luke 3:17 NLT)

[1] Chaff is the husk or shell covering something usable; think of the shells surrounding peanuts.

The first step is to decide what is important and what is not. Again, it is easy conceptually but difficult to do because it requires overriding emotions in favor of using reason and logic.

Holy Coach: A man came to Jesus and asked, "Teacher, what good thing must I do to have life forever?" Jesus answered, "Why do you ask me about what is good? Only God is good. But if you want to have life forever, obey the commands." The man asked, "Which commands?" Jesus answered, "'You must not murder anyone; you must not be guilty of adultery; you must not steal; you must not tell lies about your neighbor; honor your father and mother; and love your neighbor as you love yourself.'" The young man said, "I have obeyed all these things. What else do I need to do?" Jesus answered, "If you want to be perfect, then go and sell your possessions and give the money to the poor. If you do this, you will have treasure in heaven. Then come and follow me." But when the young man heard this, he left sorrowfully, because he was rich. Then Jesus said to his followers, "I tell you the truth, it will be hard for a rich person to enter the kingdom of heaven. Yes, I tell you that it is easier for a camel to go through the eye of a needle than for a rich person to enter the kingdom of God." (Matthew 19:16–24 NCV)

What was this man's problem? Why did he go away sorrowfully? Jesus gave him the opportunity to get his priorities right, but what he wanted outweighed what he needed. Notice that Jesus did not say he should give his wealth to Jesus but to the poor. Jesus didn't need the money; that was a test to see if the man had his priorities right. He didn't! His emotions overrode his reason. He started with the right idea—inheriting life forever seemed to be his priority—but when push came to shove he moved it to the end of the list. His things were of higher priority in his current life than his future. Living for the day or the moment dims our vision of the future. Money is often a test of a person's priorities; unfortunately, too many people fail the test.

We use an exercise with our clients to help them identify and prioritize their lives so they can assign their resources—Time, Talents, Training, and Treasures—to accomplishing what is important to them rather than wasting resources on activities that have no value. Figure 15.1 is included in the exhibit list at the end of this book. The objectives listed in the exhibit are financial, but we will add nonfinancial objectives as appropriate. For example, it might be a desire to exercise and lose weight or spend less time working and more time with the family. Whatever fits into GOALS can be added to the list.

The next step is to put checkmarks in the N, U, T, and C columns. The N is for *Necessary*. Is it absolutely necessary that this objective be accomplished? The U is *Urgent*. Even if the objective is necessary, it may not need to be accomplished immediately. An example might be buying a first home or larger home when children are born. The T is for *Tactical*. The question is whether the solution to this objective or issue is easy and can be done quickly. Will it take thirty days or thirty months? Buying a new car in the next two months is a tactical example. Buying a home in the next three years or starting a new business in five years are strategic rather than tactical objectives. The C questions whether the objective is *Clear*. Starting that business in five years may be unclear if the person doesn't know what kind of business, how much it will cost, whether to start from scratch or buy an existing business, and where to set up shop. It is not unusual for people to have goals and objectives but no clue how to achieve them. A simple example in my industry is financial planning and retirement. When new clients come to us, they will have many financial goals and no idea when they can retire, how much they will need, and how they will fund all the other goals they have. They have usually underestimated everything, including the amount and time needed to save enough to reach their unclear goals. The purpose of planning is to gain clarity on what people want, what they can realistically expect, and what actions they must take to achieve their goals.

All four of the letters will be checked if all are applicable for each objective, or only one or two. The following is the list of combinations, starting with most important at the top and least important at the bottom.

Necessary, Urgent, Tactical, Clear
Necessary, Urgent, Tactical, Not Clear
Necessary, Urgent, Strategic, Clear
Necessary, Urgent, Strategic, Not Clear
Necessary, Not Urgent, Tactical, Clear
Necessary, Not Urgent, Tactical, Not Clear
Necessary, Not Urgent, Strategic, Clear
Necessary, Not Urgent, Strategic, Not Clear Not
Necessary, Urgent, Tactical, Clear
Not Necessary, Urgent, Tactical, Not Clear
Not Necessary, Urgent, Strategic, Clear
Not Necessary, Urgent, Strategic, Not Clear
Not Necessary, Not Urgent, Tactical, Clear
Not Necessary, Not Urgent, Tactical, Not Clear
Not Necessary, Not Urgent, Strategic, Clear
Not Necessary, Not Urgent, Strategic, Not Clear

I realize this can be confusing. We have an Excel worksheet that combines and sorts the answers into the above categories and produces the report I have included as Figure 15.2. From the exhibit (the objectives were forced to fill in spaces and not necessarily reflective of being correct priorities; actual client objectives will be quite different), you can see how all objectives will fall into each category. Everything in the necessary, urgent, tactical, and clear category should be the tasks and objectives that are most important and need to be addressed first. It makes sense that if the objectives are necessary, urgent, clear, and can be solved or completed in a very short time, completing them will give you the highest return on your four Ts of True Wealth investment.

Some objectives will be classified as unnecessary and not urgent. That doesn't mean they should necessarily be ignored or dropped from the list. They may be activities that are fun, bring joy, and build stronger friendships and relationships or simply provide rest and relaxation. Of course, if objectives fall into the last category of unnecessary, not urgent, strategic, and unclear, that will probably cause you to wonder why you put them on list at all.

Once you are clear on your priorities, the next step is to develop an action plan on how and when you will accomplish your objectives. The action plan should be the result of a comprehensive plan. Since I already talked numerous times throughout this book about the value and reasons for planning, we will assume that work has been completed and your action plan can be constructed from the findings in your plan.

Holy Coach: Commit your actions to the Lord, and your plans will succeed. (Proverbs 16:3 NLT)

Six basic questions apply to almost everything we do. You know what they are: What? Why? When? Where? Who? and How? These questions can be applied when creating your action plan. You have already identified the what through the prioritizing exercise. The why is a brief statement about the benefits or results to be achieved. This is important because it will be a constant reminder as to why an objective needs to be achieved. It helps you keep your eye on the target. Achieving goals can be difficult, and there will be delays, distractions, detours, and sometimes disillusionment. If you have not written down the why, you may be tempted to give up when the going gets tough.

I am jumping to the how because the remaining w's will be a subset of how. When does this objective or activity need to be completed? We somewhat addressed this in the prioritization exercise by identifying

You Can Have It All—Wealth, Wisdom, and Purpose

the urgency and whether it is tactical or strategic. The when explains this in greater detail. It should identify specific, or reasonably specific, starting and ending dates. For example, if you need to take a class related to your work, you could write down that you plan to enroll in a class starting on June 1 and ending on September 15. Or the activity may be to research organizations that offer the class you need as the first step, in which case your when could be starting the research in April of this year and having all the information you need to make your decision by May 30.

The details and specifics should be your objective, and every major activity can be broken down into specific steps. If researching organizations is the major activity, searching the Internet, talking to people who can offer recommendations, checking out financing options, and visiting and interviewing sources would be sub-actions you would take.

The next subset under how is where. Staying with my class example, the organization you choose is the where, but that may require going to another location, which would entail travel and lodging.

The final w under how is who. Do other family members need to be involved? Do advisors need to be hired? You cannot achieve many goals and objectives on your own. I have emphasized throughout this book that having and being part of a team is critical to becoming significant— no one achieves significance by himself or herself. It is almost certain that most of your objectives will require help from one or more person.

I am not quite finished with the how. Incorporated in this step is how much of your Time, Talents, Training, and Treasures will be required. We can call this resource allocation, and almost every objective will require one or more of the four Ts. This is why it was important to go through the prioritization exercise first. Not only does prioritization identify what is most important, it also gives us clues as to the sequence of the tasks. Just like making a cake or building a house, if the work progresses in the wrong order, the results will not be what was expected and the redo will be more expensive and time consuming than necessary.

For every objective, goal, and task, you should analyze and write down specifically how much of your Time, Talents, Training, and Treasures are needed. If achieving an objective requires skills you do not have, you will need more training or will have to hire someone. Obviously, this will further impact your allocation of time and treasures. Your resources have limitations; you have only so much time, and allocating treasures to one objective means there may not be any treasures left to allocate to other objectives.

I have provided Figure 15.3, which is an Excel worksheet we use for creating our action plans. I included only one page so you can see the layout, but depending on the client's needs, there will be multiple pages. You can use whatever format is comfortable, but it should be written and contain the details I have described. If it is not written, the likelihood that your goals will be achieved goes way down.

One more note. The last column in our form is where we record the date completed. This may seem a minor issue, but it is a good idea to enter this data, especially for comparison to the target date in the preceding column. It is a little like giving yourself an "Atta boy." The emotional and psychological reinforcement will go a long way to helping you stay on track and enthusiastic about your progress.

There will effectively be multiple action plans because there should be one for every individual, one for the family holding company, and another for the family foundation.

A significant family strives to help every family member be significant. That cannot happen if the individuals do not know what significance looks like for them. Establishing priorities for the family will need to be a negotiation, realizing that everything cannot be accomplished at one time. Here again, the prioritization exercise and answering the what, why, where, when, who, and how questions will be a family activity in which every member must be heard and his or her desires carefully and thoughtfully considered.

The goal is to use the family's resources to do what is best for the entire family and not waste resources on unnecessary and unproductive activities.

Holy Coach: Why do you spend your money on junk food, your hard-earned cash on cotton candy? Listen to me, listen well: Eat only the best, fill yourself with only the finest. Pay attention, come close now, listen carefully to my life-giving, life-nourishing words. (Isaiah 55:2–3 MSG)

Prioritizing your objectives and executing a written action plan can keep you off junk food and on a healthy wealth diet.

CHAPTER 16

Balance

I will use the analogy in Chapter 2 of loading a cargo ship to demonstrate the importance of finding the right balance between the human and financial components of a family. If a ship is not balanced properly, it could sink.

The balance I am recommending means not equal in amount but equal in weight. The substance in each container and the amount and weight of that substance is synonymous with the subcategories that are important to you. A cargo ship hauls cargo containers that are all the same size and shape—these are the primary categories I discuss. However, the contents of each container, the subcategories in this case, can be very different in weight. A container loaded with gold bricks is heavier and more valuable than a container filled with bales of cotton. Only you can decide how much and what you want to load into each container or category.

There are six major categories in your life that vie for your attention and resources.

1. Physical

2. Spiritual

3. Social

4. Intellectual and cultural

5. Professional

6. Financial

This chapter explains each in more detail and their subcategories before covering resource allocation. The subcategories I have identified are only a starting point. You may have more or different subcategories and may even want to break subcategories down further.

Physical

This category is about your body. Subcategories include exercise, diet, rest, recreation, relaxation, and appearance. I want to dwell on the last two. Watching television, sitting at a computer involved in social media activities, or playing games is not what I mean by relaxation. These can become distractions, time wasters, and addictions. As I define it, relaxation includes pursuits such as hobbies, reading, walking with your spouse, playing games with your kids, and vacations and family outings to Disneyland or the zoo, plays, symphony performances, and entertainment events. Relaxation activities should be mentally and spiritually stimulating, not mind numbing.

Physical appearance is important in regard to hygiene and mental attitude. Think about those times when you felt important or special. In high school, it may have been the senior prom when you wore a tuxedo or evening gown. Maybe it was interviewing for a very important job or calling on someone to win a multimillion dollar account. Your university graduation and wedding were certainly special occasions. Or maybe you were receiving a special award.

How did you dress and look? My guess is beautiful or handsome. Every hair was in place, your shoes were shined, shirt or blouse pressed, and you smelled good! In our more casual society today, it is easy to slip into a too relaxed dress mode. Appearance affects relationships and how other people react and relate to you, but I believe how you look and take care of yourself also has a lot to do with how you perform, your attitude regarding maintaining high standards in everything you do, and your self-esteem.

Obviously, you should dress appropriately for the occasion, but significant people do not adopt slovenly lifestyles. Dressing for success has validity. Dress and take care of yourself as if you were significant, and you and others will consider you significant.

Spiritual

These subcategories will also be familiar: church, temple, synagogue, or mosque. Since I am a Christian, here are a few more subcategories familiar to me—you may have something comparable. In addition to attending church services, I am one of a group that gathers weekly to study the Bible, share challenges and family dynamics, pray together and for each other, and hold each other accountable to the standards we share and believe in. I have my individual time of Bible study and prayer, which also includes memorizing scriptures that have special meaning or applications to me. Finally, I have several ministries that require my active involvement through my church and other organizations.

Even if you do not practice a formal religion or do not consider yourself a religious person, you must feed your spiritual nature, whatever that means for you.

One important thing to understand about life is that although we want to control everything, the truth is we control nothing other than our decisions and how we deal with our circumstances. When life is out of control, and it is more often than you realize, you need to find a source of spiritual strength outside yourself. Other people will disappoint you and try to control you, and you will disappoint yourself. If we could actually control what goes on in our lives, we would have no problems. Who would purposely decide to have problems? You and I have many problems because we do not know nor can we control the future. My spiritual objective is to find my comfort and wisdom in the God I believe does know and can control the future. You will need to determine the source of spiritual peace and connection that is right for you.

Social

Relationships are a dichotomy. On one side, they are the root of most problems, heartaches, and disagreements. On the other side, they bring joy, love, companionship, communication, and service.

There may be days when being alone and avoiding people is attractive, but most people become depressed and pessimistic when they have no contact with others for extended periods. That is why we send children to their rooms when they misbehave and prisoners are put in solitary.

Separation from other humans is a form of punishment. We were created to be in relationships. Families exist because of our need for relationship. We cannot be significant by ourselves; we all need others in our lives. The novel *Robinson Crusoe*, published in 1719, is the story of a man shipwrecked and marooned on an island and his struggle to survive for almost thirty years. But the author, Daniel Defoe, did not leave him completely alone; he brought him a native to be his companion, his man Friday. We all need and need to be to others' Fridays. The subcategories include spouses, children, grandchildren, parents, grandparents, siblings, aunts, uncles, cousins, friends, neighbors, coworkers, and peers.

Intellectual and Cultural

We are the only creatures created with the ability to think, reason, create, design, solve complex problems, and teach others these skills. We are the only creatures capable of appreciating art, music, and beauty. Through our five senses, we are constantly learning, but if that were all we could do, we would not be much different from any other animal. We have elevated learning to an ability to create and develop things. What raises us above the rest of the animal kingdom is our desire and hunger to learn and know more, so we build schools and universities, museums, symphonies, theaters, trade schools, and now online educational classes. We write books, read newspapers and magazines, hire teachers and trainers, and develop computers and smartphones. Why? Partly because we understand we need to compete in this world or be left behind, but mostly because we are innately inquisitive and most of us want to improve ourselves and our families. These subcategories are education, reading, creativity, travel, experiences, and mentoring.

Professional

Professional subcategories are career, community, volunteering, and business ownership to name just a few. Society uses the word *professional* to identify those with the education, training, and experience to perform certain specialized tasks or jobs. Unfortunately, we tend to apply that title only to people with college and advanced degrees such as doctors, attorneys, accountants, and so on. I say unfortunately because I believe, and I am using it in this context here, that the cashiers, clerks, police officers, firefighters, auto mechanics, and farm workers are professionals in their jobs. I want to be assured that whoever takes my car apart and puts it back together is a professional mechanic, not a hobbyist. I have a tradesperson laying tile in two of my bathrooms as I'm writing this. He may not have a college degree or even a high school diploma, but I can assure you he is a professional when it comes to laying tile. It matters not what you do but that you enjoy what you do and are the best you can be doing it. That's a professional.

Financial

You will have no difficulty identifying with these subcategories because you know them well and I have devoted a good part of my writing to them: cash flow, assets, debt, tithing, giving, reserves, savings, taxes, retirement, disability, survivor needs, estate planning, inheritance, philanthropy, and business ownership and succession make up this group.

To enjoy life and be significant, you must find the right balance in all six of these major categories. Here we can also include two of our four Ts of True Wealth for this discussion. That would be Time and Treasures. Training obviously has a role as do Talents, but Time and Treasures are easier to quantify and adjust.

Being out of balance in one or more of these areas will have a negative effect on the others. Time is more difficult to manage since it is limited, whereas treasures are somewhat limited but more flexible because more can be acquired. Spending too much time in professional activities means less time in social activities, and that is where spouses and children often get the short end of the stick. Likewise, it may be tempting to spend more time in intellectual and cultural pursuits so you do not have to spend time in physical exercising and dieting.

I provided a Time Allocation Worksheet in Figure 11.1 to which you can refer to calculate the time you want to spend in each of the six major categories and their subcategories. Be as specific as you can, and work backward. That is, allocate time on an annual time frame and then break it into months, weeks, and days. For example, if you are in an industry like mine that requires a certain number of continuing education credits, under the category professional, you might allocate 10 percent of annual time, then identify the months you will take classes, then the weeks, and finally the day or days of the week. Under social, a goal could be having one evening a week for date nights with your spouse. Note that some activities will cross over more than one category. My example of continuing education credits could be in intellectual and professional.

Treasures too must be allocated judiciously and thoughtfully. Although treasure resources can be expanded by working more, getting better returns on investments, or reducing expenses, they still have limitations especially in the near term. It is easy to fall into the trap of thinking of wealth as a bottomless well. Just ask all those multimillion dollar lottery winners who no longer have a dime to spare or a person with a seven-figure income but no cash or liquid investments to buttress an adequate lifestyle if his or her financial world falls apart.

The problem is a complete lack of financial balance. Money can be spent on nonessentials instead of life-sustaining necessities, assets, and activities. Examples are eating rich and fat-laden food at expensive restaurants rather than spending that money on a gym membership or buying a $100,000 car instead of being satisfied with a less expensive vehicle and giving the difference to charity.

For families still in their accumulation years, finding the right balance is even more important if they want to fund homes, educations, and retirement. In financial planning, we understand it is not a question whether clients can have everything they need, it is whether they are so far out of balance by spending on their wants that they have nothing to fund what they need.

Gold miners would bring their gold to the assayer's office to convert it into cash. The assayer would dump the gold on one side of a balance and add weights to the other until the needle found the accurate balance and established the weight of the gold. However, let me again emphasize it is not your objective in life to necessarily have both plates balanced; a gold bar and an iron bar of the same weight will still not have the same value. I started this chapter by using weight as being synonymous with importance. Whatever you consider "gold" in your life should tip the scale to its favor, but your "iron" still needs to be weighed and balanced. The scale can still be in balance even when the right and left plates are at different heights. The value you offer the world depends on the degree of balance you create in your life. Time and Treasures must be properly balanced or your ship will capsize and sink.

CHAPTER 17

Family Meetings

Building trust and improving communication in your family requires coming together for common purposes. Holiday gatherings are fun and enjoyable when everyone can be together, but there will not be opportunities to actually build trust and improve communications because no one wants to spoil the festive mood by getting into bygone arguments, conflicts, and hurt feelings. In fact, trust can be strengthened only through stress. In medieval times, swords were made strong and battle ready by applying extreme heat and then quickly plunging the hot metal into cold water to create a dependable weapon. Families need ways to apply productive stress to their relationships to build trust and improve communications, which can happen only when everyone is in the same room at the same time and dealing with the difficult challenges and issues facing the family, not during holiday gatherings. We accomplish this through the structures I discussed in Chapter 13 and team building in Chapter 14. The creation and operation of these entities requires family meetings, which is the topic for this chapter.

Introducing the Concept and Gaining Buy-In

The first family meeting should take place after the patriarch and matriarch have spent time with the family coach and financial advisor and they have defined what they want to accomplish with the family wealth. There are two options: divide and dump along traditional estate planning methods or build a family legacy of significance.

With the first option, it will be a relatively short meeting; Mom and dad will tell the family what they plan to do with their wealth. Normally, the children will have no input or say in the process; they are there just to listen.

In the second scenario, the family gets to participate in developing the plan. At that point, the entities usually are yet to be created and much of the planning is still to be done and implemented. This is on purpose because we want the children involved in developing and implementing the plan they will eventually be responsible for executing and we want them to take ownership of it. It is critical that they buy into the idea they will be a team working together to build ongoing for-profit and nonprofit enterprises that will benefit the family, all family members, and the community for decades.

If the buy-in cannot be achieved by the entire family, there will be no reason to go forward even if dad and mom would prefer that. As I have said several times, it is conceivable that one or two children may not want to participate while the others do, and that is still a good reason to stay with the plan. The reluctance to buy in is often simply a case of not understanding and experiencing the benefits. After they have seen it working, they may become more inclined to participate.

Developing the Family Significance Statement

By now, you know what the family significance statement is and why it is imperative that the family has one. The first family meeting is when the family's vision, values, and mission (significance) statements are created. This first family meeting may take two or three days with most of the time dedicated to business issues but also time for fun and family enhancement activities. Again, I suggest this first meeting should be attended by everyone who can possibly make it from the family, along with the family coach/financial advisor and possibly the attorney who worked on the estate plan and will be involved in creating the family holding company and family foundation. The family's CPA may also be appropriate if there are substantial tax implications that need to be discussed.

The coach/financial advisor is the proper person to set the agenda for and conduct the meeting. He or she can keep everyone focused on the issues as opposed to going off on tangents, especially if old hurts or conflicts arise. An additional reason for including the coach/financial advisor along with the attorney and CPA is to answer questions regarding why dad and mom have chosen this path and want the rest of the family to take ownership of it.

A thought came to my mind when soccer season started recently. I have three grandchildren playing the sport, so shuttling between three and five games on Saturdays and Sundays now consumes our weekends. My thought centered on my grandkids' friendships. I reminisced about my junior high and high school days and noted that most of my best friends were on my football, basketball, and baseball teams. The same is true for my grandchildren.

Sure, it is also true that we and they attended the same school with many of these kids, but the club soccer teams on which my grandchildren play represent multiple schools. Playing on a team builds trust and requires good communications, which is why I constantly repeat the importance of the family becoming a team.

Think about your teenage years. Were you on a team? Sports is the obvious activity, but it could have been a debating team, the marching band, or a role in high school government. Were some of your best friends on those teams? You may have a cordial and caring family right now, but are they best friends? I think the statistics regarding the low levels of trust and high levels of poor or no communication suggest that, in most families, the family members are not best friends. Family meetings are when you can hopefully begin that process, and having everyone involved in creating the values, vision, and significance statements for the family will be a good place to start; it will not necessarily be dad and mom's mission statement or Jack or Jill's mission statement but the whole family's mission (significance) statement they will create.

My last comment on this since I have discussed mission statements before is that you must start with values (see Chapter 8). Allow all to volunteer what is important to them, write them down on a whiteboard or large pads, do not rule out anything until everyone's values have been written down, and then narrow them down to the top ten or twelve. Follow the procedures outlined in Chapter 8, and then construct the family values and vision statements, and finally the family significance statement.

A fun exercise is to have a professional cartoonist at the meeting drawing on a very large sheet of paper all the values and thoughts voiced by the family members with pictures and graphics depicting these values and thoughts, and in the center writing the final version of the significance statement. Some families will have it framed and display it prominently for all to see and be reminded of their family's purpose.

Committees

You will want to encourage all to be as involved as much as they choose to be, but in any organization, there are only so many positions at the top to fill. But there is also a lot of work to be accomplished. Having committees is a great way to involve more family members in important activities and decision making and building teams for which trust and good communication is imperative. Here are some committees, and their descriptions, that you may want to consider.

Education Committee: The purpose is to develop criteria and requirements for roles in the family enterprises and the educational resources to fulfill these criteria. This includes private schooling, college, and trade or vocational training. Criteria can include having and maintaining certain grade point averages, having certain levels of work experience, and having to fund some portion of the costs themselves in order to be considered for a loan or grant from the family holding company.

Investments Committee: One of the most important committees is the investments committee. While basic marketable securities would be this committee's responsibility, it is far more reaching with significant educational benefits for the participants. It may well be the incubator for major leadership roles in the family enterprises.

The primary purpose of a holding company is to own good investments, including real estate and other businesses. The future leadership of the family will require individuals who have strong business skills and experience as well as excellent people skills. Being on the investments committee also means being constantly in touch with the financial condition of the enterprise. It is the heartbeat of the family's business. The investments committee will most likely be the principal training ground for the family's future leadership.

The investments committee is charged with identifying investment and business opportunities that will grow the value of the family holding company for the benefit of all family members and future generations. That includes lending and investing in ventures family members start or buy. This committee can be likened to a bank's loan committee that establishes criteria for the investments it will consider and procedures for processing and approving investments. Family members' applications for loans or equity investments should be subject to the same due diligence as an investment or loan to a nonfamily person or enterprise. There should be no favoritism, though some latitude is normal.

The reason is to train family applicants in real-world conditions so they will be prepared to deal with other public and private institutions as necessary. If one son or daughter wants to buy a business, the family holding company may agree to provide a portion of the financing or capital but require the son or daughter to get institutional financing or private equity money for the balance. By adhering to strict guidelines and criteria, the borrower will be better able to qualify for other sources of financing.

Family Fun and Bonding Committee: All the fun lovers will want to be on this committee, whose function is to party! It can plan for birthdays, anniversaries, graduations, and special events that bring the family together simply to have a good time and to get to know each other better.

When a family meeting is to be scheduled, this committee plans the agenda that includes fun activities each day after the business portion concludes. They identify the locations and days when and where meetings will be held and make all the arrangements.

Family Enhancements Committee: Somewhat similar but different from the Family Fun committee, this committee works with the other committees to define what is needed and how it should be delivered to help all involved get what they need to personally improve and, in so doing, improve the family. This can cross over into some areas covered by the Family Fun committee, so those activities will need to be coordinated. Working this way, trust and communication can be improved. In fact, the primary objective for this committee is to find ways to improve trust and communications.

Family Financial Aid Committee: Whereas the education committee is tasked with helping family members get the education, degrees, and training they need, this committee helps with specific purchases and cash needs. Helping buy a first home or car, or possibly providing temporary income when a job is lost, or meeting some extraordinary expenses are examples. The help could be in the form of a loan or gift. This committee needs rules and guidelines but should have a degree of flexibility. However, it must also not create dependency. The ten questions to ask about giving a gift I gave in Chapter 12 should be a staple for this committee.

Rules, Procedures, and Standards Committee: The individual committees should have latitude to establish their own rules, procedures, and standards, but they must work within the overall rules, procedures, and standards of the family and the family enterprises. Think of it like our federal and state governments. Every state has laws unique to itself or that it shares with other states, but all states must adhere to federal laws, which take precedence.

Staying with my government analogy, the family needs a constitution, and this is the committee to create the first draft. Dad and mom will probably chair this committee initially since it is their wealth and vision, but it still needs to be a participatory process that allows all members to offer input and opinions and negotiate what each person feels is needed. The sons and daughters will inherit these rules and will be responsible for executing them, so they must be committed to them.

However, there needs to be a fair process for adding, modifying, and terminating rules, procedures, and standards as necessary. Obviously, this is a very important committee because it is critical that what they produce ensures no one person or group can gain unfair control or dictate what the family enterprises do or how they operate. This committee will probably meet many times before presenting the results of their efforts to the entire family, and the entire family will then ratify them. Again, consensus should be the objective to avoid dissension.

Three more points in wrapping up the chapter. If you are thinking this is a lot of work and time commitment, you are right. You are creating two major businesses, one for-profit and one nonprofit. If you are a business owner or there is an existing family business, you know how much time, capital, and interrelationships are involved, negotiated, and managed especially if there are multiple owners. Arguments, disagreements, and conflicts are normal, but discussing and negotiating those differences with care and empathy for everyone's position improves communication and builds trust.

The second point is that no wealth should transfer to anyone, the family holding company, or the family foundation until there is family buy-in. That is why the first couple of meetings are so important. The last thing you want to do is unravel what is not working. Anyone who has been through a business breakup with partners or other owners or experienced a divorce knows how traumatic and costly that can be. The goal is to unite the family, not create a situation that could destroy it and cause ill will and damage relationships.

So far, I have covered the I (Investigation) and the D (Design and Development) in my IDEA acronym. The E (Execute) and A (Administration) is my third point. The family meeting is the first step in executing the plan. Assuming there is family buy-in, the next phase in execution is formalizing and implementing the structures and then identifying and qualifying individuals for their roles; then the wealth transfer can take place.

With each family enterprise now having its vision, values, and mission (significance) statements drafted, being capitalized, and a qualified team with assigned roles in place, you are ready to open the doors for business. You are moving into the A, Administration phase.

As the family operates these entities, problems and dysfunction will become apparent, as they should. Family meetings will be the forum for improving and making the operations more efficient. Meetings can be physical or virtual as needed, depending on the magnitude, severity, and urgency of the situation. The rules, procedures, and standards will allow certain decisions to be made by the management team. More serious or difficult decisions will need entire family involvement. Like most businesses and corporations, the executives have authority to run the day-to-day operations, but major issues and changes must be brought before the board of directors.

Finally, meetings should occur at least twice a year. These are business meetings, not vacations, but fun and family enhancement activities should have some place on the agenda. They should be physical meetings with as many as possible present. As children reach ages where their attendance will not be disruptive and they would not be bored to tears, this would be a good time to involve them so they can see how the family works as a team, hopefully catch and begin to embrace the family mission, and gain training that prepares them for the day they take over. Encourage them to speak up and participate, and respect their views even if they are later discarded.

Family meetings are integral to accomplishing a successful family succession plan and achieving significance.

CHAPTER 18

Every Flock Needs a Shepherd

You likely understand by now that, because of what I do professionally, I have a bias for families utilizing a professional coach who can address the people and financial sides of a family concurrently. I will confess to being a little self-serving in my encouragement, but it is more about recommending what I know works versus what doesn't work, and I believe strongly that every flock (family) needs a shepherd (coach).

Holy Coach: Be shepherds of God's flock that is under your care, watching over them—not because you must, but because you are willing, as God wants you to be; not pursuing dishonest gain, but eager to serve; not lording it over those entrusted to you, but being examples to the flock. (1 Peter 5:2–3 NIV)

Unfortunately, too many families engage in internal warfare that could be avoided by utilizing wise counsel.

Holy Coach: Plans go wrong for lack of advice; many advisers bring success. Plans succeed through good counsel; don't go to war without wise advice. So you need advice when you go to war. If you have lots of good advice, you will win. (Proverbs 15:22; 20:18 NLT; Proverbs 24:6 NCV)

The following are just some of the benefits of having a shepherd.

Education

Financial coaches have the education, training, and experience to identify and solve the people and financial issues your family is facing and will face. That education is the result of formal schooling, reading, and work experience, but they also have the benefit of working with other families who have experienced the same challenges impacting your family. My use of the term *financial coaches* includes many disciplines such as financial planners, investment managers, insurance professionals, accountants, attorneys, and business consultants. They will have letters after their names like CFP, CLU, CPA, and JD. Although those designations imply they have the professional training and experience you need, you should also seek referrals from people you trust who have worked with the professionals you plan to use.

Although every family is unique, their problems are basically the same. The coach has been there, done that, and a good coach knows how to apply the nuances of working with the uniqueness of each family and its members. Education also includes the coach helping family members get the education, training, and experience they need.

Mediation

The *American Heritage Dictionary* defines mediation this way: "To work with two or more disputants in order to bring about an agreement, settlement, or compromise. To settle or reconcile differences." To do so requires the ability to see both sides of an argument objectively, discern a result that is acceptable to all parties, and help the individuals implement the solution. In legal disputes, arbitration is the preferred solution over going to trial and having a judge decide the outcome. In court trials, there is typically a winner and a loser. Arbitration offers the possibility that both sides could get some measure of satisfaction on a friendly basis even if they are not friends. A good coach does not implement solutions but assists the participants in implementing their shared solutions in ways that can maintain and even improve their relationship. The coach should teach skills and a process for reconciling future differences without a mediator's presence, but this will not happen unless a qualified coach is involved.

Objectivity

Family members cannot be objective. I realize that is a broad statement, but you know it is true. Husbands and wives have difficulty being objective in their relationship, so it is to be expected in other family relationships. Every family member and every nuclear family in the entire family has their own needs and wants and agendas built around their needs and wants.

It is difficult enough to achieve balance in one's own life much less in a family's life. Equality is impossible, but fairness is possible. A coach theoretically has no ax to grind, and sees no benefit in siding with one person or nuclear family over another. It might be argued that the coach will favor dad and mom since they are paying the bills. That is possible, but a good coach will not allow compensation to outweigh good judgment and doing what is right.

The coach knows dad and mom will be gone one day and his or her clients will be the children, so trying to please the parents instead of doing what is best for the family should never happen. Additionally, under our structures of the family holding company and foundation, the coach is working for the enterprise, not any one individual or family. The coach's loyalty should be to the entity, not one or more individuals in it.

Resources Sourcing

Twenty-five years ago, when you needed help or tools to complete a task, you went to the Yellow Pages or asked family and friends to recommend someone who could help. Today, the family and friends are still around, but the Yellow Pages has been replaced by the Internet, computers, and smartphones. Finding the resources your family needs to address its financial and complex people issues is not easily accomplished. In fact, the difficulty in finding the right resources is a primary reason many families never attempt to deal with these hard, complicated family dynamics. Where does one find a family coach who blends financial expertise with people skills and conflict resolution? Type "Family Coaching" into your search engine and you will likely be directed to sites for parenting or marriage counseling. Type in "Financial Coaching" and you find financial planners and institutions that will teach you about investments, insurance, budgeting, saving, and cash flow management and may offer some counseling and accountability to aid you in becoming financially literate and more efficient.

However, as I said in Chapter 4, never the twain shall meet. Because money impacts relationships and relationships impact money, family coaching can provide resources not available anywhere else. However, few families know where to go for help. Your financial planner, investment advisor, attorney, or accountant is probably not going to be much help. If they are able to provide any resources other than what they provide respectively, those resources will be financial in nature. Likewise, if you talk to therapists or relational advisors, their resources will be limited to other relational type advisors and they will likely miss the idea that money is at the root or at least a contributing factor to the family's problems. You need a coach who works with both the financial and people sides of families, and has access to the tools and personnel needed to solve the specific challenges each family needs solved. You need a one-stop shop.

Observation

Families and family members usually suffer from the "can't see the forest for the trees" syndrome. They are just too close to the problems to recognize them as problems. People do not hear themselves or how they sound to other people. They cannot see their own body language. As a result, they do not comprehend the messages they are sending. Additionally, they are so busy talking and defending their positions that they do not hear the other person's position and needs. Since we know lack of trust and poor communication are the primary reason families are in disarray, we must acknowledge that it is almost impossible for families to solve these issues without help. A coach can see and hear what family members cannot. Sometimes, just being able to create awareness can go a long way to helping individuals reconcile their differences.

Wisdom

Education is not the same as wisdom. Advisors with various degrees and licenses are well educated but may not necessarily have wisdom. In this book, I have given you wisdom, the product of knowing what is absolutely true, and I have offered you truth from what I know to be the most valid and complete source of truth.

Holy Coach: Dear friends, do not believe everyone who claims to speak by the Spirit. You must test them to see if the spirit they have comes from God. For there are many false prophets in the world, but test everything that is said. Hold on to what is good. Then he saw wisdom and evaluated it. He set it in place and examined it thoroughly. Some people may contradict our teaching, but these are the wholesome teachings of the Lord Jesus Christ. These teachings promote a godly life. Anyone who teaches something different is arrogant and lacks understanding. Such a person has an unhealthy desire to quibble over the meaning of words. This stirs up arguments ending in jealousy, division, slander, and evil suspicions. These people always cause trouble. Their minds are corrupt, and they have turned their backs on the truth. To them, a show of godliness is just a way to become wealthy. (1 John 4:1; Job 28:27; 1 Thessalonians 5:21; 1 Timothy 6:3–5 NLT)

Minimize Manipulation and Coercion

Holy Coach: Anyone who answers without listening is foolish and confused. Don't promise to pay what someone else owes, and don't guarantee anyone's loan. If you cannot pay the loan, <u>your own bed may be taken right out from under you</u>. It is not wise to promise to pay what your neighbor owes. My child, be careful about giving a guarantee for somebody else's loan, about promising to pay what someone else owes. <u>You might get trapped by what you say; you might be caught by your own words</u>. My child, if you have done this and <u>are under your neighbor's control</u>, here is how to get free. Don't be proud. Go to your neighbor and beg to be free from your promise. Don't go to sleep or even rest your eyes, but free yourself like a deer running from a hunter, like a bird flying away from a trapper. (Proverbs 18:13, 6:1–5, 17:18, 22:26–27 NCV)

What do guaranteeing or cosigning loans have to do with manipulation and coercion? There are many ways to manipulate and coerce someone into doing something he or she do not want to do or should not do. This is only one example. Offering to lend or cosign for someone's loan gives the lender leverage over the borrower. We see and read this all the time in movies, on TV, and in books. The victim borrows from the loan shark, who then offers to reduce or eliminate the debt if the victim will commit a crime for the loan shark. Or the shark offers to make the loan to accomplish the same purpose. Family members are not above employing manipulation tactics.

Holy Coach: Esau said to Jacob, "I'm starved! Give me some of that red stew!" (This is how Esau got his other name, Edom, which means "red.") "All right," Jacob replied, "but trade me your rights as the firstborn son." "Look, I'm dying of starvation!" said Esau. "What good is my birthright to me now?" But Jacob said, "First you must swear that your birthright is mine." So Esau swore an oath, thereby selling all his rights as the firstborn to his brother, Jacob. Then Jacob gave Esau some bread and lentil stew. Esau ate the meal, then got up and left. He showed contempt for his rights as the firstborn. (Genesis 25:30–34 NLT)

Isaac, the father of these two brothers, was not aware of the deal they struck. Is it apparent to you this is a case of manipulation that will have devastating consequences for everyone in the family? Is it possible you could have helped this family avoid a disaster? That is the value a coach brings to the party.

Coordination

My football analogy in Chapter 4, identified qualities, characteristics, and resources needed to win a Super Bowl. It included organization, capital, good management, experienced coaches, skilled players, lots of training and practice, a well thought-out and designed playbook, solid rules and regulations, and referees to enforce the rules. Assembling a disorganized and disconnected group of athletes, coaches, trainers, and managers who can hopefully win the Super Bowl does not happen by chance—someone must coordinate everything. Someone, or some group, coordinates the player selection, the training, the game schedule, and the travel and lodging. Families have similar coordination needs. Someone or some group in the family could do this, but it may not be the best use of their time, talents, or training.

Developing the agenda for a family meeting may best be handled by a coach who has no personal agenda and can solicit input from family members. Some members may be more willing to raise a topic or difficult issue with a coach rather than having to discuss that issue directly with dad or mom or a sibling creating the agenda. The coach may also have knowledge of issues that need to be discussed that other family members do not know about. During individual interviews it is conceivable that past hurts and abuses are still painful and unaddressed because someone fears rejection or retribution. Perhaps, a family member is having financial, career, business, or marital problems and is ashamed to discuss them because they feel they are a failure. If the coach is given permission to share these delicate and difficult topics with other family members, the coach can present them in ways that gain cooperation and commitment of the rest of the family to repairing the hurts and alleviating the shame without being judgmental.

A good coach should direct the family toward self-sufficiency, not dependence on the coach. The coach can be a resource for researching options on topics the family will be discussing so the family can make informed and effective decisions efficiently.

Mentoring

A coach can provide mentoring, but I need to draw a distinction here. A coach should not be a mentor; he or she should teach others how to be mentors and help create the family mentoring program.

I mentioned previously that everyone in the family should have a mentor and be a mentor to someone else. A mentor can provide wisdom, encouragement, positive criticism, and accountability in a loving and caring way to all of a family's members. What is said between the mentor and person being mentored must be confidential. The six requirements for building and maintaining trust—reliability, competency, sincerity, loyalty, confidentiality, and care—are the pillars of a strong and successful mentoring relationship.

A coach may have a temporary role as mentor to those who need to be taught how to mentor, but, as in everything, the objective is that the coach works himself or herself out of a job. The mentor relationship is best between different ages. For example, assume Jim is fifty-five, Jane is thirty, and Bill is sixteen. Jim should mentor someone younger who will benefit from his experience and wisdom so he could mentor Jane and she could mentor Bill since they may better relate to each other because of the closeness in their ages. Designing an effective mentoring program requires thought and insight to accommodate personalities, ages, and needs of each person and connect the right matchups.

Accountability

We all put off whatever is not urgent. This is especially true when it comes to financial planning, but it applies to many things in life. Sometimes it is fear, sometimes uncertainty, sometimes it's because the task is unpleasant, and other times it is just laziness. If we can procrastinate, we will.

I try to get to the gym four or five days a week. I always marvel at people using a trainer. Once you have learned which exercises you should do, how to do them correctly, and have done them forty or fifty times, why continue paying for a trainer? The answer must be accountability. It is hard to get out of bed at 6:00 a.m. or leave work right at 5:00 p.m. when you would rather sleep or when work puts other priorities on your time and there is no one waiting for you. When you know that trainer will get on you for being late or not showing up at all,

Kip Kolson

you go. Even more of a mystery is you go knowing that the trainer will cause you to sweat, be exhausted, and create aches and pains in parts of your body you didn't know could hurt that much, but you know a coach that holds you accountable is doing what is good for you in spite of the aches and pains.

One of my primary roles as both financial advisor and family coach is providing accountability and keeping my clients moving toward their goals and objectives in a timely and efficient manner. I can see the importance and negative outcomes of procrastination because clients procrastinate all the time. If they are saving for retirement, a specific purchase, or college for the children and they delay a couple of years, the probability of their achieving those objectives goes down significantly. Every time I ask if planning is a good idea, everyone says yes. Then I say, "Great! Let's get started," and the response is, "Things are hectic at work right now," or "We're planning a family vacation, so I'll call you in a couple of months." And they don't.

When it comes to coaching a family, the excuses are many and varied. "Everyone will be upset." "It will take too much time." "It cost too much." "It sounds like a lot of work and commitment." Yeah, so does getting to the gym. Don't do it and gain weight, experience more fatigue more often, and wear out your heart a lot sooner. Hire a coach to put you through your paces if for no other reason than for accountability and you will have more energy and stamina, lose weight, fit into those jeans you've not been able to wear for ages, and probably live another ten years. Hire a family coach and your family legacy could live for a hundred years or more.

A coach can provide accountability on financial issues as well as relationship issues. Most people avoid conflicts because they are unpleasant and difficult to address. The breakdown in trust and communication is often the result of an unwillingness to deal with unpleasantness. Hurt and pain get bottled up and trust is destroyed. A good coach will encourage the individuals to face their fears and discontent with each other in ways that can lead to resolution and reconciliation that may never happen without the accountability.

332

Holy Coach: I'm laying it all out right now just for you. I'm giving you thirty sterling principles—tested guidelines to live by. Believe me—these are truths that work, and will keep you <u>accountable</u> to those who sent you. Have confidence in your leaders and submit to their authority, because <u>they keep watch over you</u> as those who must give an <u>account</u>. Do this so that their work will be a joy, not a burden, for that would be of no benefit to you. (Proverbs 22:17–21 MSG; Hebrews 13:17 NIV)

Is having a coach absolutely necessary? No, but for most families, not having a coach is a disaster waiting to happen. Since 70 percent of wealth is lost when it transfers to the next generation, so the fourth generation is forced to start over with only the shirts on their backs, it should be obvious that families need the help. If they could successfully coach themselves, that statistic would tumble. That it stays at that level proves a coach is a necessity for the family to be significant.

CHAPTER 19

What Will Your Family's Story Be?

As this is my first book, I have come to realize how much life is like writing a book. I assume, whether in school or later, you have read a biography or autobiography of some famous person. What if you are that person? What will your family's story be? Will it be a one-book *Reader's Digest* short story or a multivolume series covering generations—children, grandchildren, great-grandchildren, and great-great-grandchildren—and depict a family dynasty that in some small or large way positively impacted society?

The best part is that you get to write it. You and your family author this incredible story as it unfolds. One difference is that books have a beginning, middle, and end. Your story will be a journey that has a beginning and middle, but you get to decide if there will be an end. There doesn't have to be. It will be part history, part reality, and part fiction in that it may describe dreams and adventures that, although they were planned and talked about, never quite became reality. Will those events you hope will come to pass when the family's heritage transfers to the next generation for safekeeping become reality or remain fiction?

There was a time when people kept diaries. I don't know if anyone still does, and that is a shame because so much history, experience, and wisdom is being lost and having to be constantly relearned.

Earlier, I described how we draft a Family Wealth Significance Statement. Essentially, it is the story of the family up to the point of drafting plus looking to the future. It chronicles the family's history and current events and where the family wants to go. I also mentioned that technology allows us to capture sight and sound so future generations can see and hear their forebears and the culture and environments that shaped and established the family's values, principles, and priorities. The adage, "If we do not learn from history, we are doomed to repeat it" can be overcome by a family that has documented its history—successes and failures alike. The Bible holds nothing back; it does not sugarcoat any of the facts or try to cover up the blemishes of the principal characters. It shows us what we should do, what we should not do, and the consequences of both.

Your family story could be its bible from Genesis, its beginning, to Revelation, its hopes and plans for the future. The Bible is God's love letter to His family. He tells us how He wants and expects us to live to get the most out of life so we can enjoy purposeful and productive lives; we will have a wonderful future if we follow His plan. A family of significance will compose its bible because it cares about the well-being of its future generations and wants them to be successful; it understands this is possible only when the good and bad are exposed and truth and wisdom are promoted.

Through my many years on this earth and observing families who have succeeded or failed, I have learned what is required to live successfully and how they composed their significant family stories. These principles have application for writing your story so I share these with you now.

Commitment

Nothing worthwhile in life will be accomplished unless there is an unwavering commitment to make it happen. Here are areas I found needed my commitment as I wrote. They are areas where you too must make a commitment.

Time: I tried to write at least one hour every day. That is nothing compared to what is required in managing a family, a family business, a family holding company, or a family foundation, so organization and coordination are paramount.

I wrote a lot about time management because you must allocate time to what is most important. I believe there is nothing more important than committing the necessary time to building a strong, unified family that allows all its members to achieve the significance they were created to accomplish.

Energy: Where would the world be without energy? No pun intended, but energy drives everything we do. Travel, feeding people, creating and distributing utilities, manufacturing, even entertainment would not exist without some form of energy. We say some people are "drivers"; that means they constantly move toward particular objectives. They are not satisfied with the status quo; they are tireless!

Everything I've discussed in this book will require tremendous energy. Anyone who is not committed to persevering through all the roadblocks, valleys, storms, and detours they will face will have difficulty becoming significant. Winston Churchill is credited with saying, "Never, never, never give up" when the Allies seemed to be losing World War II. The family and its leaders must adopt this attitude.

Patience: The most difficult commitment to make may be to develop patience; this goes against human nature. Isn't it interesting that we easily procrastinate some of our most important activities and decisions yet will be extremely impatient when it comes to minutiae and trivial pursuits? Of course, the primary problem that tests our patience is people. They just never seem to do what we want when we want and how we want them to do it. I talked about this previously when I said we get to the point of saying, "I can get it done faster if I do it myself." This attitude becomes self-fulfilling in that you will eventually be doing everything by yourself. There is no "team" in "self." No team means no significance. You will need to fight your natural instinct for impatience and replace it with grace and compassion. It will be difficult, but it will become more natural with time and experience, and you and they will grow immensely.

Resources: The three primary resources I discuss here are people, money, and having the right tools. Writing a book requires advisors, a publisher, and editor to name a few. Writing your family's story also requires people starting with yourself, spouse, children, and grandchildren. Without them, there is no story. You must be committed to doing what is right for every family member, and that means you first have to know what is right for each person.

That takes us back to trust and communication. Everyone needs to commit to communicating his or her frustrations, hurts, needs, and wants without fear of persecution or rejection. There must be a commitment to resolving problems and reconciling relationships no matter how difficult and time consuming that may be. The encouragement in marriage counseling has always been, "Don't go to bed mad at each other. Reconcile first." That is good wisdom for all relationships.

Holy Coach: Therefore, if you are offering your gift at the altar and there remember that your brother or sister has something against you, leave your gift there in front of the altar. First go and be reconciled to them; then come and offer your gift. (Matthew 5:23–24 NIV)

This also requires that commitment of patience.

Money seems like an obvious commitment. You will need to commit to spending whatever is necessary to get the help, tools, and resources you need to hold your family together and build a future that goes on for decades. Every year, new dollars must be committed to accomplishing the family's legacy and ensuring everyone has opportunities to succeed and become significant. That includes education, training, travel, funding entrepreneurial endeavors, and charity when appropriate. That said, every dollar should be treated as an investment and a return on investment identified and achieved. I do believe whatever you must spend will be the best investment you will ever make.

Finally, there must be a commitment to using the *right* tools. I emphasize *right* because there are many tools that would not be right for your family or a specific circumstance even though they could be fine for another family. Here again, the implication is that you must be communicating well with everyone so you will know what is right for them, not for you or anyone else. Tools, as I am using the word here, include utilizing the right advisors for the right purposes.

Research and Knowledge

Writing about a famous family requires an author to become knowledgeable about everyone in the family—what they said and did, whom they married, whom they birthed, the work they did, and the businesses they started and built and maybe failed at. By the time pen is put to paper (or fingers on a keyboard), the author is an authority on that family.

Your story requires you to be the authority on your family and to delegate that responsibility to someone in the next generation. I am giving this a dual meaning. For future generations to know and appreciate your family's history, someone needs to document it.

The second meaning is leadership. The author and leader may not be the same person, but the family's history will be short and the author's notes brief if leadership is not effectively transferred to subsequent generations.

Research and knowledge must also be transferred. If you do not have a formalized program and procedure for transferring knowledge to future generations, those generations will not know the family's heritage and will have nothing to pass on to their children. Doing the research requires commitment.

Outline

When I got the inspiration to write this book, I started by creating an outline that identified specific topics I wanted to discuss, reordering them into chapters to create a flow of information, and coming up with subtopics of the major topics. My outline helped me organize my thoughts in a logical sequence. In this case, my objective was to convince you that you need to protect, preserve, and promote your family in ways and with strategies that encourage involvement in service and stewardship that increases the probability that your family and its members will become significant.

An outline is simply the first step in developing and designing a formalized plan. Your family needs an outline!

The Plan

To write a piece of fiction, an author drafts an outline, writes on a consistent basis, and then edits and rewrites to make the story cohesive, believable, and entertaining. But when it comes to writing your family history, you do not get to substitute fiction for facts. You cannot make changes to your family's history if it isn't what you would prefer it was. And if the next generation has not been properly prepared to carry on the family's legacy, your story ends right there. Families have futures, not destinations. This is where writing your family's story diverges from writing fiction; there are no sequels, but there are continuances as each new generation takes the reins.

Having a plan is critical for any activity that changes and embodies uncertain results because a good plan attempts to identify all possible outcomes, dangers, and opportunities and prepare for each. Your plan A should always be backed up by a plan B and perhaps a plan C. Change is inevitable in every family, so having a plan creates a standard to measure progress and alert you when changes are happening outside the plan. That way, you will have predetermined solutions in place to quickly adjust and maintain the plan's integrity or adapt to new situations and opportunities.

Execution

If you are noticing a similarity to IDEA, that is good. Research is the investigation phase, and the outline and the plan are the design and development phase, so that brings us to execution. The biographical author must write the book and get its information into people's hands. If the book is not distributed, prospective readers will be deprived of the information, knowledge, and wisdom they might have gained.

Your story could have a major impact on not only your family but also many families, the community, and society if you set out to be significant. The Getty, Rockefeller, J. P. Morgan, Ford, and Carnegie families built empires for their families, but in doing so, the world got cars, oil, steel, and banks. The next time you slide your credit card at Walmart, remember that Sam Walton and his family made that convenience possible. What if these men had not written their family's stories?

What if one or more of your heirs makes the next great discovery in medicine, science, technology, industry, or education because you created a legacy family that provided the human, intellectual, spiritual, and financial capital and the environment, preparation, and structure for that person to succeed?

Here is an even more interesting question. What if that never happens because you did not execute the plan that created the opportunity and the world is thus robbed of that benefit? I doubt that Bill Gates's grandparents knew their grandson would develop software that drives most computers and almost every industry. You do not know the future, but you can develop the structure, foundation, resources, environment, and opportunities that increase the possibility of achieving greatness only when you execute your plan.

No book goes immediately into print and distribution without a lot of input and involvement from many people. The writer will have other people review what he or she has written, critique it, and offer suggestions. An editor will make suggestions and changes. The publisher will create a marketing plan for it. We do not think of these people as coaches, but that is what they are doing. Some writers may have someone help with their writing in terms of grammar, language, word usage, and structure and sequencing of topics or storyline while the book is being written.

Your story will be a lot better if you have the proper assistance from the right people, coaches who can help you bring your story to life and add chapters as needed, help your family craft its story, constantly editing and adding chapters to your family bible as your storyline evolves.

Holy Coach: "Fools think their own way is right, but the wise listen to others. Get all the advice and instruction you can, so you will be wise the rest of your life." (Proverbs. 12:15, 19:20 NIV)

So, what will your family's story be? The *Reader's Digest* version or your family bible?

CHAPTER 20

Step-by-Step Wrap-Up

We have covered a lot of ground. I will now simplify everything I have discussed into a list of sequential steps, but I caution you that doing so is not completely possible because many activities and tasks will normally be happening concurrently, albeit differently for each family.

I start with three major activities and provide specific functions to be completed under those.

IDEA

Investigation

- GOALS: Until you have identified and have clarity on your purpose for being on Earth and the service you provide to the world, nothing else really matters. Without clarity and commitment to your GOALS, your wealth has little meaning other than to satisfy your own desires; as long as you stay at the self level, you and your family will never be significant.

- Four Ts of True Wealth: In this step, you assess your resources in the areas of Time, Talent, Training, and Treasures. That assessment includes what you already have plus what you may need to acquire.

Design and Development (The Plan)

- Values: These are the personal character traits that you would literally die for before compromising them. Your values will be the driving force behind who you are and who you become, and how you will apply your resources to achieve significance. They are also what you will pass to your children because children learn their values from their parents, peers, education, and society. It is critical that you set a positive example and be prepared to deal with society's values that conflict with yours.

- Vision, Value, and Significance (Mission) Statements: The vision statement is a short paragraph of how your world would look if you successfully accomplished your mission statement.

The value statement is not a reiteration of your personal values as described above but a statement of your "marketability." Will people buy what you are selling? We all must sell ourselves in the marketplace of life by providing something that other people need and want. Remember that significance is bestowed on you by people who receive value from you.

Finally, the significance (mission) statement encapsulates in one sentence or a short paragraph what you understand your purpose to be that accomplishes your vision and value statements. Your mission statement is not necessarily your work, although your work could be one of the resources that helps achieve your mission.

Resources Available or Needed

- Dangers: Honestly assess anything and everything that could inhibit you from achieving your and your family's GOALS.

- Opportunities: Also identify all the opportunities you can find that will help you reach your GOALS.

- Strengths: List all the strengths you and your family have right now that increase the probability of accomplishing your GOALS.

This includes people, relationships, and financial strengths.

Financial

- Assets

- Liabilities

- Cash flow. Remember that everything emanates from having and utilizing excess cash flow properly. If cash flow is not used properly and is negative, liabilities increase and net worth declines. If that continues, bankruptcy, not significance, will be the result.

Relationships

- People: A lot of time with assistance from qualified counselors and coaches needs to be devoted to understanding each family member and building or rebuilding trust and improving communication. Since I have spoken about these already, I will simply list them here.

  - Talents

  - Training

- Needs: Every family member has different needs. If the family structure is not meeting those needs, that member will go somewhere else to get them satisfied.

- Desires: Likewise, the family must understand each person's desires and attempt to satisfy those desires. Unlike wants that are imperative, desires may not and possibly should not always be satisfied. Satisfying them could do more harm than good. Utilize the ten questions in Chapter 7.

- Roles: The objective is to find positions of responsibility in the family structures for everyone that will utilize and enhance their talents and get them the training they need to do so. The objective is that everyone takes ownership in ensuring the family is successful and significant.

Designing Your Plan

This should be done first by dad and mom and their coach and should include financial and people objectives. Once an acceptable and workable draft is ready, it can be presented to the entire family, which will open the plan up to a lot of discussion, criticism, enthusiasm, and negotiations. This is as it should be since the plan needs to be their plan too, not just dad and mom's plan being forced on them. If the attempt is to force it on future generations, it will not survive.

Finding Problems and Analyzing Scenarios

A financial plan or life plan is simply a formalized document describing where you want to go, when you want to arrive there, how you can get there, and what resources you have or need and how best to utilize those resources (the four Ts of True Wealth) to accomplish your objectives.

It is basically playing a large and important game of what if and testing the results of each what if. This is critical because each what if has consequences for many other issues in your life and family.

Identifying Solutions

A good plan develops multiple solutions so you can analyze and implement the best, most efficient, and most probable solution. Once you have a handle on the what ifs, the plan will test different solutions until you achieve the one or two that make the most sense for you, your family, and the circumstances.

Action Plan

Your action plan needs to be written and followed diligently. An action plan is an expanded to-do list. If you start each day with a list of activities and tasks that you want to complete that day (if you are not doing this, you should be), you will prioritize it and work on what is most important first.

That same discipline applies to your action plan. One reason this is important is that by checking off items as you complete them, you will feel good that you are making progress. That good feeling is a motivator for continuing to make progress and will encourage you to keep moving forward. It becomes a standard measurement of performance and a gauge for modifications and adjustments if necessary.

Execution and Administration

Structures

- Family Foundation: This entity should be created first because it is less susceptible to disagreements and a good way to begin bringing the entire family into the planning and transitioning process. It will be easier to identify common ground and shared purposes while also building a team. Additionally, it can be set up and be functional while the family continues to wrestle with other financial and relational issues, and it could even solve some of those issues.

- Family Holding Company: What is most important is adopting a change in attitude and philosophy. I use the term *Family Inc.* to describe the attitude we want the family to acquire.

When a family begins working with us, its members almost always have the attitude they are simply a group of people with individual lives that intersect only on holidays and birthdays; there are no common purposes and no team philosophy. They understand estate planning in its traditional formula of divide and dump. We know that attitude and methodology leads to shirtsleeves to shirtsleeves in three generations 70 percent of the time. We believe, and it has been the experience of many families, that aggregating the assets into a business operation that creates cash flow and builds net worth for everyone's benefit for multiple generations is a much better philosophy. I also have seen that when children understand the objectives and how building a for-profit business will benefit them more than giving them money, they become enthusiastic and committed to the family's success and significance.

Family Meeting

Again, the first family meeting after the initial planning with the patriarch and matriarch is to acquaint the children with the purposes and reasons dad and mom are doing this and why and how they want to involve all family members and get their buy-in to the process.

The objective is that they understand the planning to date is not the end but the beginning. They will be integral to the planning and execution going forward. However, this is a good time to review the Family Wealth Significance Statement dad and mom drafted with the coach's help. It is a good idea to get it into everyone's hand prior to the meeting so all will have time to read it. This will help the children understand the motives, desires, and reasons for the planning and establishment of the family foundation and holding company, and the values and principles dad and mom want the family to embrace and pass on to subsequent generations. It will provide a starting point for the family to create its vision, value, and mission (significance) statements, recognizing however that the kids play an important role in developing those statements around everyone's input and needs.

Building the Team

During the initial family meeting, roles should be identified based on needs and functions. You can also begin to formulate job descriptions and performance standards for each role. Although conversations around who should fill each role can be had, it is best to defer those decisions to the next meeting to give all involved time to think about who is best suited to fill each role and whether they are interested and qualified to fill a particular role.

Those interested in this or that role can share that with the family prior to the next meeting so others can consider it and be prepared to vote at the meeting or voice their concerns or positive comments for the group to discuss before roles are filled.

Administration (I am only listing these since they were previously discussed)

- Areas for goal setting

- Finding balance

- Establishing performance standards

- Monitoring operations

- Mentoring program

- Family enhancement

349

Shepherding Your Flock

Every flock needs a shepherd, a role a coach can play, but a coach cannot be with and engaged in the family 24/7. You must fill that role or identify someone in the family who can. A shepherd is a leader who loves and cares for the flock. You may meet the last two criteria, but you must honestly assess whether you are the right person to lead your family into the next generation. If you are the right person, you must immediately identify who the next shepherd should be, get consensus from the family about that, and start preparing for the transition even though it may be years until it happens.

Writing Your Family's Story

When reading the chapter Your Family's Story, you may have interpreted it as only an exercise in putting words on paper. That is part of it but not the most important part. Your story is unfolding and adding paragraphs and chapters every day. Yes, it is wonderful if you capture those smaller stories that make up the bigger story, but the point is to live it.

The action plan I have stressed having is a plan for living and thriving. Like writing this book, if I never got further than drafting the table of contents, you would not be reading this now. The table of contents by itself is useless. Designing a plan and creating an action plan is meaningless until you live it.

The Ultimate Gift

Several years ago, a movie was made based a book written by Jim Stovall.[1] It is a book we give to prospects and new clients as an example of what we do, what we want for their families, and the benefits that are

---

[1] *The Ultimate Gift* by Jim Stovall, Published by David C. Cook U.K. Kingsway Communications, Copyright 2001.

possible if they are willing to do what Red Stevens and Jason Stevens, the two primary characters in the book, did.

The plot in *The Ultimate Gift* centers on a billionaire who has recently passed away. Like many, in fact most, wealthy families, greed, jealousy, and materialism have infected the entire family with affluenza. Red, the deceased, realized how his wealth had already destroyed his family and feels no one deserves to inherit more than he or she already has.

Red has not done a good job of shepherding his flock, and he knows there is no one he can entrust with this much wealth. However, there is a playboy nephew he thinks could have a remote possibility of being rehabilitated but only if and after Jason, the nephew, can prove to himself and others that he is capable and worthy to receive the ultimate gift.

What Red did not do in life he attempts to do in death by speaking to Jason through a video, an attorney, and some trusted friends; but, more importantly, through some very significant gifts. I encourage you to add *The Ultimate Gift* to your reading list. Until you can read it yourself, here are the gifts you should use to write your family's story before you must film a postmortem video. I am sharing excerpts from the book not to dilute the story or keep you from reading the entire novel but to tie its message to the message I hope you have learned from this book. I encourage you to order the book on Amazon and share it with your children and grandchildren.

Gift of Work

Jason is a "trust-fund baby" who never worked a day in his life—a life filled with parties, women, and toys. But, to earn his first gift he must spend one month at a Texas cattle ranch under the tutelage of Gus Caldwell, the owner. First there is anger and resentment, and blisters and an empty stomach when Jason learns the fine art of digging postholes and mending miles of fence on this sprawling ranch. If the daily quota of poles are not standing straight and tall, no dinner! But Jason gets better and learns discipline and the value of hard work done with one's hands. Under Gus' encouragement and patience Jason has become a quality pole planter and fence mender. But it is time to go home. Gus' parting encouragement,

"Your great uncle, Red, and I discovered nearly sixty years ago that if you can do this kind of work with pride and quality, then you can do anything. Now it is time to get you back to Boston." Jason replied, "I only have a few more poles to plant to finish up this section. Why don't we leave in the morning?"

Gift of Money

Red took on a more serious expression and continued,

"Jason, you have no idea or concept of the value of money. More of the violence, anxiety, divorce, and mistrust in the world is caused by misunderstanding money than any other factor."

To earn and learn this gift Jason is given $1,500 and must use it to help five other people and accomplish some good. At the end of this month's challenge he returns to the attorney and his secretary to report. After hearing the five stories and doing some quick math, Miss Hastings says to her boss,

"Sir that seems to add up to $1,800. I believe the original document called for only $1,500." Jason seemed alarmed as he leaned forward in his chair and said, "Well, I put in $300 of my own money. Is that okay?"

How would you have answered Jason?

Gift of Friends

Jason knows a lot of people and thinks he has a lot of friends. After all, he throws the best parties and even has one lady he thinks may be the one for him. But the trust fund payments stop, which means the exotic car is repossessed, he is evicted from his plush apartment, the parties end, and that special girl walks out when Jason asks her to pay the tab for their fancy dinner because his credit card is rejected. Where are those friends now? New assignment. In the next month he must find one real friend who likes him for being himself, not for what his money can buy. Jason succeeded and shared his lesson from this gift,

---

"I thought a lot about friendship this month, and I tried to come up with the principles that define friendship. The best I can do is to say that friendship involves loyalty, commitment, and a process that includes sharing another person's life. It even goes deeper than that, but it's hard to put it into words."

I think Jason used some good words.

Gift of Learning

This gift takes Jason to a small village in South America with a little library housing one librarian and maybe four or five hundred books lining the shelves. The only customers are local natives who have little or no formal education. Schools are either nonexistent or great distances from where the people live. What could Jason possibly learn in this jungle of uneducated and backward inhabitants?

"The only thing I found out is there are good and simple people who will get up hours before daylight and walk many miles along mountain trails to get a tattered old copy of a book. The only thing I can honestly say I know that I didn't know when I left [the USA] four weeks ago is that the desire and hunger for education is the key to real learning."

Do your kids really appreciate that college diploma you paid hundreds of thousands of dollars to help them get? Did you make it too easy for them?

Gift of Problems

Red's new adventure for Jason is to find four people who have problems in each stage of life—a child, a young adult, a grown adult, and an elderly adult—and learn how they are dealing with their respective problems. Time for Jason's report.

"I have to admit that I couldn't find any young person who has learned as much from their problems as I have from mine. I have lived my whole life in a selfish and self-centered fashion. I never realized that real people have real problems. I finally realized that I have been sheltered from problems, and that

I have never learned the lessons that the people I met this
month are learning. I finally know that joy does not come from
avoiding a problem or having someone else deal with it for you.
Joy comes from overcoming a problem or simply learning to
live with it while being joyful."

Jason learned what I shared with you when I asked why you try
to protect your children from problems and failures. Teaching how to
deal with problems and failures is the best gift you will ever give them.

Holy Coach: My brothers and sisters, consider it nothing but
joy when you fall into all sorts of trials, because you know that
the testing of your faith produces endurance. And let endurance
have its perfect effect, so that you will be perfect and complete,
not deficient in anything. (James 1:2–4 NLT)

Gift of Family

Jason's next thirty-day excursion is to an orphanage where he will be
staying. Well, not just staying. Jason is assigned to a group of boys
as their houseparent for the month. What does a playboy, trust fund
baby, only child, single guy know about kids? On the thirtieth day the
attorney and Jason

"drove out of the courtyard along the gravel driveway and Jason
was turned in his seat waving to the boys until they were out

of sight. They sat in silence until Jason finally spoke. 'You know what's amazing? Not one of those boys has a family, but each of them knew more about family than I did. I think family is not as much about being related by blood as it is about relating through love.'"

Gift of Laughter

Are you able to laugh in the face of adversity, or at yourself? Jason must find and interview a person who does. He finds David, a man who lost his sight early in life and could have easily, and maybe justifiably, acquired a poor-me attitude or chosen to live off of charity or government support. David's response,

"sometimes in life, either you laugh or you cry, he said. I prefer to laugh."

Laughter and joy are a choice.

Gift of Dreams

Jason doesn't have to travel or find someone to interview to obtain this gift; he just needs to be quiet and to dream. Jason returns to the attorney's office.

"Somehow, some way, I would like to help deprived young people live a good life. I don't really mean poor young people.

I mean young people who have not learned the power and the passion and the values they can have that will make their lives worth living. Somehow I am going to do for young people what my Uncle Red is doing for me."

A dream, in itself, is not a goal, it is much bigger. Your dream should become your passion and a function of what you are passionate about. It should be unattainable on your own, requiring others to be involved, and it must positively impact other people. If you are the only beneficiary, what you desire is not a dream. It is just one item on your to-do list. Note too that Jason's dream turned out to be the same experience and lessons he has learned. Dreams are usually aligned with how God SHAPEs the person. Hopefully, this book has helped you begin to dream if you are not already a dreamer. That has been my intent.

Gift of Giving

New instructions:

"Every day for the next thirty days, I want you to give something to someone else that is a gift from you." 'I don't have anything,' Jason mumbled."

Or did he? He had no treasures. They were taken away when the trust fund payments stopped. But he had something better that only he could give. He still had his Time, Talents, and Training. I won't go through all thirty days, but he shared his umbrella, gave up a good parking spot, carried an elderly man's groceries, read articles to blind people, baby sat for free, volunteered at the Salvation Army, delivered meals to the disabled, helped build a house with Habitat for Humanity, and even helped bake cookies for an elementary school bake sale. Giving money would have been too easy and uninvolved. Giving Time, Talent, and Training is much more valuable for the recipient and the giver.

Gift of Gratitude

Red shares a personal story about his Golden List and tells Jason that every day for the next thirty days he should create his Golden List: a list of ten things he is grateful for. Starting tomorrow morning, before getting entrenched in your busy day, write out your Golden List with the ten things you can be grateful for. Like Jason, do it for the next thirty days and see how it will change your life. It is impossible to be thankful and unhappy at the same time. Joyful people have learned and practice an attitude of gratitude.

Gift of a Day

I suspect you will relate to Jason's eleventh gift challenge because someone somewhere has probably suggested this challenge to you. If you knew tomorrow is your last day on earth and your life ends the day after, how would you spend your last day? Jason must spend thirty days contemplating this question and writing down his answer. Jason would start his last day writing out his Golden List, but with a lot more than ten items. Then he would spend time with family and friends, telling them how important they have been in his life and how much he loves them. He would find a quiet spot somewhere in nature to take in the beauty of God's handiwork, and finally he would spend his last hours doing something to help someone or some cause that would benefit from his Time, Talents, and Training. You know this, but when people are facing eminent death and are asked if they had any regrets, their answers are always about spending more time with their children; being a kinder, more patient, and compassionate person; and doing more to help others. No one ever says they wish they had worked more, purchased more stuff, made more deals, or went more places. But what was the lesson Red wanted Jason to learn? <u>Today may be your last day</u>! Tomorrow is not guaranteed and every day is a gift. Live today like it is your last day.

Gift of Love

The video is turned on and Red's image appears to give Jason his final challenge.

"I want you to explore how love is involved in all the other gifts, and prepare to share that with Mr. Hamilton [the attorney]."

When Jason reports on the last day of the month he revisits each gift and explains how each affected him and changed his life forever. He didn't say it, but I will. It was not the gifts in themselves that changed Jason from a self-absorbed playboy type into a responsible, grateful, and compassionate young man, it was that Red loved him enough to make him go through a process that taught Jason how to develop and use his Time, Talents, and Training to create a purposeful and joyful life. It was difficult, stressful, frustrating, and unpleasant at times, but I know Jason would tell you it was well worth it.

The Ultimate Gift

So, after all that, what was this ultimate gift Red promised Jason if he successfully fulfilled the requirements of the previous twelve?

I will let Jason tell you what he said right after Red, on the video, tells Jason how proud he is of him and his satisfaction that Jason persevered through all twelve gift challenges to become the excellent man he believed Jason could be.

"I'm going to do it, I'm going to use every element of the ultimate gift, and I'm going to find a way to pass it on to deprived people who are as I was a year ago. I had no idea that the greatest gift anyone can be given is an awareness of all of the gifts he or she already has. Now I know why God made me and put me on this earth. I understand the purpose for my life and how I can help other people find their purpose."

That has been the goal of this book. I wrote it and I do what I do because I share Jason's understanding of the ultimate gift. Now I know why God made me and put me on this Earth. I understand the purpose for my life and how I can help other people find their purpose. My prayer is that this will be your purpose also and that you will pass it on to your children, grandchildren, great-grandchildren, and many generations to come. By the way, Jason was also put in charge of the $1 billion Red Stevens Foundation!

This was Jason's story. It is a good story, a story he will be able to pass on to his children and grandchildren. Fortunately, he learned in time how to redirect his life from Uncle Red, who made many mistakes, was someone who loved Jason and could see the talent and abilities that no one else could see, not even Jason, and who had the wisdom and faith to take what was broken and turn it into a work of art. What will your family's story be?

CHAPTER 21

The Last Word Is One Word

I previously referenced Adam and Eve as being the first family. That is technically true from the human perspective, but there is a family that existed before them, a perfect family that set the example for what all families are supposed to be. In the prologue I identified this perfect family as the *Father, Son, and "Holy Coach,"* the latter being the Holy Spirit. There's is no perfect family other than this one. It is the premier family legacy that endures forever, so making the Father, Son, and Holy Coach family the standard to emulate is really the only way to achieve family significance.

Holy Coach: For the Father loves the Son and shows him all he does. Yes, and he will show him even greater works than these, so that you will be amazed, and the Holy Spirit descended on him in bodily form like a dove. And a voice came from heaven: "You are my Son, whom I love; with you I am well pleased." (John 5:20; Luke 3:22 NIV)

Will you be able to say of your children, "With you I am well pleased"?

If you visit www.familywealthleadership.com or see our business card or letterhead, you will notice these words as part of our logo: Service • Stewardship • Significance. Let me remind you of the formula one last time: Service + Stewardship = Significance. Service applies to how you will deal with the GOALS you choose. Stewardship is about how you will manage your four Ts of True Wealth. That formula is the essence of this book. But I can condense it even further into one word. Service to your GOALS is service to people you care about. So, let me replace the word *service* with the word *love*. Now, the formula is Love + Stewardship = Significance. If you love people, you will steward your True Wealth in ways that benefit the people you love and, in return, you will gain significance and benefit yourself. The one word that will change your life and create your family's legacy is *love*.

Holy Coach: Jesus replied, "'You must love the Lord your God with all your heart, all your soul, and all your mind.' This is the first and greatest commandment. A second is equally important: 'Love your neighbor as yourself.' The entire law and all the demands of the prophets are based on these two commandments." (Matthew 22:37–40 NLT)

I draw your attention to the last sentence, which says every law we have could be eliminated if we could get the first two right: love God and love your neighbor. Neighbor in this context means everyone other than yourself. It includes your family, your friends, your coworkers, boss, employees, and everyone with whom you come in contact.

Holy Coach: I tell you, make friends for yourselves using worldly riches so that when those riches are gone, you will be welcomed in those homes that continue forever. (Luke 16:9 NCV)

The problem is that we have difficulty loving our neighbors because we love ourselves more. Throughout this book, I have tried to convince you to properly steward your four Ts of True Wealth to serve others rather than self.

In GOALS, the Giving to those in need, Own family, Affinity groups, and Legal agencies is addressed by "Love your neighbor as yourself." Those four are about people. The Spiritual addresses the Greatest Commandment, "Love the Lord your God." You have a choice: you can love your wealth, but that will keep you in the Self box, or you can love everything GOALS represents. If the former, your wealth will take precedence over people and you will use people to satisfy your pursuit of wealth. If the latter, you will use wealth to satisfy people and significance will be in reach. In my logo in Figure 1.1, there is a reason GOALS is on one side and True Wealth the other separated by "Service" and "Stewardship"—think of it as a balance beam. If you raise the right side, moving people toward the Significance box, the wealth side moves down, indicating that people are more important than things. Raising the wealth side means things are more important than people.

I will leave you with a final legacy story. There was a man who had great wealth. His wife had been unable to conceive, so at age seventy-five, he had no heirs.

Holy Coach: God told Abram: "Leave your country, your family, and your father's home for a land that I will show you. I'll make you a great nation and bless you. I'll make you famous; you'll be a blessing . . . All the families of the Earth will be blessed through you." . . . he took him outside and said, "Look at the sky. Count the stars. Can you do it? Count your descendants! You're going to have a big family, Abram!"

Fast forward twenty-four years. When Abram was ninety-nine, God told him, "I'll make a covenant between us and I'll give you a huge family. This is my covenant with you: You'll be the father of many nations. Your name will no longer be Abram, but Abraham, meaning that 'I'm making you the father of many nations.' I'll make you a father of fathers—I'll make nations from you, kings will issue from you. I'm establishing my covenant between me and you, a covenant that includes your descendants, a covenant that goes on and on and on, a covenant that commits me to be your God and the God of your descendants. And I'm giving you and your descendants this land where you're now just camping, this whole country of Canaan, to own forever. And I'll be their God. And Sarai your wife: Don't call her Sarai any longer; call her Sarah. I'll bless her—yes! I'll give you a son by her! Oh, how I'll bless her! Nations will come from her; kings of nations will come from her." Abraham laughed, thinking, "Can a hundred-year-old man father a son? And can Sarah, at ninety years, have a baby?" "Your wife, Sarah, will have a baby, a son. Name him Isaac. I'll establish my covenant with him and his descendants, a covenant that lasts forever."

Abraham and Sarah were old by this time, very old. Sarah was far past the age for having babies. Sarah laughed within herself, "An old woman like me? Get pregnant? With this old man of a husband?" Wait a minute. This couple should be in an assisted living community eating soft food and playing canasta or bridge. No one who is a hundred is going to have one child, much less be the father of a great nation. This is a fictional story, right?

God did to Sarah what he promised: Sarah became pregnant and gave Abraham a son in his old age, and at the very time God had set. Abraham named him Isaac. When his son was eight days old, Abraham circumcised him just as God had commanded. Abraham was a hundred years old when his son Isaac was born. The baby grew and was weaned. Abraham threw a big party on the day Isaac was weaned. Okay, sounds like a happy ending, but what has this to do with legacy?

After all this, God tested Abraham. God said, "Abraham!" "Yes?" answered Abraham. "I'm listening." He said, "Take your dear son Isaac whom you love and go to the land of Moriah. Sacrifice him there as a burnt offering on one of the mountains that I'll point out to you." What! The guy waits 100 years to have one son, and now he is supposed to kill him! Not only is that wrong, it pretty well puts an end to the "father of a great nation" promise.

Abraham got up early in the morning and saddled his donkey. He took two of his young servants and his son Isaac. He had split wood for the burnt offering. He set out for the place God had directed him. On the third day he looked up and saw the place in the distance. Abraham told his two young servants, "Stay here with the donkey. The boy and I are going over there to worship; then we'll come back to you." Abraham took the wood for the burnt offering and gave it to Isaac his son to carry. He carried the flint and the knife. The two of them went off together. Isaac said to Abraham his father, "Father?" "Yes, my son." "We have flint and wood, but where's the sheep for the burnt offering?" Abraham said, "Son, God will see to it that there's a sheep for the burnt offering." And they kept on walking together. They arrived at the place to which God had directed him. Abraham built an altar. He laid out the wood. Then he tied up Isaac and laid him on the wood. Abraham reached out and took the knife to kill his son. Just then an angel of God called to him out of Heaven, "Abraham! Abraham!" "Yes, I'm listening." "Don't lay a hand on that boy! Don't touch him! Now I know how fearlessly you fear God; you didn't hesitate to place your son, your dear son, on the altar for me." Abraham looked up. He saw a ram caught by its horns in the thicket. Abraham took the ram and sacrificed it as a burnt offering instead of his son. God never intended that Isaac would actually be sacrificed. That is not His nature. It was a test for Abraham's benefit so he would know for sure that the promise he would be the father of many nations would be fulfilled. Still not seeing what this has to do with legacy? Read on.

Isaac marries Rebekah. Rebekah became pregnant. But the children tumbled and kicked inside her so much that she said, "If this is the way it's going to be, why go on living?" She went to God to find out what was going on. God told her, <u>two nations</u> are in your womb, <u>two peoples butting heads</u> while still in your body. <u>One people will</u> <u>overpower the other, and the older will serve the younger</u>. When her time to give birth came, sure enough, there were twins in her womb. The first came out reddish, as if snugly wrapped in a hairy blanket; they named him Esau (Hairy). His brother followed, his fist clutched tight to Esau's heel; they named him Jacob (Heel). Isaac was sixty years old when they were born. One day Jacob was cooking a stew. Esau came in from the field, starved. Esau said to Jacob, "Give me some of that red stew—I'm starved!" That's how he came to be called Edom (Red). Jacob said, "Make me a trade: my stew for your rights as the firstborn." Esau said, "I'm starving! What good is a birthright if I'm dead?" Jacob said, "First, swear to me." And he did it. On oath Esau traded away his rights as the firstborn. Jacob gave him bread and the stew of lentils. He ate and drank, got up and left. That's how Esau shrugged off his rights as the firstborn. So begins a web of deceit and an example of how ignorance when it comes to managing wealth leaves a child vulnerable to being taken advantage of, even by a brother. The plot thickens.

Rebekah was eavesdropping as Isaac spoke to his son Esau. As soon as Esau had gone off to the country to hunt game for his father, Rebekah spoke to her son Jacob. "I just overheard your father talking with your brother, Esau. He said, 'Bring me some game and fix me a hearty meal so that I can eat and bless you with God's blessing before I die.' Now, my son, listen to me. Do what I tell you. Go to the flock and get me two young goats. Pick the best; I'll prepare them into a hearty meal, the kind that your father loves.

"Then you'll take it to your father, he'll eat and bless you before he dies." "But Mother," Jacob said, "my brother Esau is a hairy man and I have smooth skin. What happens if my father touches me? He'll think I'm playing games with him. I'll bring down a curse on myself instead of a blessing." "If it comes to that," said his mother, "I'll take the curse on myself. Now, just do what I say. Go and get the goats." So he went and got them and brought them to his mother and she cooked a hearty meal, the kind his father loved so much. Rebekah took the dress-up clothes of her older son Esau and put them on her younger son Jacob. She took the goatskins and covered his hands and the smooth nape of his neck.

Then she placed the hearty meal she had fixed and fresh bread she'd baked into the hands of her son Jacob. He went to his father and said, "My father!" "Yes?" he said. "Which son are you?" Jacob answered his father, "I'm your firstborn son Esau. I did what you told me. Come now; sit up and eat of my game so you can give me your personal blessing." Isaac said, "So soon? How did you get it so quickly?" "Because your God cleared the way for me." Isaac said, "Come close, son; let me touch you—are you really my son Esau?" So Jacob moved close to his father Isaac. Isaac felt him and said, "The voice is Jacob's voice but the hands are the hands of Esau." He didn't recognize him because his hands were hairy, like his brother Esau's. But as he was about to bless him he pressed him, "You're sure? You are my son Esau?" "Yes. I am." Isaac said, "Bring the food so I can eat of my son's game and give you my personal blessing."

Jacob brought it to him and he ate. He also brought him wine and he drank. Then Isaac said, "Come close, son, and kiss me." He came close and kissed him and Isaac smelled the smell of his clothes. Finally, he blessed him. Ahhh. "The smell of my son is like the smell of the open country blessed by God. May God give you of Heaven's dew and Earth's bounty of grain and wine. May peoples serve you and nations honor you. You will master your brothers, and your mother's sons will honor you. Those who curse you will be cursed, those who bless you will be blessed." And then right after Isaac had blessed Jacob and Jacob had left, Esau showed up from the hunt. He also had prepared a hearty meal. He came to his father and said, "Let my father get up and eat of his son's game, that he may give me his personal blessing." His father Isaac said, "And who are you?" "I am your son, your firstborn, Esau." Isaac started to tremble, shaking violently.

He said, "Then who hunted game and brought it to me? I finished the meal just now, before you walked in. And I blessed him—he's blessed for good!" Esau, hearing his father's words, sobbed violently and most bitterly, and cried to his father, "My father! Can't you also bless me?" "Your brother," he said, "came here falsely and took your blessing." Esau said, "Not for nothing was he named Jacob, the Heel. Twice now he's tricked me: first he took my birthright and now he's taken my blessing." He begged, "Haven't you kept back any blessing for me?" [A blessing in those days was not simply words, but an inheritance of the father's estate and wealth. Traditionally, the firstborn received the larger share. In this case, Esau should have inherited two thirds, and Jacob one third. Now, Esau gets nothing and Jacob gets everything.] Isaac answered Esau, "I've made him your master, and all his brothers his servants, and lavished grain and wine on him. I've given it all away. What's left for you, my son?" "But don't you have just one blessing for me, Father? Oh, bless me my father! Bless me!"

Esau sobbed inconsolably. Isaac said to him, "You'll live far from Earth's bounty, remote from Heaven's dew. You'll live by your sword, hand-to-mouth, and you'll serve your brother. But when you can't take it any more you'll break loose and run free." Esau seethed in anger against Jacob because of the blessing his father had given him; he brooded, "The time for mourning my father's death is close. And then I'll kill my brother Jacob." When these words of her older son Esau were reported to Rebekah, she called her younger son Jacob and said, "Your brother Esau is plotting vengeance against you. He's going to kill you. Son, listen to me. Get out of here. Run for your life to Haran, to my brother Laban."

Family competition and envy is old as humanity. There is much more to this story, and I encourage you to explore the intrigue and deception in Genesis 12–32, but I need to get you to the finale. Jacob gets married, starts a family, but not without in-law problems, and is returning to his mother and homeland when this event takes place.

Holy Coach: But Jacob stayed behind by himself, and a man wrestled with him until daybreak. When the man saw that he couldn't get the best of Jacob as they wrestled, he deliberately threw Jacob's hip out of joint. The man said, "Let me go; it's daybreak." Jacob said, "I'm not letting you go 'til you bless me." The man said, "What's your name?" He answered, "Jacob." The man said, "But no longer. Your name is no longer Jacob. From now on it's Israel (God-Wrestler); you've wrestled with God and you've come through." Jacob asked, "And what's your name?" The man said, "Why do you want to know my name?" And then, right then and there, he blessed him (Genesis 12–32 MSG summarized).

God changed Jacob's name to Israel; that is the genesis of the nation of Israel today. All ethnic Jews are in the family of Israel. Abraham has assuredly become the father of several great nations with descendants as numerous as the stars. Likewise, Esau was promised to also father a great nation. The banished half-brother, Ishmael is the father of the Islamic nations. Today, in the Middle East, the Arab and Palestinian nations (descendants of the older Esau) and the Israeli nation (descendants of the younger twin, Jacob) and the Islamic nations (descendants of Ishmael) wage a war that started at their birth.

As I mentioned when I reported the blunders and escapades of King David's family, the lesson is that it is dangerous to assume your family is exempt from issues such as these. Abraham, and later King David, were God's handpicked servants. If their families had these problems, yours is potentially no exception. If you do not prepare because you believe your family is different, the odds are you will not be. The good news in these stories, in spite of their faults, is that we know who they are and their legacy because they somehow overcame their problems, due in part to documenting their stories so future generations would know their heritage and hopefully but not always learn from their family's mistakes.

Jealousy, greed, deceit, and revenge destroyed a family. Sibling rivalry turned into a war between nations that has lasted more than 4,000 years, with no end in sight. On the other hand, Israel has become a beacon of freedom and opportunity in that region. Finally, these two nations have had strife and tribulations within their own nations as well as with each other for thousands of years.

Holy Coach: I said to myself, "Come on, let's try pleasure. Let's look for the 'good things' in life." But I found that this, too, was meaningless. So I said, "Laughter is silly. What good does it do to seek pleasure?" After much thought, I decided to cheer myself with wine. And while still seeking wisdom, I clutched at foolishness. In this way, I tried to experience the only happiness most people find during their brief life in this world. I also tried to find meaning by building huge homes for myself and by planting beautiful vineyards. I made gardens and parks, filling them with all kinds of fruit trees. I built reservoirs to collect the water to irrigate my many flourishing groves. I bought slaves, both men and women, and others were born into my household. I also owned large herds and flocks, more than any of the kings who had lived in Jerusalem before me. I collected great sums of silver and gold, the treasure of many kings and provinces. I hired wonderful singers, both men and women, and had many beautiful concubines. I had everything a man could desire! So I became greater than all who had lived in Jerusalem before me, and my wisdom never failed me. Anything I wanted,

I would take. I denied myself no pleasure. I even found great pleasure in hard work, a reward for all my labors. But as I looked at everything I had worked so hard to accomplish, it was all so meaningless—like chasing the wind. There was nothing really worthwhile anywhere. (Ecclesiastes 2:1–11 NLT)

No family is immune from problems. I offer these not as examples of what or what not to do but as forewarning of what you should expect so you will not be caught off guard. Your family will leave a legacy. The question is whether it will be a legacy of destruction or a legacy of positive significance built on love and stewardship. The miracle of love is that it never runs out when you give it away. The more love you give, the more you get. Love is the one word, the last word.

Holy Coach: Now these three remain; faith, hope, and love; but the greatest of these is love. (1 Corinthians 13:13 NIV)

Here is the irony! The best way to love yourself is to love God and love others more than you love yourself. You will always get more in return than you give away. Love is how you and your family will be significant.

Holy Coach: Friends love through all kinds of weather, and families stick together in all kinds of trouble. (Proverbs 17:17 MSG)

Suggested Reading

Buford, Bob. *Halftime.* Grand Rapids, MI: Zondervan; 1994.

Collier, Charles W. *Wealth in Families,* 3rd ed. Cambridge, MA: Harvard University; 2012.

Hughes Jr., James E. *Family Wealth: Keeping it in the Family.* New York: Bloomberg Press; 2004.

Reeb, Lloyd. *Success to Significance.* Grand Rapids, MI: Zondervan; 2004.

Stovall, Jim. *The Ultimate Gift.* Colorado Springs, CO: David C. Cook; 2001.

Warren, Rick. *Purpose Driven Life.* Grand Rapids, MI: Zondervan; 2002.

Williams, Roy, and Vic Preisser. *Preparing Heirs: Five Steps to a Successful Transition of Family Wealth and Values.* Bandon, OR: Robert D. Reed Publishers; 2012.

Bible Versions

GW: God's Word (Baker Publishing)
KJV: King James Version (public domain)
NASB: New American Standard Bible (Lockman Foundation)
NET: New English Translation (Biblical Studies Press)
NKJV: New King James Version (Thomas Nelson)

NIV: New International Version (Biblica)
NLT: New Living Translation (Tyndale House)
NCV: New Century Version (Thomas Nelson)
MSG: The Message (NavPress)
TLB: The Living Bible (Tyndale House)

Scripture Verse
References by Chapter

Prologue

Source of wisdom (Prb. 9:10 NCV)
Source of wisdom (Prb. 2:6–11 NIV)
Purpose of wisdom (Prb. 1:2–7 NLT)
Truth, wisdom, discipline, and good judgment (Prb. 23:23 NLT)
Scripture is inspired by God (2 Tim. 3:16–17 NLT)
Holy Spirit's role (John 16:13 NLT)
Truth equals freedom (John 8:32 NIV)

Chapter 1: Significance

My version of significance (Luke 12:15 NLT, Proverbs 22:1 NLT,
    Proverbs 3:9–10 NASB)
Sorry! It really is not about you! (Ephesians 2:10 NLT)
What is significance again? (Luke 12:23–24 NLT; Psalm 139:13–14 NLT)
Service (Mark 10:43–44 NCV)
Prodigal Son: (Luke 15:11–32 TLB)
Purpose (Ephesians 2:10 NCV)

Wealth (2 Chronicles 32:26–29; Ecclesiastes 5:19, 6:2 NLT; Deuteronomy 8:12–14, 18a NLT)

Purpose (Jeremiah 29:11 NIV)

Discontent (Ecclesiastes 5:10–11, 6:3 NLT; Proverbs 30:15a NLT; Hebrews 13:5 MSG; Philippians 4:11–13)

Deceit (Proverbs 14:8; Matthew 13:22 NIV)

Desires (James 4:1–3; 1 Peter 1:13a, 14 NLT)

Irresponsibility for our actions (Genesis 3:12–13 NASB)

Jealousy (Genesis 4:1–8 GW; Proverbs 27:4 GW; James 3:14 NASB; Exodus 20:17 GW; Ecclesiastes 4:4 NLT)

Lack of trust (Proverbs 28:20 NLT; Proverbs 14:22 GW; Joshua 2:12 GW; Jeremiah 9:4 GW; Isaiah 30:5 GW)

Poor communications (Mark 4:23; Proverbs 8:1; John 8:43; Ecclesiastes 9:17; Job 18:2; 32:16–21, 33:3 NLT)

Self-centeredness (Proverbs 18:12 NIV)

Breaking the rules (Proverbs 16:20 TLB; Proverbs 10:17, 15:40, 29:18; 30:17 NLT; Micah 6:13–15 NLT; Job 27:13–19 TLB; Luke 7:46–49 NLT; Genesis 3:1–19, 23 NLT)

Pride (Proverbs 11:2; 16:18; Ezekiel 28:4; Proverbs 29:23 NLT; 1 Corinthians 4:7 NCV; Ecclesiastes 4:4 NLT)

Presumption (James 4:13–17 NCV)

Gossip (Proverbs 16:28, 11:13 NLT; Proverbs 13:3; 29:20 NLT; Job 4:8 NLT)

Greed (Proverbs 28:22 NLT; Philippians 2:3–4; Luke 12:15–21 NASB; Proverbs 30:15–16 MSG; Proverbs 15:27; Luke 6:38 NLT)

Immediate gratification (1 Timothy 6:9–10 NCV; 2 Samuel 11:2–27 NASB; Genesis 3:6, 12–13, 16–19, 23–24 NASB; Proverbs 25:28 NLT; Psalm 73:7 NCV)

Lack of discipline (Proverbs 13:1, 13:24, 18:18, 29:15, 17, 19, 21, 15:32 NLT)

Overspending (Romans 12:2a NCV; Proverbs 22:7 NCV)

Fear (Matthew 6:24–34 NLT)

Lack of wisdom (Proverbs 6:1–6 NCV)

Competition (Matthew 5:24 NLT; Luke 10:38–42 NLT)

Hypocrisy (Matthew 7:3–5 NIV)

Worry (Luke 12:22–31 NASB)

Procrastination (Ecclesiastes 11:4 NLT)
Ungratefulness (Proverbs 30:11–14 NLT)
The Remedy (2 Peter 1:5–9; Ephesians 6:1–3 NLT; James 4:11 NLT; sow = reap)

Chapter 2: Your Family's Story

Where have you been, and what have you experienced? (Joshua 4:4–7; Joel 1:3 NLT; Deuteronomy 6:6–9 NCV)
Strengths (Colossians 3:21 NCV)
What is important to you about wealth? (Ecclesiastes 4:4, 9–12 NCV; Proverbs 14:12 GW; Matthew 7:13–14 NIV)
How do you feel about your heirs inheriting wealth? (Matthew 20:1–15 NLT; Proverbs 20:21, 13:11 GW; Luke 16:11–12 NCV [substitute child for *servant*]; Matthew 25:14–29 GW)
The law of entropy (Proverbs 27:23–27 TLB)

Chapter 3: Your Family's Conflict

God created the first family and immediately there was conflict (Genesis 1:26–27, 2:15–18 NIV)
Wealth creates worry (Proverbs 13:8 MSG)
Worry (Matthew 6:19–21, 24–34 NLT)
Deception (Matthew 13:22 NIV; Exodus 20:15–16 NLT)
Quick riches (Proverbs 28:20 NLT)
Lack of trust (Psalm 55:20 NCV; Jeremiah 9:4 GW; Isaiah 30:5 GW; Ecclesiastes 5:5 NCV; Proverbs 14:22 GW; Joshua 2:12 GW)
Good listening skills (Mark 4:23 NLT; Proverbs 8:1 NLT; Ecclesiastes 9:17 NLT; John 8:43 NLT; James 1:19–20 NIV; Job 18:2, 32:16–21, 33:3 NLT)
Gossip (Proverbs 11:13, 13:3, 29:28 NLT; Job 4:8 NLT)
Discontent (Ecclesiastes 5:10–11)
Greed (Proverbs 30:15 NLT); Hebrews 13:5 MSG, Proverbs 15:27; 29:22 NLT; Luke 12:15–21 NASB)
Contentment (Philippians 4:11–13 NIV)

Quarrels and fighting (James 4:1–2 NLT)

Discipline and self-control (1 Peter 1:13a, 14 NLT; 1 Timothy 6:9–10 NCV; Psalm 73:7 NCV)

Generosity (Luke 6:38 NLT, Philippians 2:3–4 NASB)

Story of King David and Bathsheba (2 Samuel 11:2–7 NASB)

Ingratitude (Proverbs 30:11–14 NLT; Luke 17:11–19 NCV)

Story of King David and his son, Absalom (2 Samuel 13:1–5, 11–12, 14–15, 21–23, 26–29; 14:5–8, 10–14; 16:15, 20–22; 17:1–4, 11–14; 18:1–4a, 6–15, 31–33 NCV)

Jealousy (Exodus 20:17 GW; Ecclesiastes 4:4 NLT; Genesis 4:1–8 GW; Proverbs 27:4 GW; James 3:14 NASB; Luke 10:38–42 NLT)

Competition (Galatians 6:4–5 NLT; Luke 6:37–38, 41–42 NLT)

Getting wisdom (Proverbs 6:1–6 NCV)

Obeying or disobeying rules (Proverbs 16:20 TLB; Genesis 3:1–19, 23 NLT, Job 27:13–19 TLB; Proverbs 10:17 NLT; 30:17 NLT; 15:5, 10, 32 NLT; 29:18 NLT; Micah 6:10a, 13–15 NLT)

Arrogance and pride (Proverbs 18:12 NIV; Matthew 5:5 NIV; Proverbs 11:2; 16:18, 29–23 NLT; Ezekiel 28:4–5; 1 Corinthians 4:7–8 NCV)

Hypocrisy (Matthew 7:305 NIV)

Why discipline is necessary and important (Proverbs 13:1; 15:31–32; 13:24; 19:18; 29:15, 17, 19, 21; 21:20; Ecclesiastes 5:11 NLT)

Procrastination (Proverbs 22:7 NCV)

The antidote to affluenza (2 Peter 1:5–9; Ephesians 6:1–3; James 4:11 NLT)

Chapter 4: Why Is This Happening to My Family?

The value of having shepherd (John 10:2–4 NCV)

Rules are necessary and important (Matthew 22:37–40; Romans 3:23 NIV)

Chapter 5: IDEA (Proverbs 24:27 NLT; Romans 5:3–4 NCV)

Investigation (Deuteronomy 13:14; Proverbs 27:23–24 NET; Luke 14:28 NLT)

Chapter 12: Preparing for the Transfer (Proverbs 13:22, 20:21; Galatians 4:1–2 NCV; Ecclesiastes 2:18–19 NCV)

Taxes (Matthew 22:19–21; Romans 13:6–7 NLT)
Cash flow (Acts 19:25 NIV; Ecclesiastes 5:10–11 NLT)
Control (James 2:6b NCV)
Giving gifts while alive (Matthew 7:11 NLT)
How much? (Proverbs 20:21 NCV)
When? (Jeremiah 17:9a NLT)
After death (Proverbs 13:22 NLT)
Estate planning (Ecclesiastes 6:2 NLT)
Investment management (Ecclesiastes 5:13–14 NLT, 11:2 NCV; Proverbs 21:5 NCV)
Preparing people (Proverbs 1:2–7 NLT)

Chapter 13: Backbone Required

Service and stewardship (Luke 6:48; Proverbs 15:22 NIV)

Chapter 14: Building the Team

What is a team? (Romans 12:5–6a, 7–11 [Christ body = team], 15–18 TLB)
Trust and communication (Daniel 6:4; Luke 16: 9–13 NLT)
What roles are needed? (Ecclesiastes 3:13 NCV; Proverbs 28:19 NLT, 6:6–11 NCV; Ecclesiastes 11:6 NLT; Proverbs 10:5 NCV, 12:27 NLT, 14:23 NCV)
Helping your children find their significance (Proverbs 22:6 NLT)

Chapter 15: Priorities

Separate the important from the unimportant (Matthew 19:16–24 NCV; Luke 3:17 NLT)
Having an action plan (Proverbs 16:3 NLT) Individually (Isaiah 55:2–3 MSG)

Chapter 16: Balance

Chapter 17: Family Meetings

Chapter 18: Every Flock Needs a Shepherd (Proverbs 15:22, 20:18 NLT, 24:6 NCV; 1 Peter 5:2–3 NIV)

Wisdom (1 John 4:1; Job 28:27; 1 Thessalonians 15:21; 1 Timothy 6:3–5 NLT)
Minimize manipulation or coercion (Proverbs 18:13 NCV; Proverbs 6:1–5, 17:18, 22:26–27 NCV; Genesis 25:30–34 NLT)
Accountability (Proverbs 22:17–21 MSG; Hebrews 13:17 NIV)

Chapter 19: What Will Your Family's Story Be?

Resources (Matthew 5:23–24 NIV)
A coach (Proverbs 19:20, 12:15 NIV)

Chapter 20: Step-by-Step Wrap-Up

Gift of problems (James 1:2–4 NLT)

Chapter 21: The Last Word Is One Word (John 5:20; Luke 3:22 NIV)

One word: love (Matthew 22:37–40 NLT; Luke 16:9 NCV)
Abraham, Isaac, Jacob, and Esau, a family conflict (Genesis chapter 12–32 MSG)
Worldview (Ecclesiastes 2:1–11 NLT)
Significance view (Matthew 22:37–40; 1 Corinthians 13:1–13 NLT)
Love = Significance (Proverbs 17:17 MSG)

Your True Wealth

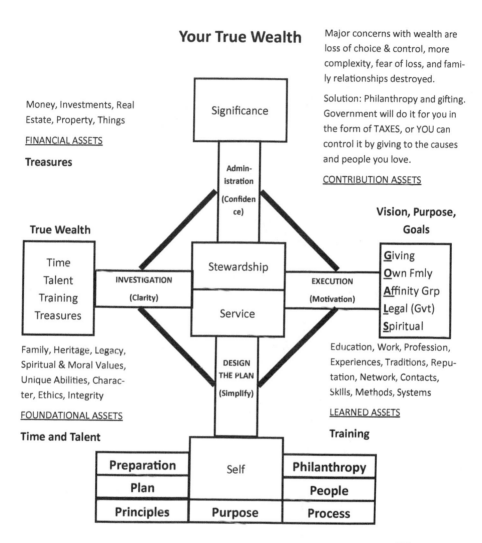

Major concerns with wealth are loss of choice & control, more complexity, fear of loss, and family relationships destroyed.

Solution: Philanthropy and gifting. Government will do it for you in the form of TAXES, or YOU can control it by giving to the causes and people you love.

CONTRIBUTION ASSETS

Money, Investments, Real Estate, Property, Things

FINANCIAL ASSETS

Treasures

Significance

Vision, Purpose, Goals

True Wealth

Time
Talent
Training
Treasures

INVESTIGATION
(Clarity)

Admin-
istration
(Confiden
ce)

Stewardship

Service

EXECUTION
(Motivation)

Giving
Own Fmly
Affinity Grp
Legal (Gvt)
Spiritual

Family, Heritage, Legacy, Spiritual & Moral Values, Unique Abilities, Charac- ter, Ethics, Integrity

FOUNDATIONAL ASSETS

Time and Talent

DESIGN
THE PLAN
(Simplify)

Education, Work, Profession, Experiences, Traditions, Repu- tation, Network, Contacts, Skills, Methods, Systems

LEARNED ASSETS

Training

Preparation	Self	**Philanthropy**
Plan		**People**
Principles	**Purpose**	**Process**

Figure 1.1

AREAS FOR GOAL SETTING

SPIRITUAL	PHYSICAL	INTELLECTUAL & CULTURAL	PROFESSIONAL	SOCIAL	FINANCIAL
Church	Exercise	Reading	Career	Spouse	Tithing & Giving
Small Group	Diet	Education	Community	Children/Grandchildren	Cash Flow
Ministry	Rest	Creativity	Volunteering	Parents/Grandparents	Assets
Prayer	Relaxation	Travel	Business Ownership	Siblings	Debt
Bible Study	Recreation	Mentoring		Aunt/Uncle/Cousins, etc	Reserves
Memorization	Appearance			Friends	Disability
				Neighbors	Survivor
				Co-Workers	Savings
				Peers	Taxes
					Retirement
					Estate Planning
					Philanthropy
					Business Succession

Figure 6.1

Personal Goals Worksheet

Name

6/6/15

	What	When	Time	Talent	Training	Treasures	Progress
				Resource Allocations			
	Enter a detailed description of your goal and objective. Be specific, using measurable metrix	Identify a date or time frame for achieving this objective	How much time will you allocate to this objective on a daily, weekly, monthly, annual basis	What innate abilities can you use to help you achieve this objective	What training do you already have, or do you need to get, to help you achieve this objective	What financial resources will you allocate to achieving this objective	Record your progress in reaching this goal or objective
SPIRITUAL							
Church							
Small Group							
Ministry							
Prayer							
Bible Study							
Memorization							
PHYSICAL							
Exercise							
Diet							
Rest							
Relaxation							
Recreation							
Appearance							
INTELLECTUAL & CULTURAL							
Reading							
Education							
Creativity							
Travel							
Mentoring							
PROFESSIONAL							
Career							
Community							
Volunteering							
Business Ownership							

Figure 6.2

385

Life Values for Name as of Date

[Underline your top 10, then circle the top 5 of the 10, then list the top 3 of the 5]

Acceptance
Accomplishment
Adaptability
Adventure
Assertiveness
Availability
Balance
Beauty
Belonging
Caring
Commitment
Community
Compassion
Confidence
Conviction
Courage
Creativity
Decisiveness
Dependability
Determination
Dignity
Diligence
Discipline
Diversity
Duty
Effectiveness
Encouragement
Entrepreneurship
Equality
Equity
Ethics
Excellence
Fairness
Faith
Faithfulness
Family
Forgiveness
Freedom
Friendship
Generosity
Gentleness
Goodness
Grace
Gratitude
Harmony
Health

Honesty
Honor
Hope
Humility
Humor
Independence
Innovation
Integrity
Involvement
Joy
Justice
Kindness
Knowledge
Leadership
Listening
Love
Loyalty
Mastery
Mercy
Modesty
Obedience
Objectiveness
Opportunity
Optimism
Patience
Peace
Personal Growth
Power
Pragmatism
Productive
Punctual
Purpose
Reliable
Respect
Responsible
Security
Self-control
Self-sufficient
Sensitive
Service
Significance
Simplicity
Teachable
Teamwork
Tolerance
Tradition

Trust
Truth
Wisdom

Top Three

Figure 8.1

386

MY LIFE VALUES AND VISIONS

For: _____

Date: _____

___ Priority   Highest Life Value (One Word):

                Action Phrase (Short action statement using above word):

                Value Statement (Short paragraph defining why this is important and what value it has for you and others):

___ Priority   Highest Life Value (One Word):

                Action Phrase (Short action statement using above word):

                Value Statement (Short paragraph defining why this is important and what value it has for you and others):

___ Priority   Highest Life Value (One Word):

                Action Phrase (Short action statement using above word):

                Value Statement (Short paragraph defining why this is important and what value it has for you and others):

> Vision Statement (Answer the following questions as to how you see these values impacting each of the five major areas of your life listed below. How would it make others feel significant and how would it make you feel significant? Attempt to include all three values into one paragraph.)

Spirituality in Your Life:
     Desired Outcome (How would this look three years from today?):

     True Wealth Application (State how you will apply your Time, Talents, Training and Treasures to implementing these values in this area of your life.):

Family:
     Desired Outcome (How would this look three years from today?):

     True Wealth Application (State how you will apply your Time, Talents, Training and Treasures to implementing these values in this area of your life.):

Figure 8.2

UNIFYING VALUES OF CLIFFORD R. KOLSON

1. PUT MY FAITH IN GOD
Pray and study the Bible daily. Attend church and church functions regularly and provide service to my church by donating my time and abilities. Tithe. Associate with other Christians and participate in Christian activities. Set a Christian example for my family, friends, and associates. Seek and implement God's plan for my life through a personal ministry utilizing the talents and abilities He has given me. Be active in a small group.

2. LOVE MY FAMILY
Wife: Spend quality time. Demonstrate more personal affection by showing and telling her now much I love her and do it more often. Leave her love notes. Encourage her personal growth in all areas but especially the strengthening of her faith in God. Respect her viewpoint, ask for it, don't discourage it through my actions and speech. Listen better by giving her my full attention, maintaining eye contact, and being quiet. Include her in all decisions and don't demand my way all the time.

Children: Encourage them to have high self-esteem and achieve their goals. Help them to set goals. Spend at least one hour per week on an individual basis. Continue to teach them responsibility and how to handle it. Prepare them for adulthood. Encourage their faith in God.

3. HAVE A PURPOSE
Seek to identify, refine, and fulfill God's purpose for my life. I will set long-range and intermediate goals and plan my activities to achieve those goals. I will also establish a measure of performance to which I will compare my actual performance and make corrections as needed to achieve excellence.

4. BE THANKFUL
Everyday thank God for his many blessings, my good health and the good health of my family, and the good fortune He has bestowed upon me and my family.

5. ` BE HEALTHY
I will maintain a diet of low-fat, low-cholesterol food; maintain my weight at around 160 pounds, and exercise at least 4 days per week. I will get between 6 to 8 hours of sleep each night. Spend at least one hour per week in a relaxing and enjoyable activity, or for time alone for contemplation and mediation. I will take one week off per year for a family vacation, and one week for a personal vacation.

6. CULTIVATE FRIENDSHIPS
Make a list of those people in my life that I enjoy and call them, or drop them a note monthly to let them know I'm thinking about them and that they are an important part of my life. Meet with one couple for a night out each month. Invite them to church if they are not already attending somewhere. Seek new friendships. Be a friend by accepting others unconditionally; encouraging them, especially to know Christ, and by being available when they need someone. Associate with people that will build me up, not tear me down.

7. CARE ABOUT OTHERS
I will take the time to understand other persons' points of view and respect their opinions. I will help others to achieve their goals and self-esteem. To care about others requires me to tell them about Christ. I will voice my beliefs and opinions but will not impose them on anyone else. I will not hurt anyone else to benefit myself. I will have empathy.

8. HAVE HIGH SELF-ESTEEM
Continually develop and maintain a strong sense of personal worth as I relate to myself and others. Strive for self-actualization. Remember that my value as a person is in direct relationship to the value I provide to God.

9. ACHIEVE EXCELLENCE

Figure 8.3a

MY LIFE VALUES AND VISIONS

For: Kip Kolson

Date: 5/22/14

___ Priority   Highest Life Value (One Word): **Faith**

Action Phrase (Short action statement using above word): **Put my faith in God, my wife, my family, and people who have proven to me to be trustworthy.**

Value Statement (Short paragraph defining why this is important and what value it has for you and others):

God is the only one who can meet my needs because He loves me, He knows me better than I know myself, He knows all my tomorrows, and He will always do what is best for me even if it means experiencing difficulties, trials, and tribulations. He will never abandon me, He will never fail me, and He will never stop loving me. On earth, I must have people around me who I trust, so I must identify those people who care about me and put my trust in them.

The value for me is I can have hope, optimism, love, peace, joy, and calm knowing that God is in control. The value for others is that I will be a more positive and pleasant person to be around, and be an encouragement to others who are struggling by being a good example and supporter. Having confidence in the people I love, and who love me, removes worry and tension from my life.

___ Priority   Highest Life Value (One Word): **Love**

Action Phrase (Short action statement using above word): **Love God, love my family, and love others. Embrace and live Matthew 22:37-40, which says, "Love the Lord your God with all your heart, all your soul, and all your mind. This is the first and greatest commandment. And the second is like it. Love your neighbor as yourself. All the laws and prophets hang on these two commandments."**

Value Statement (Short paragraph defining why this is important and what value it has for you and others): **Love is the only commodity that increases to me the more I give it away. The best way for me to love myself and to be significant is to love God and love others. By loving others I will acknowledge their importance and value as a person and their value to God. The best way for me to help others be significant, is to treat them as already being significant.**

___ Priority   Highest Life Value (One Word): **Purpose**

Action Phrase (Short action statement using above word): **Seek to identify, refine, and fulfill God's purpose for my life. I will set long-range and intermediate goals and plan my activities to achieve those goals. I will also establish a measure of performance to which I will compare my actual performance and make corrections as needed to achieve excellence, not perfection, which is impossible. I believe it is my purpose to help others identify and live out God's purpose for their lives.**

Value Statement (Short paragraph defining why this is important and what value it has for you and others): **By helping other people achieve significance, as defined by them, I will achieve significance, as defined by me and what I believe God's purpose is for my life. A person's value in life is dependent on the value they bring to others. By helping other people identify the value they bring to the world, they, the people they touch, and the world will be a better place.**

___ Priority   Highest Life Value (One Word): **Gratitude**

Action Phrase (Short action statement using above word): **Everyday thank God for his many blessings, my good health and the good health of my family, and the good fortune He has bestowed upon me and my family. Every day look for opportunities to tell my wife, my children, my friends, my peers,**

Figure 8.3b

CRAFTING YOUR PERSONAL VISION AND MISSION STATEMENT

Client's Name

April 7, 2014

If you had the resources of a Bill Gates or Warren Buffet, how would you use those resources? (Be specific. "World peace" or "make the world a better place," is too ambiguous) __

How would you complete this statement? I feel I will have been significant and had a significant life if:

__

When you read the paper or hear the news on television or the radio:

What makes you mad?

1. __
2. __
3. __

What makes you sad?

1. __
2. __
3. __

What makes you glad?

1. __
2. __
3. __

How would you complete this sentence? I really care about _____ (Could be people or causes)

1. __
2. __
3. __

If you had the power to change anything in the world and make the world a better place, what would you change?

1. __
2. __
3. __

Why would you make these changes? __

How would you make the changes? __

Who would you hope to impact with your changes? __

Where would you implement these changes? __

Figure 9.1

390

CRAFTING YOUR PERSONAL VISION AND MISSION STATEMENT

Kip Kolson

April 7, 2014

If you had the resources of a Bill Gates or Warren Buffet, how would you use those resources? (Be specific. "World peace" or "make the world a better place," is too ambiguous) **I would teach, coach, and mentor high net worth families in how to use and transfer their wealth for hundreds of years in ways that create responsible and educated generations that will continue to use the family wealth wisely and charitably.**

How would you complete this statement? I feel I will have been significant and had a significant life if _____. **I have been happily married to the same woman until the day one of us dies. My children are responsible adults and raising responsible children of their own and all are involved in some type of charitable activities. My friends and clients consider me to be honest, trustworthy, of high integrity, and available whenever they needed me. My clients have discovered and are developing their own purpose and significance for themselves and their families because I have been able to guide and encourage them. Finally, and most importantly, to have the confidence that when I stand before God, He will say, "Well done, good and faithful servant."**

When you read the paper or hear the news on television or the radio:

What makes you mad?

1. **Abuse of children**
2. **Abuse of women**
3. **Moral decay of our society**
4. **Government intrusion in our lives, causing loss of freedom**

What makes you sad?

1. **Broken families**
2. **Children growing up in foster care or government facilities**
3. **Parents not raising their children to be good citizens and independent**
4. **Abortion**
5. **Greed**

What makes you glad?

1. **Seeing and hearing about people who give of themselves to help others**
2. **Strong families and children giving of themselves to help others. Kids intelligently demonstrating service and stewardship.**
3. **Families with a strong spiritual foundation**

How would you complete this sentence? I really care about _____ (Could be people or causes)

1. **Encouraging families to maintain a strong, unified purpose and mission to benefit the family, all family members, and society.**

Figure 9.2

ALLOCATING TIME TO PERSONAL GOALS
Clients' Name
11/09/15

[Enter the Percentage of Time You Would Like to Spend in Each Area]

SPIRITUAL	Percentage	Hours /Year	Aver. Hrs /Week
าurch		0.00	0.00
nall Group		0.00	0.00
inistry		0.00	0.00
·ayer		0.00	0.00
ble Study		0.00	0.00
emorization		0.00	0.00
		0.00	0.00

PHYSICAL			
‹ercise (Non-Recreation)		0.00	0.00
eals		0.00	0.00
est		0.00	0.00
elaxation		0.00	0.00
ecreation (Other than vacations)		0.00	0.00
ppearance		0.00	0.00
acation (Deduct meals & rest)		0.00	0.00

INTELLECTUAL & CULTURAL			
eading		0.00	0.00
ducation		0.00	0.00
·eativity		0.00	0.00
·avel		0.00	0.00
		0.00	0.00

SOCIAL			
)ouse		0.00	0.00
าildren/Grandchildren		0.00	0.00
arents/Grandparents		0.00	0.00
blings		0.00	0.00
int/Uncle/Cousins, etc		0.00	0.00
iends		0.00	0.00
eighbors		0.00	0.00
)-Workers		0.00	0.00
eers		0.00	0.00
		0.00	0.00

FINANCIAL			
anning		0.00	0.00
anaging Cash Flow		0.00	0.00
anaging Investments		0.00	0.00
·operty Maintainance		0.00	0.00
ิilanthropy		0.00	0.00
		0.00	0.00

PROFESSIONAL			
areer		0.00	0.00
ommunity		0.00	0.00
ตlunteering		0.00	0.00
vic		0.00	0.00
ission/Purpose		0.00	0.00

·tal	0.00%	ი	ი

Figure 11.1

Time Log 12/13/2007 Kip Kolson

Start	End	Activity		Duration
8:30 AM	9:45 AM	RE affinity group	Education	1:15
9:45 AM	10:30 AM	Kevin: LMU meeting/Possible new business/general	Business Dev.	0:45
10:30 AM	10:40 AM	To list and time log	Organizing	0:10
10:40 AM	11:05 AM	emails	Communications	0:25
11:05 AM	11:20 AM	In box	Administration	0:15
11:20 AM	11:30 AM	Client CRT funding at Crowell Weedon	Client Planning	0:10
11:30 AM	12:30 PM	Client Review valuation proposals	Client Planning	1:00
12:30 PM	12:45 PM	Client CRT funding at Crowell Weedon	Client Planning	0:15
12:45 PM	1:35 PM	Flight reservation for PCG Jan 2008 meeting in Phx	Administration	0:50
1:35 PM	1:50 PM	Personal accounting	Personal	0:15
1:50 PM	3:50 PM	Psomas: Contract for legal coordination on dynasty trust	Client Planning	2:00
3:50 PM	5:00 PM	Lunch		1:10
5:00 PM	5:10 PM	Client Phone & email Grace Lee on LOC documents	Client Planning	0:10
5:10 PM	5:25 PM	emails	Communications	0:15
5:25 PM	5:35 PM	Review employee emails	Compliance	0:10
5:35 PM	6:10 PM	Client Contract for legal coordination on dynasty trust	Client Planning	0:35
6:10 PM	7:45 PM	Small Group		1:35
7:45 PM	8:20 PM	Client Contract for legal coordination on dynasty trust	Client Planning	0:35
8:20 PM	8:40 PM	Review Voorhees planning website-IDIT	Client Planning	0:20
8:40 PM	9:30 PM	Computer stuff	Administration	0:50
9:30 PM				0:00
12:00 AM				0:00
12:00 AM				0:00
12:00 AM				0:00
12:00 AM				0:00
12:00 AM				0:00
12:00 AM				0:00
12:00 AM				0:00
12:00 AM				0:00
12:00 AM				0:00
12:00 AM				0:00
12:00 AM				0:00
12:00 AM				0:00
12:00 AM				0:00
				13:00

Administration	1:55	18.70%
Business Dev.	0:45	7.32%
Client Planning	5:05	49.59%
Communications	0:40	6.50%
Compliance	0:10	1.63%
Education	1:15	12.20%
FWL Planning	0.00	0.00%
Insurance	0:00	0.00%
Investments	0:00	0.00%
Marketing	0:00	0.00%
Organizing	0:10	1.63%
Personal	0:15	2.44%
Training	0:00	0.00%
	10:15	100.00%

Figure 11.2a

Time Log Summary
Kip Kolson

	Target	Allocation	10/31/07	11/30/07	12/31/07	Totals
Administration	10%	14.99%	15:50	11:30	16:35	19:55
Business Dev.	25%	16.42%	3:05	1:10	0:25	4:40
Client Planning	20%	22.48%	8:30	22:45	10:35	17:50
Communications	10%	10.59%	21:15	23:40	20:00	16:55
Compliance	5%	4.92%	21:55	5:40	2:35	6:10
Education	5%	10.18%	15:55	10:00	12:30	14:25
FWL Planning	5%	0.41%	0:00	0:10	2:20	2:30
Insurance	5%	0.86%	1:55	2:15	1:05	5:15
Investments	5%	6.32%	18:25	10:50	9:30	14:45
Marketing	5%	4.88%	16:20	9:10	4:25	5:55
Organizing	2%	4.55%	6:10	10:20	11:25	3:55
Personal	2%	3.40%	3:05	3:45	14:00	20:50
Training	1%	0.00%	0:00	0:00	0:00	0:00
Totals	100.00%	100.00%	12:25	15:15	9:25	613:05:00
						6:39
		Days >	31	30	31	92
		Hours per day based on a five day work week >				9:43

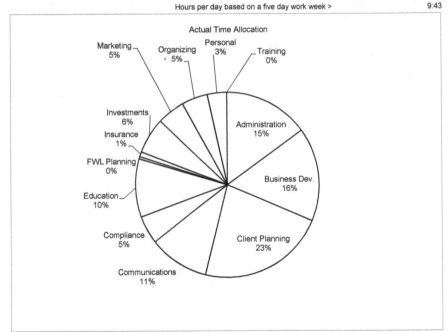

Actual Time Allocation

Figure 11.2b

CASH FLOW

Please complete the following with approximate amounts and round to the nearest whole number.

To the extent possible, list income and expenditures by the individual. This will be necessary for survivor and disability projections.

List income or expenses received or paid jointly under the "Joint" column.

You need NOT provide a total in the "Annual" column for monthly items. Rather, indicate joint amounts for items that are received or expended other than monthly. For example, property taxes, insurance payments, gifts paid or received, etc.

Items marked with an asterick (*) indicate discretionary expenses.

CASH FLOW	Date Prepared:			
Clients:	Monthly			
	Client	2nd Person	Joint	Annual
INCOME				
Taxable Income				
Consulting Income				
Self-Employment/Business Income				
Total Self-Employment Income				
Employment Income				
Bonus				
Commissions				
Employee Expense Reimbursements				
Other Earned Income				
Less: Union/Other Dues/Tax Ded Expenses				
Total Earned Income				
Interest				
Dividends				
Notes Receivable				
Pensions				
IRA Distributions				
Social Security (Taxable Portion)				
Alimony				
Ltd. Partnerships (Public)				
Ltd. Partnerships (Private)				
Annuity Income				
Investment Real Estate (Net Before Debt Service)				
Business Income (Net Before Debt Service)				
Awards/Prizes/Winnings				
Earned Income not subject to FICA				
Other Taxable Income				
Total Taxable Income				
Non-Taxable Income				
Social Security (Non-Taxable Portion)				
Child Support				
Municipal Bond Interest				
Other				
Other Non-Taxable				
Total Non-Taxable Income				
TOTAL BEFORE TAX INCOME				
Income Taxes Withhold				
Federal Income Tax				
State Income Tax				
F.I.C.A				
Self-Employment Tax				
Total Taxes				
TOTAL AFTER TAX INCOME				

Figure 11.3

Enter a "y" in columns C - F if the statement is true. Leave blank if false. Add additional objectives at the end of the list if they are not included in this list. When everything is prioritized, go to the Final and Copy to Word tab.

	Objectives	Rating > 8 Necessary	4 Urgent	2 Tactical	1 Clear
1	Ensuring sufficient cash and cash equivalent reserves are available to meet emergencies				
2	Paying off or reducing debt to a manageable level				
3	Directing a portion of your personal savings or investment portfolio to a tax advantaged vehicle				
4	Having all of your portfolios consolidated and analyzed to make sure your overall plan is on track				
5	Matching your risk tolerance to that of your investment portfolio				
6	Creating and building a diversified investment portfolio				
7	Reviewing your investment performance against your plan				
8	Gaining more control over spending habits				
9	Receiving current income from my investments		y	y	y
10	Incorporating tax management strategies throughout your financial plan to minimize or reduce income taxes whenever possible		y	y	
11	Minimizing the taxes on your investment accounts		y		y
12	Reviewing techniques to save income tax and estate taxes on deferred money		y		
13	Minimizing estate taxes			y	y
14	Assuring adequate funds are available to meet the educational needs of your family			y	
15	Providing cash for specific capital expenditures				y
16	Attaining a level of financial independence that provides the lifestyle of your choice without having to rely on earned income				
17	Reviewing alternative retirement methods	y	y	y	y
18	Generating a guaranteed retirement income stream	y	y	y	
19	Asset protection in the result of serious illness	y	y		y
20	Protecting assets in the event that you require Long Term Care in the future	y	y		
21	Receiving adequate income in the event of disability during your working years	y		y	y
22	Planning for income for your spouse in the event of your premature death	y		y	
23	Planning income for your children in the event of your premature death	y			y
24	Providing a smooth and orderly transfer of your estate to your heirs while minimizing costs and estate taxes and the time delays of probate	y			
25	Reviewing your current will structure to eliminate unnecessary taxes		y	y	y
26	Distributing assets fairly to your children		y	y	
27	Protecting your assets transferred to your children from creditors, divorce, and bankruptcy		y		y
28	Reviewing different methods of meeting your estate tax liabilities		y		
29	Creating a family bank structure with my children involved as directors and in management decisions			y	y
30	Charitable planning to your estate's planning			y	
31	Contributing annually to charity				y
32	Maintaining control of your business throughout your lifetime				
33	Eliminating the need to liquidate your business to pay estate taxes	y	y	y	y
34	Passing your business in a manner where it is sold to key employees	y	y	y	
35	Creating a business-planning concept that can help you sell your business to key employees in an efficient manner	y	y		y
36	Providing incentives to your key employees with non-stock compensation alternatives	y	y		
37	Having your key employees own stock in your company	y		y	y
38	Protecting your business from the death of a key employee	y		y	
39	Protecting your key employees and their families from serious illness and disability	y			y
40	Protecting your company from serious illness and disability of your employees	y			
41	Finding key employees for the continued success of your company		y	y	y
42	Passing your business in a manner that maintains family ownership and control		y	y	
43	Maintaining family harmony after your estate has been settled		y		y
44	Having your spouse take an active/ownership role in the business plan after you pass		y		
45	Creating a business planning concept that shows you how to gift/sell/bequest your business to your children/heirs			y	y
46	Balancing the inheritance for your children not active in the business			y	
47	Leaving the business only to active children/heirs versus all children/heirs				y
48	Having your children/heirs active in the business with regards to the future success of your business				
49	Passing your business in a manner where it is sold to a third party	y	y	y	y
50	Buying out a partner's interest in the event of his or her death	y	y	y	
51	Reviewing your business' property and casualty coverage every two years	y	y		y
52	Reviewing alternative sources for your existing line of credit	y	y		
53	Reviewing the efficiency of your existing long term debt structure	y		y	y
54	Additional Objective				
55	Additional Objective				
56	Additional Objective				
57	Additional Objective				
58	Additional Objective				
59	Additional Objective				
60	Additional Objective				
61	Additional Objective				
62	Additional Objective				
63	Additional Objective				
64	Additional Objective				
65	Additional Objective				
66	Additional Objective				
67	Additional Objective				
68	Additional Objective				
69	Additional Objective				
70	Additional Objective				
71	Additional Objective				
72	Additional Objective				
73	Additional Objective				
74	Additional Objective				
75	Additional Objective				
76	Additional Objective				
77	Additional Objective				

Figure 15.1

TRUE WEALTH DISCOVERY SUMMARY
Larry and Jane Sample

Your Stated Objectives Prioritized (Number indicates your order of priority)   5/22/2007

Necessary, Urgent, Tactical and Clear
__ Ensuring sufficient cash and cash equivalent reserves are available to meet emergencies

__ Reviewing alternative retirement methods

__ Eliminating the need to liquidate your business to pay estate taxes

__ Passing your business in a manner where it is sold to a third party

Necessary, Urgent, Tactical and Not Clear
__ Paying off or reducing debt to a manageable level

__ Generating a guaranteed retirement income stream

__ Passing your business in a manner where it is sold to key employees

__ Buying out a partner's interest in the event of his or her death

Necessary, Urgent, Strategic and Clear
__ Directing a portion of your personal savings or investment portfolio to a tax advantaged vehicle

__ Asset protection in the result of serious illness

__ Creating a business-planning concept that can help you sell your business to key employees in an efficient manner

__ Reviewing your business' property and casualty coverage every two years

Necessary, Urgent, Strategic and Not Clear
__ Having all of your portfolios consolidated and analyzed to make sure your overall plan is on track

__ Protecting assets in the event that you require Long Term Care in the future

__ Providing incentives to your key employees with non-stock compensation alternatives

__ Reviewing alternative sources for your existing line of credit

Necessary, Not Urgent, Tactical and Clear
__ Matching your risk tolerance to that of your investment portfolio

__ Receiving adequate income in the event of disability during your working years

__ Having your key employees own stock in your company

Figure 15.2

Family Wealth Leadership

Wealth Management Issues Analysis and Action Plan

Larry and Jane Sample

September 8, 2011

	Investigation Phase		Design and Development Phase				
Topics and Activities	Issues Identified	Outcome if Status Quo Maintained	Recommended Solutions	Benefits if Implemented	Action Plan	Target Date to Implement	Date Implemented
Business Planning and Business Succession Planning							
Review and Update Business Succession Plan							
Review and Update Buy/Sell Arrangements							
Key Executive Compensation							
Merger, Acquisition, and Disposition Consulting							
Risk Management							
Review and Maintain Employee Benefit Programs							
Assist with Business Loans and Financing as Requested or Required							
Review and Coordinate Tax Strategies with Tax Advisors							
Review and Coordinate Legal Structures and Asset Protection Strategies with Legal Advisors							
Compliance Review of Legal Entities (Client Responsible for Taking Actions)							

Red = High Risk, Immediate Action Needed; Blue = Moderate Risk, Action Needed; Green = No Action Needed at this time

Figure 15.3a

Family Wealth Leadership

Wealth Management Issues Analysis and Action Plan

Larry and Jane Sample

September 8, 2011

	Investigation Phase		Design and Development Phase			
Topics and Activities	Issues Identified	Outcome if Status Quo Maintained	Recommended Solutions	Benefits if Implemented	Action Plan	Target Date to Implement	Date Implemented
Charitable Giving While Alive and at Death						
Compliance Oversight for Family Foundation (Client Responsible for Taking Actions)						
Oversight of Donor Advised Funds, CRTs, and Other Charitable Entities						
Due Diligence on Charities as Requested by Client						
Due Diligence on Trustee Providers and Community Foundations Offering Trustee Services						
Review Investments in Charitable Entities not Included in FWL Investment Management Services						
Coordination with Trustees, Legal and Tax Advisors, Charities, and Family						

Red = High Risk, Immediate Action Needed; Blue = Moderate Risk, Action Needed Green = No Action Needed at this time

Figure 15.3b

399

About the Author

Kip Kolson entered the financial services industry in 1967. His experience includes tenures in banking, commercial real estate development, and financial planning; at a leading business and personal financial planning corporation as well as ownership of his own real estate company; and now his own family wealth leadership company.

Kip started his own company in 1988 as owner of Kolson Investment Property Advisors. It was during these six years that he developed a better understanding of the wants and needs of the average business owner and its employees. Feeling a need to have a greater impact on helping others, Kip decided to pursue his financial planning career with IDS Financial Services, but knew he needed to associate with an independent firm to achieve his goal of being a client advocate. In 1992, he joined Advantage Financial Advisory Group, the predecessor of Family Wealth Leadership, and over time acquired the firm. As owner and president, he guides all aspects of the firm to ensure it achieves its mission of optimizing a family's true wealth in order to prepare the next generation as responsible stewards and to leave a legacy for future generations.

Kip Kolson lives Orange County, California, with his wife of 52 years. When not helping other families, he is spending time with his three grandchildren, two sons and daughters-in-law, and volunteering in ministries and charities, and attending the kids' soccer, flag football, basketball, and baseball games. He also speaks at events and on radio on the topics in this book: investing, financial, estate and business planning, and family coaching.